For Him Who
Has Eyes to See

For Him Who Has Eyes to See

Beauty in the History of Theology

EDMUND J. RYBARCZYK

CASCADE *Books* • Eugene, Oregon

FOR HIM WHO HAS EYES TO SEE
Beauty in the History of Theology

Copyright © 2016 Edmund J. Rybarczyk. All rights reserved. Except for brief quotations in critical publications or reviews, no part of this book may be reproduced in any manner without prior written permission from the publisher. Write: Permissions, Wipf and Stock Publishers, 199 W. 8th Ave., Suite 3, Eugene, OR 97401.

Cascade Books
An Imprint of Wipf and Stock Publishers
199 W. 8th Ave., Suite 3
Eugene, OR 97401

www.wipfandstock.com

PAPERBACK ISBN: 978-1-4982-7942-0
HARDCOVER ISBN: 978-1-4982-7944-4
EBOOK ISBN: 978-1-4982-7943-7

Cataloguing-in-Publication data:

Names: Rybarczyk, Edmund J.
Title: For him who has eyes to see : beauty in the history of theology / Edmund J. Rybarczyk.
Description: Eugene, OR: Cascade Books, 2016 | Includes bibliographical references.
Identifiers: ISBN 978-1-4982-7942-0 (paperback) | ISBN 978-1-4982-7944-4 (hardcover) | ISBN 978-1-4982-7943-7 (ebook)
Subjects: LCSH: 1. Aesthetics—Religious aspects—Christianity. | 2. Philosophical theology. | 3. Title.
BT 55 R625 2016 (paperback) | BT 55 R625 2016 (ebook)

Manufactured in the USA.   09/27/16

Dedication

Across my life beauty has gently but gradually interposed herself into my own reality. Well, she was always there, but recently she has made herself known to me in intentional and even assertive ways. Primarily, I owe my awareness of beauty to my mother, Valerie Tenney. When I and my younger siblings—Jim, Bill, and Susan—were young, my mom would variously take us to cross-cultural celebrations, enormous but delicate gardens, Willamette Valley farms, the Pacific Ocean on the Oregon Coast, home-spun music concerts, college plays, movies and art shows. She was constantly exposing us to the beautiful world around us and although I did not know it then, an innate sensitivity toward and appreciation of beauty was being woven into my soul.

Some twenty-five years ago my mother and her husband, Michael Tenney, converted to Eastern Orthodoxy. In 1992 they invited me to attend a Russian Orthodox liturgy in St. Spyridon's Cathedral in Seattle, Washington. It was there that I was enchanted by the beauty of a service that was strange to me. And yet, I encountered the Lord's Spirit therein, and in very sensory ways at that. My nose smelled gentle but holy scents. My ears heard the priest's haunting chants. My eyes observed both the people's sincere kinesthetic adorations of the triune God and the visually stunning cadre of Russian icons. All in all I was introduced to a profound presence of beauty in Christian worship. That seminal experience opened my imagination to theological possibilities. What might beauty mean for we who proclaim Christ our Lord?

Today Valerie and Michael continue to bless me with beauty through their love of gardening and guitar playing. To you I dedicate this study. More, I extend my most sincere appreciation to both of you for having enriched my life with beauty!

This is an appropriate place for me to also thank the eminent scholar of theo-aesthetics Jeremy Begbie, Professor of Theology at Duke University, for his review of my list of chosen theologians. Mike Beals, President of Vanguard University, himself a philosophy professor, was also very kind to have reviewed my chapter on Kant. I am grateful for the help of these keen minds.

Contents

1. Introduction
   The Evangelical Problem with Beauty | 1
2. Gregory of Nyssa (c. 330–395) | 10
   The Beauty of the Infinite God
3. Augustine of Hippo (c. 354–430)
   Ascetic Wariness and Worries | 34
4. Pseudo-Dionysius the Areopagite (5th–6th Centuries)
   The Porous Nature of God's Beauty | 56
5. The Medieval Era and Thomas Aquinas (1225–1274)
   Beauty in Our Eyes and Minds | 80
6. Post-Patristic Interlude
   An Explosion of Christian Art and Aesthetic | 101
7. The Reformation
   Correcting and Overcorrecting Aesthetic Abuse | 111
8. Jonathan Edwards (1703–1758)
   The Wonder of God's Beautifying Beauty: The Holy Spirit | 138
9. Immanuel Kant (1724–1804)
   The Beauty of the Human Person's Ability to Perceive Beauty | 158
10. Paul Evdokimov (1901–1970)
    Beauty through Iconic Lenses | 182
11. Hans Urs von Balthasar (1905–1988)
    Jesus Christ: The Supreme Source of All Beauty | 205

Bibliography | 237

I

Introduction
The Evangelical Problem with Beauty

OUR VOCABULARY IS OFTEN powerful. In many ways, we become the words we use. With our words we taste the recipe of reality. Using words, we sample together life's peace, play, delight, humor, irony, toil, frustration, alienation, and wounding. And the words we use to process all those qualities actually shape the flavor of each. Or, to use another analogy, words are like automobiles: they take us places. Just like an automobile enables us to go and see things beyond our own neighborhood—the ocean, a mountain, a redwood forest, or an old college friend—words enable us to see more crisply life's experiences.

With only that bit of setup at hand, here's my premise: Evangelicals[1] have failed to employ the word *beauty* in our daily vocabulary. And that means we have failed to incorporate beauty variously into our everyday conversations, how we treat others, the way we navigate daily life, and our own lives in Christ. Frighteningly, it might mean we ourselves are not purposefully beautiful.

1. Evangelical is a sociological descriptor, not necessarily a specific Protestant denomination. Evangelicals traditionally emphasize the inspired truthfulness of the Bible, God's sovereignty, the exclusive salvific nature of Jesus Christ, the need for personal conversion, preaching the gospel, the reality of the afterlife (heaven and hell), and the bodily resurrection. Those categories at work, there are Roman Catholics, Eastern Orthodox, and Protestants who are all Evangelical in orientation. My critique in this chapter primarily concerns low-church Protestants: those who do not have priests, sacraments, or follow the liturgical calendar.

For Him Who Has Eyes to See

Oh, we like beauty. Some Evangelicals, owing to family proclivities or a personal sense of space, know how to decorate their homes with beauty. Regularly we enjoy the beauty of a well-crafted piece of furniture or jewelry. But when it comes to our faith, presumably that value above all others in our lives, we bar beauty. We don't know how to include her. When we do think about including her our thoughts are clunky and jumbled. If that seems overstated, just think of the Evangelical church buildings you have attended. They are consistently clean but bare. Designed for utility, they enable crowds of Christians to sing, pray, and chiefly listen together. Some of those buildings might intrigue us with their sheer size or their reputation, but beauty is rarely one of their celebrated features. Frequently built on shoestring budgets, they are functional—lights, heating, sometimes comfortable seating, and visually clear lines of sight are consistently present—but aesthetically they are boring. They rarely have an intentionally beautiful aspect to them. They are too often merely gathering spaces, auditoriums, or worse, theaters for a kind of Christian show. Nobody thinks to go to an Evangelical auditorium just to be there, to pray or to contemplate God there, or to seek personal solace inside the walls. Yet it is just not natural to have worship spaces that are functional but aesthetically stark. Excepting Islam, which consistently forbids any aesthetic design other than two-dimensional painted geometric designs, all of the world's religions intentionally employ beautifully designed sacred space to shape the experience of the religious concelebrant. More, the sacred space of those religions is consistently a mirror of ultimate and true reality (however understood) itself; sacred space design thus exemplifies something important about the world view, of the metaphysic, and of the ultimately valuable for those who spend time inside the walls.

The point here is, our very worship spaces—the very places we assemble to disciple, shape, renew, and enliven ourselves as we worship and glorify the triune God—betray the Evangelical inability to incorporate beauty into our way of being.

Concerning beauty and aesthetics we Evangelicals have an imaginative and theological vacuum. Vacuums do not cause anything. Rather, vacuums are empty spaces that are quickly filled with other things. Not surprisingly then we Evangelicals sate that hunger-for-beauty vacuum, that our attention must go toward something dynamic in church with substitutes: pastors as heroes, or worship bands as superstars. Outside of churchly space, we fill our beauty vacuums with items from pop culture, historical artifacts,

Introduction

antique furniture, trophies from our travels, the latest fashion fads, or even national symbols. Personally, I'm not against the collection of display of any of those things. (Please, Christians need not only have or collect "Christian" art!) It's just that we do not think of or appreciate or speak together about the beauty in our lives either as a blessing from God himself or as a way to bless God and others.

Concerning beauty, we have a stunted theological vocabulary. Beauty is not a regular feature of our daily conversation. Beauty is not woven into the lyrics of our churchly music. Beauty is not integrated into our life and thought and prayer as Christians. My argument here, again, is that we Evangelicals do not know how to talk, think, or live for beauty in the affirmative. We do not have a vocabulary that roots beauty in and through our daily lives as Christians.

Our vocabularic stuntedness is one thing, but our prejudicial attitude is another. Evangelicals seemingly have a theological bias against beauty.[2] We are afraid beauty will distract from God's word, preached or written; as will be shown in our chapter on the Reformation, that fear has historic, if unevenly understood, roots. We worry that beauty will become an idol; as our chapter on Gregory of Nyssa will reveal, that worry has ancient Christian historic roots. We shudder to think that beauty—merely a matter of "personal preference" as we believe it is, something addressed in our chapter on Immanuel Kant—might deter people from the more important matters of life: preaching the gospel, developing Christian character, ethics, justice, and communal responsibility. I am going to suggest, both implicitly and explicitly through the theologians surveyed herein, that all of those "weighty" matters are even more important, more truly themselves, more accurately understood, and more deeply loved and thus eagerly embraced, when beauty is folded into their mixture. Beauty is indeed a spice of life; beauty makes absolutely everything better. Yet, beauty is more than mere spice.

Beauty stems indirectly but purposefully from the very being of God. Yes, God is truth and light and life and love. But God himself is beautiful. Beauty exists because God exists. *Beauty is an oversplash of God's glory and love.* As such beauty whispers to us something about God. It reminds us that God loves to share. Beauty, spilling onto the simplest of creatures, tells

---

2. The Roman Catholic theologian Balthasar calls us out on this: "Contemporary Protestant theology nowhere deals with the beautiful as a theological category." Balthasar, *Seeing the Form*, 55.

us that God is not a glory hog. Truly, God enjoys our enjoyment of his beautiful creation. If Genesis is correct, God made the entire cosmos for us! God exuberantly surrounds us with beauty almost every single day, if only we will train our eyes, or our mind's eye, to see it and celebrate it. Beauty is God's way of saying, "There is so much more. This life is sometimes wonderful, but in me there is always more." Beauty is regularly present, but *only for him who has eyes to see*.

And that, too, is part of the Evangelical problem: we have not trained our eyes to see beauty. In truth, as William James once argued, our eyes require more than mere seeing.[3] We need to know how to look, and for what to look. Our seeing itself is pre-shaped by our outlook on life, and some outlooks are more prone to recognizing and appreciating beauty than others. For instance, frequently beauty is subtle; we can travel right past it every day and miss its tender greeting. Beauty is unusual to our Western, rational souls precisely because the human perception of it is innate. We often feel it before we know how to articulate its presence. Yes, for some personality types, apparently trained from birth to be sensitive toward it, beauty gives deep joy. But for many Evangelical Christians beauty is not on our horizon precisely because it is less rational, or what I prefer to call *a-rational*: that quality which is decidedly indifferent to whether something makes sense. The a-rational in life is not predisposed against reason. The a-rational is not in a fight with reason! Yet, the a-rational elements of life just are not bothered to make immediate sense. Here are just a few things that don't make immediate logical sense about Christianity:

- God is both three and one
- the eternal God became finite in Jesus
- the fountain-of-life God died in and as Christ Jesus
- each of us gains eternal life by dying to our former selves
- we are asked to cast our future and our entire identity on a God we cannot see
- God the Holy Spirit prays through us to God
- we can pray to God by speaking in unknown tongues

Each of those truths are resolutely biblical, but they only make sense after we give ourselves to the "theo-logic," to quote Balthasar, the logic which

---

3. James, *Principles of Psychology*, vol. 1, 443.

Introduction

ultimately transcends and frequently defies human logic, the logic of biblical revelation, or simultaneously of that which stems from God's own being. The same is true with how we view beauty: we need some theo-logic.

And yet beauty doesn't seem to concern herself with making logical sense. Frankly, sometimes her appearance at odd times is nonsensical! True, we can touch upon beauty with our words; I mean to do that in this study. Yet, beauty smiles without any defensive challenge toward her friend reason. Reason too is a God-given gift but beauty delights in not being imprisoned by reason. Beauty—that a-rational, elusive, peaceful, delightful, mysteriously oversplashing quality present in so many things, people, and places around us—is frequently free from reason, even though she has no war with reason.

The human nervous system structured the way it is, we often feel things profoundly faster than we can think about them. My contention is that we feel or intuit beauty before we know how to process or explain it. Beauty, because it is usually perceived before understood, can leap into our souls faster than we can reason or reflect upon it.[4] Rationalists may not like beauty for that very cause: it is more felt than analyzed. Rationalists, God bless us, want to understand. Contrastingly, beauty frequently defies logic. Consistently, beauty eludes analytic certitude. Myself, I am a Pentecostal. Raised to be mindful of the presence and leading of the Holy Spirit, Pentecostals value intuition. We know the Holy Spirit can communicate with our souls in a-rational ways: he can speak to our hearts, give us dreams and visions, and even emotively motivate us to do good works. Nevertheless, for all that intuitive awareness, we Pentecostals too are sadly stunted when it comes to our vocabulary and sensitivity to the presence of beauty.

Oriented to words—itself a marvelous proclivity that has grown from the Reformation's emphasis on reading the Bible and listening to sermons—our Evangelical souls are rather icy toward the warm embrace of beauty. We don't understand it, or don't want to understand it, so for generations on end we have taught ourselves that beauty is unimportant. We are like horses with blinders on; we have excellent direct-ahead foveal vision, but no peripheral vision. The problem is that beauty frequently comes to us from the peripheries, from the fringes of our awareness, so to speak. With foveal vision we look directly and narrowly forward to see the details of

---

4. Nemoianu, "An Appreciative review of Peter Kivy," 445–47. Our perception as innate and beauty as leaping were taken from page 446. My thanks to Jerry Camery-Hoggat, my fellow colleague at Vanguard University for this lead.

life. Foveal vision enables us to read books and think in reasoned ways. Less direct than foveal vision, peripheral vision makes us sensitive to the more nuanced matters of life. Beauty often comes to us from the edges, the less-direct places in life. But if we haven't trained our peripheral vision, or perhaps more accurately if we have not trained our intuition, we will only be able to perceive what's directly ahead.

Beauty invites. She never forces herself upon the human will. Praise God for truth and goodness, beauty's two other ancient sisters! But both goodness (ethics, morals, behavior) and truth (philosophy, science, engineering, accordance with life) can be very coercive, very overpowering. For example, good deeds can win over people's hearts and attitudes even when performed by ill-motivated government officials. Or to offer a personal example, when I was an eleven-year-old boy, the thrown softball that hit me square in the temple both knocked me onto the outfield grass and stung whether or not I had previously believed the truth that it would do so! Truth can hurt. Goodness and truth constantly have an either-or effect to their presence. The good can shape us even when we are not aware of it. Truth naturally pierces and divides even though many assume that truth is always beneficial. Beauty is a different kind of gift. Beauty, even though she can be overwhelming and even euphoric, consistently comes in peace.

And so, for me, beauty is a cause of both wonder and gratitude. How can something so profound be so peaceful? How can something that so marvelously fills me with hope have been so freely offered? How can something so transfixing daily surround me?

We do not perceive life from either nowhere or everywhere. All people "do" life from somewhere, from some time-bound, geographically situated, acculturated, linguistically informed, and world view-anchored vista. Christians, or so this historical theologian believes, ought to perceive life from, in, and through the God of their salvation. Still more carefully put, following Jesus Christ is not just a means to an end. God did not simply give us his Son so that when we die we can go to heaven (thank you, Father, for the hope of heaven!). Being a Christian is about all of life. This Christian way is not a private affair. (Private Christians were called "heretics"—alone ones—by the ancient church.) Private Christians unwittingly are practicing their faith in un-Christian ways. Being a theologian, or even being theologically minded, is about taking all of life and assessing that through the revelation of God. And that reception, that assessment, should include beauty.

Introduction

At a minimum I want Evangelicals to declare a truce with beauty. I want us to stop being so suspicious of beauty. But I hope for far more: *that we open our souls to beauty's presence, and that precisely as an offering from God*. As our chapters on Augustine, Edwards, and Balthasar will exemplify, beauty can beautify. If we will allow beauty into our way of being—and not just into our churchly space—and especially if we will allow beauty to serve as a signpost, a down payment, and a love offering from the triune God we ourselves may be beautified. On the lookout for beauty we can become aware of life's delicate matters. Aware that beauty may just be around the corner we can train our souls to be open to life's complexities, joys, and surprises. God is a transcendent God: he towers above and beyond our creation. Yet, he is so transcendent that he delights to shine in and through his creation. Our souls open to the beauty of God, we may find ourselves more alive, more full of peace, and therefore able to in turn offer the life and peace of Christ to others.

And that sentiment begs still further qualification. Aware that discussions about embracing and celebrating beauty can make one seem like a flight-of-fancy thinker, or a butterflies and daisies empath, I want the reader to understand my own biases. My own greatest theological commitment is to the triune God: Father, Son, and Holy Spirit. This God has revealed himself in history. Most preeminently, that same living God sent his fierce-yet-peaceful Son to rescue, redeem, and restore both those whom will be saved and with them the entire earth. The authoritative treasure store of that historical revelation is the Bible, a collection of holy-if-earthy documents that are inspired of the Holy Spirit, the continually abiding presence of God who both lives inside a believer's innermost self and who sustains our every breath of life. In short, I affirm the collective wisdom of the church's confession of the eternally wise God. In that light, I am not seeking to supplant the long-standing theological categories of truth, goodness, grace, redemption, or holiness with beauty. I'm not arguing that beauty should trump love, though the two are inextricably woven. Beauty does not save. Only Christ does. Yet, as the chapters on Evdokimov and Balthasar especially will exclaim, Christ himself is beautiful.

And so I write first to share the insights of some of church history's most formative theologians, but also to encourage the injection of beauty into our collective Christian imagination, world view, and action. We will be more effective in our grand mission, not less, for embracing beauty. Yes, beauty can be elusive. Yes, beauty is hard to describe and harder still to frame in some intellectual way. But my belief is that if Evangelicals perceived beauty as a godly attribute, if we could see that beauty is most accurately perceived from—not against—a biblical world view, we would more readily incorporate its presence into our daily lives, our sacred worship, and our gospel service.

In this study we will survey four Protestants: Martin Luther, Huldrich Zwingli, John Calvin, and Jonathan Edwards. Three Eastern Orthodox will be examined: Gregory of Nyssa, Pseudo-Dionysius, and Paul Evdokimov. We will also survey three Roman Catholics: Augustine, Thomas Aquinas, and Hans Urs von Balthasar. And because he so profoundly changed the aesthetic game, we will study Immanuel Kant, himself representing the dawn of a muted Christian take or even an agnostic perspective within Christendom, and a subjectivizing turn. Modernity, and with it now postmodernity, still have not recovered from Kant's "eye of the beholder" position.

In order to denote some historical flashes of theo-aesthetic reflection I will follow a chronological order, but in the chapter surveys herein I do not force these theologians to fit either my own questions or some preconceived theological system. I also do not at all presume any kind of development of aesthetic theology over the centuries; there is no continuous progression of theologians who reflect on beauty.[5] What I do herein is arrange the chapters around the three broad rubrics of God's beauty, the beauty of or made by humankind, and nature's beauty; after all, we consistently encounter beauty in those categories. Yet, I have diligently sought to allow each theologian to speak about beauty as he desired. There were times when I was surprised by the perspective of one of our theologians. Frequently I was delighted in how a theologian wove beauty into his perception of a given rubric. All along I myself learned deeply about beauty and the ways it appears in both life and in theology.

The reader should know this book is chiefly about visual beauty. There is almost no effort herein toward analyzing a theologian's literary or poetic quality, although frequently I found myself being moved by a thinker's prose. It also deserves clarifying that my first interest is to learn how these eminent theologians framed beauty. In other words, I wanted to learn about the lenses, the theological means of filtering beauty from our chosen theologians. There will be little examination of how a theologian's thoroughgoing system or systemization was itself inherently beautiful. Similarly, I will not compare how perspectives vary between beauty through

---

5. Cf. Balthasar, *Clerical Styles*, 20–22.

Introduction

creational versus christological versus eschatological lenses. Beauty comes to us multi-formed so I am happy to consider it herein from varied and multi-formed Christian theological perspectives. Again, as a committed Christian disciple, I believe beauty makes the most sense inside a biblically informed and theologically cast world view, but this study is no comparison of theological systems and their ability to most accurately perceive, describe, and celebrate beauty. In all of this, the reader may decide on my accuracy and assessment of each theologian. The same is true of what I offer to Christians for whom beauty is mostly a foreign category; they may decide if what is suggested aligns or not with a fitting vision of God and his creation.

2

Gregory of Nyssa (c. 330–395)
The Beauty of the Infinite God

CHRISTIANS HAVE USED ART in their worship for some eighteen hundred years. The catacombs[1] in the outskirts of Rome reveal that Jesus' Gentile followers painted religious artwork in the places where they buried their dead, and held occasional worship services, at least as early as the end of the second century.[2] While it is true that history's early Christians did not build church buildings as such until around the year AD 230,[3] archaeology

---

1. Paul Evdokimov, *The Art of the Icon*, 173, notes that the biblical art in the catacombs was of three kinds: 1) water signs, such as Noah's Ark, Jonah, Moses, the fish, and anchors; 2) bread and wine signs, such as the multiplication of bread; 3) salvation signs and signs that refer to saved persons like Daniel.

2. Sister Charles-Murray, "Art and the Early Church," 303. Margaret R. Miles argues that the Gentile Christian use of imagery was not a break from earlier Jewish Christian practices. Historical evidence suggests that the second commandment against the use of images was not understood as entirely forbidding imagery, even in first-century Judaism. It was accepted that art could be used in non-idolatrous ways. Miles, *Image as Insight*, 43–44.

3. Rodney Stark argues that it was not until the third century that the Christians as a group began to feel safe enough that they could build public structures without opprobrium. Stark, *The Rise of Christianity*. Prior to AD 200 Christians were not a large or influential enough collective presence to challenge the politico-religious power or architectural dominance of Rome. Krautheimer, *Early Christian and Byzantine Architecture*, 24. Constantine's blessing of the Church in AD 315 provided new opportunities for Christianization. Before Constantine, "Christianity had left no visible trace in Rome," but after he legitimized Christianity, "the leading features of Constantinian church building

shows that ancient believers decorated their private dwellings and physical worship spaces with different biblical symbols representing Jesus—arks, shepherds, lambs, loaves of bread, and fish; over time ancient Christians also took pre-existing themes from pagan culture and "Christianized" those.[4] Theirs was not artwork for the sake of evangelism, rather it was to shape, inform, and reinforce an understanding of their invigorating new way of life.[5] So then, in the first couple centuries, whereas many church leaders, most famously the Latin father Tertullian (c. AD 160–225), were opposed to the use of images because images abounded in pagan religion;[6] Christians were nevertheless immediately making biblically themed art following the apostolic era. In part, they made and used art for spiritual reasons; they were competing for people's souls. In part, they wanted to be diligent to secure people's allegiance to Christianity through images.[7] And yet, careful reflection on beauty and aesthetics took a few centuries to burst forth. Why the discursive dearth? Why the lacuna concerning an element of human existence—beauty—that is central to so many cultures?

[were] hugeness, a simple plan and exterior, and a gorgeous interior" wherein churches were "flooded with light, filled with beautiful and precious tapestries, vessels, sculptures, and decorations." Krautheimer, *Rome*, 18–19. Miles, in *Image as Insight* 45, reasons that said churches "designed for maximal visual engagement" were soon filled with worshippers, and that such structures were built with the approval of church leaders.

4. Among these were included peacocks as symbols of eternal life, palm leaves as symbolizing Christ's victory on the cross and the Christian's salvation, and goldfinches as symbols of Christ's passion and resurrection. See Ferguson, *Signs and Symbols in Christian Art*.

5. Timothy Potts wrote, "Before being objects of beauty or admiration, Early Christian images were expressions of faith." "Director's Foreword" in Spier, ed., *Picturing the Bible*, xii.

6. Barasch, *Icon*, 113–16. Tertullian, in a way that influenced much subsequent Western formulation, interpreted Old Testament passages prohibiting images to preclude all art and image, not just that about God. Barasch, 115, notes that Tertullian even believed that it was the devil, not God, who invented the artist. In Exodus 20 and Deuteronomy 5 God prohibits making images, but the context pertains to the worship of said images. Barasch, 14–20, believes that these passages in specific are, like the Old Testament in general, characterized by ambiguity about images. He also reveals that debates about images predated the Bible. In Greco-Roman antiquity there was also divergence on images, some believing those conveyed the god portrayed with possibility of miraculous benefit and others believing that wood or stone were always only wood and stone and never a locus for a god. By way of contrast, the great theo-aesthetic giant, Han Urs von Balthasar, a figure whom we cover in a chapter herein, believed the Old and New Testaments clearly ban the use of images. Balthasar, *Seeing the Form*, 40.

7. Phillips, *The Reformation of Images*, 11.

For Him Who Has Eyes to See

Certainly this absence of reflection on beauty is not due to scriptural portrayals. The Bible itself, besides being a stunning collection of glorious—if also poignantly earthy—literature, variously celebrates the beauties of God, physical creation, and human existence. There are several direct examples in this regard. The beauty and goodness of God's creative handiwork are emphasized (Gen 1 and 2). There are descriptions of beauty regarding the Jewish community's heartfelt construction of the tabernacle (Exod 35–40), followed by the richly detailed and elaborate accoutrements of the temple (1 Kgs 5–7, 1 Chr 28–29, 2 Chr 2–7); strikingly, Moses's sanctuary (Exod 25:8–9), the ark of the Covenant (Ex. 35:34–5), and Solomon's temple (1 Chr 28:19) are all built with design and beauty following God's own directions. We should not miss the point regarding those Jewish worship sites: they were meant to be locations for a visual experience of the holy.[8] The Psalms repeatedly note that God and his beauteous workmanship are a cause of rejoicing and prayerful reflection (27:4; 50:2; 96:11–13; 104:24–34). Jesus commented on the simple beauty of God's creative and providential enterprise, "even Solomon in all his glory was not clothed like one of these [lilies]" (Matt 6:29–30). Later, he let us in on something of the kingdom's impending beauty when he said, "the Son of Man will come in his glory and he will sit on his glorious throne" (Matt 25:31). And the Revelation, rife with Jewish apocalyptic symbolism, isn't the least embarrassed to describe both Jesus himself (1:12–16; 19:11–16; 22:1–2) and the eschaton (21–22:6) in categories bursting with beauty. All this to say, the centuries-later iconoclastic (Orthodox and Protestant) impulses to the contrary, the Bible is not against beauty or beauty's use; it *is* against turning anything into an idol.[9] The pagan world of Christian antiquity was replete with tactile images that were worshipped as gods, and so biblical prohibitions against idolatry were formative on the early Christian imagination.

And yet the primary reason the first Christian generations overlooked beauty in their theological and spiritual writings is simple: they had bigger fish to fry. In scattered places across the Roman Empire they were enduring severe persecution; that heart-wrenching challenge led to all manner of practical questions and pastoral crucibles to be resolved. In more peaceful times literate Christians spent their energies building apologetic bridges to the truths they discerned in Greek philosophy; they were evangelistically minded and wanted to show the glory of Christ to anyone who would stop,

---

8. This visual emphasis is decisively made by von Balthasar, *Seeing the Form*, 325.

9. E.g., Exod 20:4–6; Lev 19:4; 1 Cor 10:14; 1 John 5:21.

discern, and turn. Questions outside the Lordship of Christ, his divinity, his salvific ability, and God's redemptive action in history[10] were largely relegated to the back shelf. The time for reflection on beauty would have to wait for a different context.[11] Moreover, beauty did not pose a philosophical problem for the early Christians. "There is no major controversy about divine beauty in the early church; so there is no need for the Fathers to reach maximal clarity."[12]

We see the dawning of relational interface between theology and beauty with Gregory of Nyssa.[13] Together with his brother Basil and his friend Gregory of Nazianzus, Gregory is known as one of the three Cappadocians: Eastern empire developers and defenders of Trinitarian theology. Their insistence on the simultaneous threeness and oneness of God was victorious at the Council of Constantinople (AD 381), a gathering of bishops where the Nyssan was regarded as a leading theological authority.[14] Less pronounced across Christian history have been Gregory's reflections upon beauty. This disconnect is interesting precisely because his Trinitarian reflections were based upon a certain aesthetic understanding of God. Robert Payne summarized Gregory's perspective: "to the end he persisted

---

10. Incidentally, these questions and lines of thought were precisely what led the Christians to discern and develop Trinitarian theology. It is very difficult to read the New Testament and not see that God converses with, works together with, and relates to himself as Father, Son, and Holy Spirit. It was not Greek philosophy, but the apostolic witness, that gave rise to Trinitarian doctrine. True enough, that doctrine was subsequently developed using categories and terminology from Greek philosophy, but it is critical to understand the historical context and development.

11. Stephen Gero's understanding is that "No theological consensus evolved for, or against, image-worship during the patristic period." Gero, "Byzantine Iconoclasm and the Failure of a Medieval Reformation," 51. This parallels Judaism of the same era: "A review of the Talmudic (rabbinic) commentaries of the Greco-Roman period suggests that the Jews did not, in fact, believe that pictorial images were necessarily idolatrous." Spier, ed., *Picturing the Bible*, 3. By the fourth century many early Christian suspicions against arts were laid to rest. By the sixth century Christian images were being treated much like relics: both were understood as implements to help bridge the gap between sense and spirit. Phillips, *The Reformation of Images*, 3.

12. Louie, *The Beauty of the Triune God*, 21.

13. Gregory was not the first leader to reflect on beauty. Earlier fathers like Justin Martyr, Hippolytus, Clement of Alexandria, Origen, Tertullian, and Irenaeus had touched upon images and beauty. Spier clarifies about those fathers, "Some modern scholars have assigned to the Early Christian theologians an antipathy, or even hostility, to the visual arts, but careful interpretation of their work suggests that this supposed hostility has been exaggerated." *Picturing the Bible*, 4.

14. Copleston, *A History of Philosophy*, book 1, vol. 2, 31–32.

in seeing all things in the mirror of God, a mirror of crystal purity, tenuous and dazzling."[15] For Gregory, God was nothing if he was not beautiful.

Born into a privileged Christian family in Cappadocia (modern-day Turkey), Gregory was educated by his intensely devout older sister, Macrina, and then later by his older brother, Basil the Great, Bishop of Caesarea.[16] Not much is specifically known about Gregory's schooling, but his own writings manifest a vast knowledge about then regnant contemporary philosophy; like many of the educated Christians of the Roman Empire he thought it made sense to employ Greek philosophy to elucidate truth, even though it was finally God's revelation that held authority over human reasoning. A man of his own historic context, Gregory clearly had read Plato, the Stoics, the Jewish Neoplatonist author Plotinus, and the Alexandrian theologian, Origen. Some twentieth-century scholars accuse Gregory of too readily repeating the ideas of Greek philosophers.[17] More recently, however, there is consensus that Gregory was taking Greek philosophical terms and categories and filling them with new meaning.[18] This recontextualizing method is particularly evident in Gregory's theology concerning God and creation and the doctrine of the image of God—two ever interrelated themes that the Nyssan interweaves with beauty and to which we now turn.

GOD AND CREATION

Among Westerners today there are broad assumptions about the Judeo-Christian God. Many folks who don't follow Jesus Christ know that "God," even vaguely stated, is eternal, omnipresent, and holy.[19] Put in ridiculously

---

15. Payne, *The Holy Fire*, 137.

16. Kannengiesser, "The Spiritual Message of the Great Fathers," 62.

17. Campenhausen, *The Fathers of the Greek Church*, 115–25. Adolf von Harnack, *History of Dogma* (1897) also read the early church fathers as having too readily capitulated to Hellenistic categories.

18. Particularly I follow the interpretations of David Bentley Hart, *The Beauty of the Infinite*; Morwenna Ludlow, *Gregory of Nyssa*; and eds. Lucas Francisco Mateo-Seco and Guilio Maspero, *The Brill Dictionary of Gregory of Nyssa*. It was first Jean Daniélou in *Platonisme et Théologie Mystique* who argued that Gregory should be seen as a man who related to his context in the language of his day but who nevertheless remained committed to biblical categories.

19. Stereotypically, many tend to think of him primarily as a judge who zealously waits to condemn every "sinner"; this portrayal stems from a truncated churchly witness

Gregory of Nyssa (c. 330–395)

simple terms, many contemporary Western citizens would agree that the Christian God is a big God; he's not a human being, he's greater than the earth and its weather patterns, he's larger even than the universe. What Westerners do not imagine much, if at all, is that *God is himself beautiful*. Gregory of Nyssa did envision that, and did so on the basis of God's own infinite nature. It is critical that we understand at least a summary of the philosophical tradition that Gregory inherited if we are to understand how unique and nuanced he was on God being both creator and beautiful.

Neoplatonism, a philosophical body of thought that had evolved prior to Gregory's era, had envisioned the whole of reality in dualistic fashion: there are material things and then there is the absolute One that made them, but those are not the same. The logic worked like this: the One and all the separate things cannot be ultimately the same; if they are the same then there truthfully are no real distinctions in life. Envisioning that everything was ultimately One was terribly difficult to maintain since it defied everyday experience. People knew that canaries were not artichokes, and that artichokes were not people, and that persons were not themselves the Absolute One. In short, a seamless pantheism was a postulation breaking with people's everyday experience. Moreover, it was just too fantastic to believe that the One directly caused the things themselves to exist. The One, Plato had taught, was far beyond materiality. Materiality was characterized by constant change, and constant change led to dissolution and collapse, and those in turn led to death; the transcendent and perfect One was not, and could not be, sullied with a connection to materiality.[20] And, the logic continues, since materiality/matter is the furthest emanation away from the One,[21] and since matter is most prone to change, alteration, and collapse,

---

about God's holiness. Conversely, many are prone to conceptualize God primarily as a divine butler who exists mostly to make people happy and ease life's travails; that goes to the church's syrupy witness regarding God's love.

20. One wonders, at the psychological level, did belief in the constancy, the immutability, of the absolute One offer some tidbit of hope in a transient, collapsing, and disease-ridden existence?

21. *Stanford Encyclopedia of Philosophy*: "The causality of the One was frequently explained in antiquity as an answer to the question, 'How do we derive a many from the One?' Although the answer provided by Plotinus and by other Neoplatonists is sometimes expressed in the language of 'emanation,' it is very easy to mistake this for what it is not. It is not intended to indicate either a temporal process or the unpacking or separating of a potentially complex unity. Rather, the derivation was understood in terms of atemporal ontological dependence."

matter then is viewed as problematic and even the principle of evil itself.[22] The One was beyond the universe, not immanent. The One was infinite, but whereas that infinity was characterized by limitless plenitude and simplicity it was also perfectly static and unmoving, since movement implied change that in turn implied imperfection.[23] After some five centuries that traditional stream of logic was ensconced in the world view of those who thought using Greek categories.

Modifying Plato's own scheme, the founder of Neoplatonism,[24] Plotinus (d. AD 270), reasoned that the One, an entity beyond being itself[25] had emanated—a metaphor to suggest a mysterious putting forward—*Nous* or "Intellect." Variegated as Thought or Mind or Beauty, *Nous* is the source of all particular forms and distinctions in the universe. *Nous* is not itself the One but is expelled from the One like rays which issue forth from the sun all the while without diminishing the sun, or is like the reflection of a face in a mirror that does not thereby diminish the face. Next Plotinus posited that out of *Nous* proceeded the World-Soul. Itself without physicality or division, the World-Soul is the bridge, the connecting link, between the spiritual world of the One-and-*Nous* and the material world of the universe. (It might be helpful if grossly simplistic to hold that *Nous*, through the World-Soul, did the physical-material work for the One.) Plotinus could neither stomach the possibility of creation *ex nihilo* (entirely out of nothing) on the part of the One nor could he accept a simple monistic pantheism, where the One directly caused existence or is thoroughly all existence. Both creation *ex nihilo* and monistic pantheism would imply change in the One, alternately named the Good. Thus, Plotinus, following in Plato's wake, wrought a kind of sophisticated pantheism, one that he believed accounted for the

---

22. Copleston, *A History of Philosophy*, book 1, vol. 2, 464–70.

23. Hart, *The Beauty of the Infinite*, 151.

24. Sometimes Neo-Platonism is alternately called Mystical Platonism. Cf. Thomas Hopko, "The Trinity in the Cappadocians," 261, following the lead of Jean Daniélou. Historians first coined the phrase Neo-Platonism in the early nineteenth century as a way to help understand the succession of Western thought. *Stanford Encyclopedia of Philosophy*, http://plato.stanford.edu/entries/plotinus/.

25. Plotinus did not believe either that the One (the first god, as he called it) was conscious or thought thoughts, since both of those would imply change: consciousness would mean it could distinguish itself from itself and thereby be limited, and thinking would mean that it didn't think and then it did, again implying change. The One, for Plotinus, is beyond being but it is not nothing. Copleston, *The History of Philosophy*, book 1, vol. 1, 465; see also Bernard McGinn, *The Foundations of Mysticism*, vol. 1 of *The Presence of God*, 49–51.

Gregory of Nyssa (c. 330–395)

distinctions in life between spirit and matter, without the former being an immediate cause of the latter.[26]

Envisioning reality thus, we would expect Plotinus to have viewed reality as rather drab. After all, if the One is so transcendent that it is both beyond matter and removed from human experience, what delight could it elicit in human hearts? Or, if physicality and materiality are mired in evil and viewed contemptuously for their constant change what joy might their beauty finally evoke? Remarkably, Plotinus appreciated beauty and goodness in everyday life because he saw those stemming from the cosmos' unity and harmony. Frederick Copleston notes that that is an intriguing disconnect from the intrinsic logic of Plotinus' own position,[27] but then the history of human thought is ever remarkable in its ability to ignore lacunae, leaps of logic, and obvious fallacies.

A FRAMING FORAY: WHY SUCH DISDAIN FOR PHYSICALITY?

One of the constants of both Greek philosophy and some of the Eastern religions is the broadly held view that physicality/materiality is a tremendous and vexing problem, if not the very human problem itself. Plato (427–342 BC) believed in reincarnation and longed for the soul's eventual and final return to the spiritual and transcendent One. Hinduism (1500 BC) seeks not only to be finally delivered from physical existence, an existence repeating itself in a cyclic reincarnational fashion, but from existence altogether. Similarly, Buddhists yearn for nirvana: an euphoric blowing out, a cessation of existence that brings final peace. The Buddha (d. 483 BC) sought neither rebirth nor an eternal heavenly existence, but nonexistence.[28] Why this widespread human mistrust, disdain, and disgust concerning physicality?

To ask that question very much locates us as people of our own historical era. We Westerners enjoy the benefits of anesthesia—to my mind, the greatest of all human inventions, next to television digital recorders—and antibiotics, electric and hydraulic and combustion engine powers, soap, labor and delivery rooms, clean running tap water in our homes, vaccines, x-rays, MRIs, dentists, lab technicians, access to clean and healthy food, and

26. Copleston, *A History of Philosophy*, book 1, vol. 1, 467, notes that contemporary philosophers might not agree with Plotinus hereon.

27. Ibid., 470.

28. Prothero, *God Is Not One*, on Hinduism 136–39, Buddhism 171–77.

a myriad of specialty doctors. As of 2011 in the United States the average expected mortality rate at birth for men was age 76.3 and for women was 81.1.[29] True, we've all suffered and we all know friends and family who've suffered greatly, but compared to the bulk of humans who've lived through history we flourish in health.

Contrastingly, in Jesus of Nazareth's era, some 300–500 years *after* the advents of Greek philosophy and Buddhism, in the Roman Empire the average mortality rate at birth was less than thirty years; that atop the brutal percentage who died in childbirth.[30] Reasons for these high death rates are varied but interrelated: life was septic. There were no sewer systems. This meant that human waste had to be carried away in buckets or on carts, when it wasn't simply thrown into a pile or left in a ditch in the road. People who lived in the higher levels of tenement buildings would not uncommonly dump their chamber pots out the window onto the street rather than make the arduous trek out to the sewer pit. No wonder cities often emitted a putrid stench. Not surprisingly, this unsanitary situation affected water usage. In *some* ancient Roman cities water was piped to fountains and to public buildings and baths, and some of the rich even had piped water in their homes. But for most urban dwellers the water was often contaminated, especially since it often came from underground cisterns. K. D. White said, "untreated water . . . when left stagnant, encourages the growth of algae and other organisms, rendering the water malodorous, unpalatable, and after a time, undrinkable."[31] Furthermore, the non-rich had to carry their water home in jugs; given the laborious nature of hauling water it is not likely that much of it was used for scrubbing floors or washing clothes or bathing; this increased the unsanitary quality of life.

Stemming from their view of human flesh, care of bodies following death was uneven. Jews and Christians did bury their dead, but lower-class Romans frequently dumped bodies outside of cities. Sometimes families would burn their deceased relatives but it was not uncommon that they would be discarded in and alongside roads. We can only imagine how this

---

29. *National Vital Statistics Reports*, Volume 61, Number 6, "Deaths: Preliminary Data for 2011." The U.S. Center for Disease Control and Prevention. This is the most recent posting from the CDC.

30. Stark, *The Rise of Christianity*, 155. Infants died at a brutal rate. Stark, 160, estimates that at a city like Antioch of Syria would have had an infant mortality rate of near 50 percent.

31. Ibid., 152–53, quoting K. D. White, *Greek and Roman Technology*, 168.

would have attracted flies, mosquitoes, and other vermin, and how this would intensify the grotesque ancient living conditions.

The majority of the urban populace packed into apartment buildings, structures that were hard to heat. Similarly, cooking was difficult and was done with crude wood or charcoal braziers. Windows were closed from the external air by hanging cloths or animal skins across openings in the wooden walls. And, because these apartments lacked chimneys, the rooms were always smoky in winter. Folks were careful to manage the airflow in and out their crude windows so as not to asphyxiate themselves. The danger in this, though, was that the drafts could cause a fire. "Dread of fire was an obsession among the rich and poor alike."[32] Added to this ill-formed matrix, people shared their living quarters with livestock, including horses and oxen. Because of this tremendous overcrowding, it seems very likely that most people spent most of their days at the public spaces, and only used their tenements to sleep and store possessions.

"Ordinary life under any circumstances was often cruel, plagued by epidemics, unrelieved pain, and constant uncertainties about life itself. Many essential tasks were painfully difficult and time-consuming."[33] So wrote historian George Marsden about eighteenth-century America at a time—some 1,450 years after Gregory's own era—when the Enlightenment was underway! Lacking what we contemporaries would consider even a shambled medical capacity, ancient people were commonly disfigured by accidents, maladies, physical violence, and life's hardships. The cities were not infrequently overridden with crime and rioting. Life in the country had its own struggles: hardship concerning food production and familial protection; marauders, bandits, and armies could trample one's crops and wipe out one's family. We could go on by describing the physical and life-style effects of epidemics and natural disasters, but the point is that life was brutal, ugly, and commonly disgusting.[34]

That brief foray in mind, we can sympathize with people who reflected on life's meaning and purpose—people who like us would wonder what it all meant, and who in reductionistic fashion saw materiality and physicality as themselves the primary evils confronting existence. Viewing the everyday languishing, brokenness, and handicap of human existence they understandably could conclude, in geographic and cultural contexts that were

---

32. See Stark, *Rise of Christianity*, 151.
33. Marsden, *Jonathan Edwards*, 3.
34. Stark, *The Rise of Christianity*, 147–62.

separate and quite diverse, that the physical-material quality of life is something one finally wants to escape. It was into that context that Christianity was birthed. With its doctrines of the goodness of physical creation, the enfleshment of God himself, the shameful crucifixion as God's very means of salvation, and the resurrection as the grand telos for creation, Christianity surely looked like "foolishness to Gentiles" (1 Cor 1:23) and a cause of derision among Athenian philosophers (Acts 17:32). Biblical teachings on physicality and materiality flew in the face of established Greek philosophy, and that held true 300 years after Jesus into Gregory of Nyssa's era.

In understanding the biblical world view and the resurrection of Jesus Christ, we must see that Christianity, though opposed to *worldliness* (sinfulness and idolatry), is a *this-world–affirming* religion. Sincere is the far-reaching piety that slogans, "this world is not my home," or "we're all just'a passing through," or which prays, "Come, Lord Jesus and deliver us from this sinful existence." Well-intended, that piety is affectively directed toward the things of God, but it is nevertheless theologically problematic because it variously denies the goodness of God's creation, God's love for his creation, and the Holy Spirit's eschatological aim of resurrection and more than restoration in the pattern of Jesus' own resurrection and more than restoration.[35] Put simply, God does not intend on abandoning his creation but redeeming it![36] True beauty, God's beauty, does not abandon physicality, it loves it for its own sake as his own, the handiwork of God.

Gregory of Nyssa inherited Plotinus's philosophic pastiche and was so familiar with it that he could dialogue with it as a first language. Indeed, he so regularly writes using Neoplatonic terms and categories that many historical theologians believe he was simply another Neoplatonist himself. However, Gregory took that framework and injected biblical teachings

---

35. See Gregory's *On the Holy Spirit*, 23 (per Hopko, "The Trinity in the Cappadocians," 273. Gregory called the Spirit the kingdom of God).

36. Resurrection is not simply restoration. The New Testament shows that the resurrection implies both continuity and discontinuity with what went before. After his resurrection Jesus was still Jesus, but he was transformed. He exhibited a mysterious ontological capacity (Mark 16:12; Luke 24:30–31), one moving toward glorification (John 20:14–29). Paul makes several analogies to express this continuity-and-discontinuity dynamic (1 Cor 15:35–55). The Revelation (21) looks for the new heavens and the new earth, that is the existing heavens and earth made brand new; "Behold, I am making all things new," 21:5 (NASB). For a vivid unpacking of this theme read Wright, *Surprised by Hope*.

therein in such a way as to produce a new and fresh vista.[37] Gregory was a person who knew that beauty mattered. Working a theo-aesthetic formulation that would rarely be equaled in Christian thought, Gregory agreed with antiquity's values on beauty. He was "not simply indulging [himself] in [his] portraiture of beauty." Gregory was one who "sensed that beauty was the soul of the real."[38]

Against Neoplatonist formulations Gregory argued creation *ex nihilo*: God created all there is from absolutely nothing. Paul Evdokimov, restating patristic teaching, said, "Nothing existed outside of God, not even an empty space outside of God."[39] Rather, Genesis 1:1, 3 says, "In the beginning God created the heavens and the earth. . . . then God said, 'Let there be light,' and there was light." Matter was not coeternal with God (the One), as Aristotle had argued. Matter was not preexistent. Matter did not emanate across a spiritual-to-material bridge, as Plato and Plotinus argued. Gregory knew the Scriptures do not worry about "protecting" God from materiality. It was God, not an intermediary, who "formed man of dust from the ground, and breathed into his nostrils the breath of life" (Gen 2:7). Gregory knew biblical logic teaches that in the beginning there was only God, and after he spoke there was *other than* God. With Neoplatonism Gregory agreed that the One—God—was utterly transcendent: he is before and above and beyond all being. God infinitely exceeds all human ability to describe him or attain to knowledge of him; God's essence is a mystery that is finally both "inconceivable and incomprehensible."[40] Certainly, we can know important things about God owing to his self-revelation, but that leaves us forever away from knowing God exhaustively. In his treatise *On Virginity* Gregory wrote that although the created world exudes beauty we must be careful in not equating that beauty to God's own. King David had, in a state of "blessed ecstasy" granted by God's Spirit,

> glimpsed God's infinite and incomprehensible beauty. He saw as much as a mere mortal can see, leaving the covering of the flesh, and by thought alone entering into contemplation of that immaterial

---

37. The Eastern/Greek fathers of the church did this on a constant basis. John Meyendorff held that this contextualization of Hellenic philosophy with Christian theology is what makes the Fathers to be the Fathers, the ones who blessed the future church with philosophically penetrating, intellectually sturdy, and abiding theology. Meyendorff, *Catholicity and the Church*, 79.

38. O'Donohue, *Beauty*, 39–40.

39. Evdokimov, *The Art of the Icon*, 101.

40. Hopko, "The Trinity in the Cappadocians," 262.

and spiritual realm. And though yearning to say something which would do justice to his vision, he can only cry out (in words that all can echo after him): *Every man is a liar* (Ps 115:11). And I take this to mean that anyone who attempts to portray that ineffable Light in language *is* truly *a liar*—not because of any abhorrence of truth, but merely because of the infirmity of his explanation.[41]

Gregory was convinced on the transcendence of God, and still, Gregory knew, this transcendent and eternal one himself deigned to create and deigned to allow other to freely exist as other. Why is this? Because God is good. We saw above that Plotinus alternately called the finally transcendent entity the One, or the Good, but Plotinus's One does not deal with or relate to the physical realm. In an enormous shift, Gregory has the good one—God himself—creating, sustaining, and loving his creation. The Bible regularly describes God as good. In the Septuagint, the version of the Bible that Gregory read, *kalos* appears 236 times, *agathos* appears 548 times, and in the New Testament both terms appear 102 times each.[42] Gregory, following sustained biblical teaching, understood that what God created is good because God is himself good. God is the archetype of beauty and the essence of beauty, but God didn't cling to that beauty as his sole possession, something to be guarded. God unselfishly shared that because it is God's nature to love.

Paul the apostle wrote about a profound humility that characterized the second person of the Trinity, Jesus Christ, "who, although He existed in the form of God, did not regard equality with God a thing to be grasped, but emptied [*ekenosen*] Himself, taking the form of a bond-servant, and being made in the likeness of men" (Phil 2:6–7). The whole of Greogry's subsequent Eastern Orthodox tradition emphasizes the self-emptying, the letting go, the *kenosis*, that God's Son voluntary underwent for the purposes of the Father. Often the Christian East speaks hereon of the condescension of God: he came down to our level in order to raise us up to his level, he was "obedient to the point of death . . . on a cross . . . that at the name of Jesus every . . . tongue should confess that Jesus is Lord," (2:8–11).[43] David Bentley Hart, working from Gregory's theology, rightly believes that this

---

41. Gregory of Nyssa, *Song of Songs*, 105, original italics.

42. Ramelli, "Good/Beauty."

43. Athanasius (296–373) is particularly famous for having written, "He was made man that we might become god." "The Incarnation of the Word of God," 54, in *Patrologiae Cursus Completus, Series Graecae* (hereafter cited as *PG*).

self-giving is evinced in God's free act of creation: God lovingly, tenderly, and generously created others to exist, and to exist freely, even such that it could say no to God.[44] "The self-emptying of God in his creature is not a passage from what he is to what he is not, but a gracious condescension by which the infinite is pleased to truly disclose and express itself in one instance of the finite." Elsewhere Hart noted, "God's power is manifest most profoundly in the Son's *kenosis* because God's power is the infinite peace of an eternal venture of love, the divine ecstasy whose fullness is the joy of an eternal self-outpouring."[45]

By speaking God created out of his abundant self. Creation, rather than a second- or third-tier dimension in a lessening hierarchy of existence, is itself an expression of God's bounty. This is a substantial divergence not only from Neoplatonism but also with different Eastern and Western pantheisms. Rather than apologize for physicality or materiality, Gregory held that creation's glory stems from God's glory, indeed it participates in God's glory. Beauty is not merely the result of the universe's harmony, nor is it some vague gestalt of matter interacting with Plato's unseen forms. Beauty isn't necessitated by the existence of the One that indirectly emanates the material realm.[46] Rather, beauty is really and truly present in each creature's existence and form; every creature, every plant, and every physical thing has its own beauty. But it is a beauty that is *given freely* from the living God. The nuance cannot be missed here: God created beings, the universe, people, and nature to exist as other-than-him even though he sustains their every movement and breath. God is not the universe for Gregory. Instead, God joyously brought and brings the universe to be out of nothing; that act in itself is beautiful, but the creation itself exhibits beauty too. Yes! Life *is* beautiful, but life is so because the infinite and ineffable God has made himself known as the supremely good one, the ineffably beautiful one. This good God, this beautiful God wants to share his delight with creation in a participatory manner.

To express this participatory interplay, this mutual relationship, Gregory used music as an analogy. The first true music is God's Wisdom, God's Logos: a song God sings and which sings back to himself, as himself, the second person of the Trinity.[47] Music is a powerful analogy because whereas

---

44. Hart, *The Beauty of the Infinite*, 247.
45. Ibid., 357, see also 323.
46. Ibid., 191.
47. Neoplatonism's bridge, the World-Soul, is replaced by Gregory with the New

one can hear music, be moved by its motion, melodies, and harmonies, it is consistently mysterious to describe. So it is also between God and his creatures; we can feel him, sense him, and know full well that he is among us, and yet putting that into words is toilsome, indeed. And still the cosmos's beauty is itself a kind of music that expresses the music of God's own self. Hart put it eloquently, "Creation . . . is a song" full of rhythm and diversity and motion that sings back to the "archetypal music," God himself. People, too, "are music moved to music."[48]

> According to Gregory of Nyssa, creation is a wonderfully wrought hymn to the power of the Almighty: the order of the universe is a kind of musical harmony, richly and multifariously toned, guided by an inward rhythm and accord, pervaded by an essential "symphony" the melody and cadence of the cosmic elements in their intermingling sing of God's glory, as does the interrelation of motion and rest within created things; and in this sympathy of all things one with the other, music in its truest and most perfect form is bodied forth.[49]

Very carefully stated, creation does not *add to* God but is *an expression of* God's superabundance. "True beauty," Hart asserted,

> is not the idea of the beautiful, a static archetype in the "mind" of God, but is an infinite "music," drama, art, completed in—but never "bounded" by—the termless dynamism of the Trinity's life. . . . God is boundless, and so is never a boundary; his music possesses the richness of every transition, interval, measure, variation—all dancing and delight. And because he is beautiful, being abounds with difference: shape, variety, manifold relation.[50]

And, to continue unpacking Gregory's complex views, there is interplay between God and creation, and beings and beings, and creatures and creatures, precisely because God himself is characterized by interplay. God is a Trinity. This, too, is a remarkable divergence from Neoplatonism with its static and singular absolute deity.

Testament's outlandish (to Greek philosophers) but nuanced teaching on the Son of God as Logos: God created in and through his Logos, with the Logos as the source and aim of creation.

48. Hart, *The Beauty of the Infinite*, 194–95.
49. Ibid., 194–95, 275, referencing Gregory's *In Inscriptiones Psalmorum*, 1.3:3–33.
50. Ibid., 177.

Gregory of Nyssa (c. 330–395)

Neoplatonism envisioned the material world as a shadow of the spiritual world. In that ancient Greek outlook there were enormous distinctions between the One and physicality, distinctions only traversed by emanations. This harmonized with people's general disdain for physicality. By way of contrast in the kind of perspective which the Nyssan developed Christianity was, Hart exclaims, "an undeniable assault upon pagan values: a certain Jewish subversion, a rejoicing in the order of creation as gift and blessing, an inability to grow too weary of the flesh, and abiding sense of the sheer weightiness—*kabod*—of God's glory and the goodness of all that is."[51] This goodness, this beauty, is given by God, extended into physical existence because God himself is an active giver. Again, this portrayal of God as an active God, a God who creates, sustains, and is invested in creation's direction and eventual future *omega* is completely biblical yet divergent from Greek philosophy. For contemporary Christians Gregory's portrayal of God as creator, sustainer, and eschatological redeemer may seem obvious, but that is precisely because we benefit from the insights of Gregory and many other theologians like him. Truly, as Didacus Stella put it in the first century, "Pygmies on the shoulders of giants can see farther than the giants themselves." Today we benefit from nineteen hundred years of theological reflection. Because of Gregory of Nyssa we can see more of the beauty of God in life, if we are willing and if we are looking.

THE DOCTRINE OF THE IMAGE OF GOD

What makes people most like God? Our faculty for language? Our creativity? Our altruistic ability? Many Western theologians who followed in Augustine's psychologizing path (see our next chapter) said it was our intellectual capacity. Gregory said it is our free will.[52] Of all earth's creatures we can choose. Gregory echoed Aristotle's position that we become like the things that we love. This ability *to become* is an innate element of the image of God. In fact, Gregory was renowned for emphasizing the doctrine of the image of God. Compared to the bulk of the much later Protestant tradition—one that followed Augustine's total depravity constructs—Gregory's anthropology was very optimistic. Fully aware of the Bible's teaching on human sinfulness, he nevertheless did not emphasize our essential fallenness nearly to the extent that Western theologians do. This more optimistic

---

51. Ibid., 107.
52. On this point I follow Daniélou, ed., in *From Glory to Glory*, 12.

perspective stems from his ardent commitment to humanity having been created in God's image. Near the end of his life, in his *Commentary on The Song of Songs*, Gregory poetically wrote that God created humankind to shine forth God in a manner that surpasses the sun, the moon, and the whole created universe. Indeed, Gregory added about man, "nothing in creation can equal your grandeur."[53]

To early twenty-first-century Western secular eyes a claim like that is outlandish. Increasingly, we are taught that we are just animals; we are more sophisticated animals to be sure, but in the end we are simply electrochemically charged matter that will one day return to the stardust of our origins. Gregory would have none of that. Committed to the biblical world view, Gregory was adamant that we are unique. Yet he was careful. We are not unique owing to our own doing. We have no immediate claim to self-induced exalted capabilities. Gregory was a theologian: he related everything in life to God's own self. It follows that we are powerfully capable of either magnificent knowledge or insidious evil because of what God did when he made us: he granted us free will. We are not merely the products of our genealogy, our DNA, or our culturally constructed realities. *We can choose.* (Later Eastern Orthodox theologians will aver that God thus took a risk when he created: we might not choose God's own self.)[54] God's gift of free will makes possible an ability to have a genuinely loving relationship with both God and others. Gregory put it like this:

> Human nature is in fact like a mirror, and it takes on different appearances according to the impressions of free will. If gold is held up to the mirror, the mirror assumes the appearance of gold and reflects the splendor of gold's substance. If anything abominable is held up, its ugliness is impressed on the mirror—for example a frog, toad, centipede, or anything unpleasant to behold. Thus, the mirror represents in its own being whatever is placed before it. So too the soul, when cleansed by the Word from vice, it receives within itself the sun's orb and shines with this reflected light. Therefore, the Word says to his bride: "You have become beautiful by approaching my light; by drawing near to me, you have

---

53. Ibid., 162.

54. Ware, *The Orthodox Way*. Ware said, "Without freedom there would be no sin," said Ware, "but without freedom . . . man would not be capable of entering into communion with God in a relationship of love" (58–59).

Gregory of Nyssa (c. 330–395)

attained communion with my beauty." "Behold, you are fair, my companion."[55]

We can become evil or we can become good, but we have a choice.

Centuries after Gregory Eastern Orthodox theologians will make much of the two Hebrew synonyms "image" and "likeness" (*selem* and *demut*, Gen 1:26). They will argue that image implies potentiality and that likeness implies realization. Their argument runs that God made people uniquely to reflect him, all while he gave us the ability to do so more and more; this allows for process and sustains the Eastern Orthodox doctrine of *theosis*: that we can, by the grace of God, become like God. Gregory did not argue his position on the basis of a specific theological interpretation of image and likeness.[56] His argument is more simply psychological: free will makes us become like that which we choose. We are in fact mirrors: we reflect that to which we attend. When we attend to purity, we become pure. When we attend to owning things we become covetous. But what we choose to focus upon is our own choice. We are free to choose our own focus. Again, this is very optimistic (Augustine, and later Martin Luther, held that the unrighteous cannot help but choose unrighteousness) but it is repeated in Gregory's teachings.

What then of beauty? Here's where Gregory made an enormous shift away from the Neoplatonist philosophical heritage of his day. As noted above, change was a profound problem for ancient Greek philosophers. Daniélou noted, "For the Platonist, change is a defect; and the intelligible world is superior to the world of the senses insofar as it is immutable." Change implied imperfection, inconsistency, and eventual collapse. Gregory, committed as he was to the biblical narratives, argued conversely that change was *precisely* what it meant to be a creature. Only God is eternal and eternally perfect. As finite creatures with physical bodies, *we must change*. But still more carefully Gregory argued that change can occur for the ill or change can occur for the good.[57] Human beings are not animals. We are indeed, by God's intention, capable of moving toward God's own self. "What

---

55. Gregory of Nyssa, *Song of Songs*, 92.

56. Daniélou, *From Glory to Glory*, 10. David L. Balas, "Deification," 210–13, in *The Brill Dictionary of Gregory of Nyssa*, notes that Gregory cautiously used the terminology about deification/divinization because he was too committed to the distinction between created being and uncreated being.

57. Following the same kind of logic, and also in dialogue with Neoplatonism, Pseudo-Dionysius will argue that limits and finitude are not themselves evil. Cf. Balthasar, *Clerical Styles*, 194–96.

appears so terrifying (I mean the mutability of our nature)," argued Gregory, "can really be a pinion in our flight towards higher things, and indeed it would be a hardship if we were not susceptible of the sort of change which is towards the better."[58] The beauty in this is that we can be transformed "'from glory to glory' [2 Cor 3:18], and thus always improving and ever becoming more perfect by daily growth, and never arriving at any limit of perfection. For that perfection consists in our never stopping our growth in good, never circumscribing our perfection by any limitation." "Perfection is progress itself," Daniélou interacted with Gregory, "the perfect man is the one who continually makes progress. And this cannot have a limit." The beginning of acquiring the good "is merely the beginning of a new acquisition. In this way, the notion of change, which is essential to the human condition, can take on a wholly positive aspect."[59] Hart summarized, "for Gregory change is simply constitutive of created nature.... if it ceased to change it would cease to exist."[60] To encapsulate, free will enables change for the good. We ought be careful here; Gregory did not argue that people can save themselves—only the grace of God through Jesus Christ brings us into relationship with the living God. And yet, free will, this profound God-given capacity to choose and interact with life and then change for the good, enables a process that makes transformation become a God-blessed enterprise. We should see the beauty in this both because God wants us to change, to become more virtuous and more like himself, and because our becoming like him will make us more beautiful.

This progress in the soul's beauty Gregory likens unto creation itself. In the beginning God did not take preexistent matter and shape it into the universe. He spoke it into existence. It was not and then it was. This bringing into being, this act of calling to be out of nothing is creation, *ktisis*: an absolute beginning. Similarly, God did new things across the sweep of salvation history, things stemming from his infinite possibility to transform and renew. And just as creation had a beginning, Gregory taught that each person has new and absolute beginnings, seasons and trajectories that take new paths from the former new seasons and trajectories. Besides taking the former Neoplatonist worry about change leading to collapse and overturning it, this becomes a vision of hope and beauty for the believer. God is not stuck in the past, even though he builds on his past works of redemption

---

58. Quoted in Daniélou, *From Glory to Glory*, 51.
59. *On Perfection* (PG 46.285B-C), quoted in Daniélou, *From Glory to Glory*, 51–53.
60. Hart, *The Beauty of the Infinite*, 189.

and transformation. God is ever drawing us to the next season, the next beautiful appropriation of grace and goodness in our lives. This moves us from theology to spirituality (not that those two are ever distinct for the Nyssan), from ideas about reality into a whole way of life. For Gregory, this whole way of life involved an ever-increasing form of hunger.

Only a few years after Gregory's death and hundreds of miles away in Egypt Augustine of Hippo (AD 354–430) will famously write, "Thou has formed us for thyself, and our hearts our ever restless till they rest in Thee."[61] Gregory believed similarly that we were made expressly for God, and that we find meaning and satisfaction in God, but he made a critical shift because he believed we would *never be finally satisfied*. The logic of such a position seemingly would indicate a dynamic of perpetual aggravation but Gregory saw it as a beautiful dynamic rooted in the infinity of God's own glorious self. Stated more precisely, *each new resting in God would produce still more hunger for God*. God implanted in the human self a desire that corresponds to God's own infinite self; this is not a prison of ongoing frustration, it is a beautiful relationship of joy, one open to giving and receiving that will continue into eternity.[62] On this dynamic Gregory loved to quote the Apostle Paul, "If anyone supposes that he knows anything, he has not yet known as he ought to know" (1 Cor 8:2), and "We all, with unveiled face beholding as in a mirror the glory of the Lord, are being transformed into the same image from glory to glory, just as from the Lord, the Spirit" (2 Cor 3:18), and again, "I do not regard myself as having laid hold of it yet; but one thing I do: forgetting what lies behind and reaching forward to what lies ahead, I press on toward the goal . . ." (Phil 3:13). In each of these verses Gregory understood Paul to be touching upon and teaching the notion of eternal growth, *epektasis,* in and toward Christ. Prior to Gregory *epektasis* meant "straining forward," "tension," and "expansion."[63] In his own teaching the Nyssan believed that God was himself boundless and since that is true we can never exhaust him! If God is infinite how could we ever deplete our relationship to and with him? Gregory reasoned that "every desire for the Beautiful which draws us on in this ascent is intensified by the soul's very progress toward it. And this is the real meaning of seeing God: never to have this desire satisfied." For Gregory the theologian, visible things suggest

---

61. *Confessions*, 1.1. Augustine wrote the *Confessions* between 397 and 398. Gregory wrote his Commentary on the *Song of Songs* in the late 380s or early 390s.

62. Hart, *The Beauty of the Infinite*, 288.

63. Daniélou, *From Glory to Glory*, 57. Cf. Sherry, *Spirit and Beauty*, 157.

invisible things, and both should make us hungry to always see still more. And yet in the end, "no limit can be set to our progress towards God: first of all, because no limitation can be put upon the beautiful, and secondly because the increase in our desire for the beautiful cannot be stopped by any sense of satisfaction."[64]

God is the beautiful one who is "ever more beautiful," who imparts beauty to his creation.[65] On into eternity and into the eternal One, we will always want more and more of God. In his teaching on *epektasis* Gregory posits eternal tensions between seeing and not seeing, knowing and not knowing, apprehending but always pursuing. Each stage suggests both delight and the yearning for more.

> One who gazes at that divine and infinite Beauty, since what appears each time is more surprising and wonderful than what has already been seen, admires what appears each time, and his or her desire to see never ceases, because what is expected is surely more magnificent and divine than what has already been seen.[66]

Had he the opportunity the Nyssan might have taken Augustine's "our hearts are ever restless till they rest in Thee," and edited it to say, "our hearts are ever filled and then starved again as we are drawn to Thee, O unbounded and beautiful One." In Gregory's spiritual theology, we will always be becoming more like God, ourselves being stretched out in an eternal tension wherein stages of growth are followed by more growth, of beauty surpassed by still more beauty! This is not an eternal cycle of repetitive quicksand within which we remain stuck; rather, it is a path that constantly drives us higher and higher into the infinite reaches of God's beauteous love. "God becomes ever more intimate and ever more distant."[67]

Gregory did not word it so, but his ideas hereon make room for imagining how our resurrected eternal life in God will always be new. Each new chapter of growth after God's own self will make us more capable of moving on to the next chapter, each new beautiful discovery opens up the possibility of yet another beautiful discovery, each new surge of divine love through our hearts and minds will expand our capacity to know and be

---

64. Gregory, *The Life of Moses* (397D–405A), quoted in Daniélou, *From Glory to Glory*, 147–48.

65. Hart, *The Beauty of the Infinite*, 188.

66. Gregory, *Song of Songs*, 11, quoted in Ramelli, "Good/Beauty" in *The Brill Dictionary*, 362.

67. Daniélou, *From Glory to Glory*, 54.

known (1 Cor 13:12) in the eternal and infinite love that is the Trinity. To personalize this, over past decades I have dearly loved hiking California's High Sierras with my father-in-law, Dennis McNutt. Every trail is its own adventure. One is constantly yearning to see what is up around the next chiseled-granite bend, one delights in the fresh-aired trek toward the next beautiful vista. Applying Gregory's concept of *epektasis* to that analogy, our own existential-spiritual-resurrected mountain hike won't be increasingly beautiful simply because there will always be more of Christ Jesus into the future (which there will be), but because one will, with ever perfected ability owing to one's relational knowledge of God, be able to more acutely discern and appreciate God, to constantly be seeing, experiencing, and sensing more of God *where one is*. One will see more beauty in the beautiful One than in previous stages, one will know deeper love than one did in times prior. The newness, the *kainos*, is always replacing the past with what is new, while not denigrating or rejecting what went before.[68]

In the next life the beatific vision will be, Gregory asserted, a ceaseless and ecstatic experience of God's own endless love and delight. But we can enjoy something of that vision now through, among other ways,[69] enjoying and celebrating God's goodness and beauty. Thus, for the Nyssan, beauty is a means of participation in the glory and gift of God himself, though God's essence is eternally beyond our capacity to understand or possess. In his *Song of Songs Commentary* Gregory links divine beauty to human yearning. Children, Gregory notes, are attracted to beautiful trinkets. For instance, the beauty of gold chains and flowers, "draws the child by yearning and desire to participate in the good. The description of beauty somehow attracts the desire of the young to what is shown, fanning their desire for a participation in beauty." The goal of this participation is neither crassly for the sake of experience nor does Gregory equate such participation as a one-for-one with salvation. Instead, participation in God's beauty is a means of

---

68. Ibid., 59, noted, "Thus each stage is important: it is, as Gregory says, a 'glory'; but the brilliance of each stage is always being obscured by the new 'glory' that is constantly rising. So too the sun of the new creation, the New Testament, obscures the brightness of that first sun, the Old Law. . . . And yet this is by no means to depreciate the value of each particular stage—all are good, all are stages of perfection. But the mistake would be to try to hold on to any one of them, to put a stop to the movement of the soul. For sin is ultimately a refusal to grow." On *kainos* see Bauer, *A Greek-English Lexicon of the New Testament*, 394.

69. Gregory noted many means of a sharing participation in and with God: prayer, practicing virtue, receiving the mysteries (a.k.a. sacraments), living in/as the church, becoming like God through Jesus Christ.

shaping and training the soul. This sharing, this participation is an avenue for moving into the wisdom, righteousness, and goodness of God.

At more mundane levels Gregory enjoyed good literary prose and had an eye for the beauty of nature.[70] He appreciated good Christian art, remarking once that "he could not contemplate a particular depiction of the sacrifice of Abraham without tears."[71] He looked for beauty and paid attention to beauty.

> The river Halys gleams like a ribbon of gold through a deep purple robe, and scarlet sand is washed down from the bank to touch the river with redness. High up lie the oak-crowned ridges of the hills, all green, and worthy of some Homer to sing their praises; and as the oaks wander down the slopes they meet the saplings planted by men. All over the foothills are vines, some green, others ripe with grape clusters. Here at Vanota the fruit is ripe, but it is otherwise in the nearby villages. . . . Homer never saw the apple trees with such gleaming fruit as we have here, the apples themselves almost the color of the apple blossom, so white and shining. Have you ever seen pears as white as newly polished ivory? And what shall we say of the immense heaps of peaches? And what of the pathways beneath the climbing vines, and the sweet shade under the clusters of grapes, and the new wall where the roses climb and the vines trail and twist and form a kind of protecting fortress against invaders, and what about the pond which lies at the very top of the pathway and the fish that are bred there?[72]

Gregory appreciated the beauty of nature, but that paled in comparison to the beauty he both saw and yearned for in his soul, one that followed hard after God.

WRAP-UP

Physical, earthly beauty was meaningful for the Nyssan, but by and large his was an aesthetic of the spiritual, of the divine. The nuance here is subtle but significant: Gregory did not disdain physical or creaturely beauty but his constant and repeated emphasis is upon the beauty of God, or even more carefully the beauty of God which can be discerned. Umberto Eco

---

70. Mateo-Seco and Maspero, eds., "*Epistulae*," in *The Brill Dictionary of Gregory of Nyssa*, 272.

71. Miles, *Image as Insight*, 44.

72. *Epistulae* 15, VIII/2, PG 46, col. 1,000, as quoted in Payne, *The Holy Fire*, 142.

Gregory of Nyssa (c. 330–395)

notes that this preference for the divine over the material, the eternal over the finite, and the creator over the creature, is an ancient aesthetic that prevailed into the medieval period. Things were valued more for how they suggested the divine or for how they pointed to eternal significance more than for how they themselves were in themselves beautiful,[73] and this was true from classical Greek philosophy hundred of years before Christ into the thirteenth century. Our next theologian, Augustine, will be far more conflicted about the goodness and beauty of things in themselves than was Gregory.

WHAT GREGORY TEACHES US TO SEE:

- God himself is beautiful
- God is humble
- Creation *ex nihilo* is a beautiful doctrine and frames beauty as a gift
- Creation, as an expression of God's goodness and glory, is beautiful
- Creation is like a musical expression of God
- The image of God involves our ability to become and choose
- We will hunger, be satisfied, and hunger still again for God through eternity

---

73. Eco, *The Aesthetics of Thomas Aquinas*, 137–44.

3

Augustine of Hippo (c. 354–430)
Ascetic Wariness and Worries

SHOULD CHRISTIANS ENJOY BEAUTY? If so, how much aesthetic pleasure is healthy? If not, why not? Some of the most stringent historic opposition to the pleasure of beauty (*aesthesis*, in ancient Greek) has come from the realm of asceticism. From the Greek *askesis*, asceticism seeks to discipline the body for the sake of the higher good. The Apostle Paul presented a nascent Christian asceticism when he wrote, "I discipline my body and make it my slave, so that, after I have preached to others, I myself will not be disqualified" (1 Cor 9:27, *NAS*). Ascetics believe both that they are pursuing a better reality and that that pursuit often involves sacrifice. Most ascetics have defined and loved the beautiful according to their own values. Others have shunned both beauty and the beautiful as distractions at best; beauty, for them, must be sacrificed for the ultimate aim and that ultimate aim consistently involves the denial of the physical, bodily, material world of shapes and forms.

Most of the world esteems costly sacrifice. For example, through fasting and peaceable demonstration Mahatma Gandhi helped end the British Empire's grip over India. Martin Luther King Jr. showed an entire American generation that enormous social change can be wrought through peaceful and selfless civil resistance. On the personal level, over millennia billions of people around the world have esteemed the sacrifices of religious ascetics. In China there are myriad legends about the powers of Daoist *Xians*, ascetics who can cast magical spells, walk on water, and run at superhuman

Augustine of Hippo (c. 354–430)

speeds. Evangelicals often forget that Jesus himself was a great archetype for later Christian monastic practice: he remained a lifelong celibate, owned only a cloak, obeyed only God the Father, and died a martyr for his way of life. My own Evangelical students stood in awe and listened to a bearded thirty-something-year-old Greek Orthodox monk who, atop one of the limestone styla of Meteora in Greece, told them his personal story of being called to the monastic lifestyle. He was joyful to serve God in a centuries-old monastery that rested on only a few acres of an austere fingerlike peak of rock. Standing outside the monk's little soot-laden ancient Orthodox church, and with the populated valley far below, the students felt very constricted. In that rather claustrophobic context students in turn asked the monk, "Do you ever go down and visit family?" "Do they allow you to take vacations?" "Can you go somewhere else on retreat to study?" After pausing the monk answered matter-of-factly, "I will be on top of this rock until they carry my body off of it in a wooden box." The resulting silence was as thick as San Francisco fog; the students were stunned. They were awestruck at the prospect of having as one's vocation forty to fifty years of praying on the top of that limestone pillar. Truly, it's almost encoded in our DNA to respect those who suffer for what they believe. When sacrifice is variously tethered to belief in some higher good, or a rebellion against a perceived systemic evil, the allure of asceticism is quite dramatic.

Why make that excursion into the ramifications of asceticism upon the collective human imagination? Because for more than 2,000 years now asceticism has had a profound impact upon Christian views of beauty. Christians of all stripes have been taught that beauty, especially religious beauty, is simply wasteful if not openly idolatrous. (The irony is that we often then turn to secular forms of beauty for our enjoyment. How is that less problematic?)[1] If we are luxuriating in nature's beauty, or admiring the fine arts, or marveling the symmetry, muscular structure, and curves of human bodies we may even feel a twinge of guilt. Shouldn't Christians be *in* but *not of* the world? Truly, those anti-positions owe more to asceticism than they do to biblical teaching. One aim of this book is to assert this maxim: *Christianity is a this-world–affirming religion.* Jesus came to save the world—he didn't come to save us *from* the world. But let us not rush ahead.

Enter Aurelius Augustine. He knew what it meant to be an ascetic. Not only was asceticism widespread among both Greek philosophers and

---

1. For a penetrating critique of this dynamic see Ugolnik, *The Illuminating Icon.*

Christians in his day,[2] as a young man he converted to Manicheaism, a syncretistic pastiche of Christian teaching, Middle Eastern practice, and Greek philosophy. The Manichees, vegans who practiced fasting, variously prayed daily prescribed prayers, prohibited marriage, and espoused that the human body was evil while the soul/spirit was good;[3] the latter classic dualism. At first, a young man from North Africa (today's Algeria), Augustine was attracted to this way of spiritual and ascetic life. Manicheaism's dualistic teachings were rather black and white and this accorded with Augustine's yearning for certitude. Understanding Manicheaism's world view made him feel superior, lofty even. And yet, across his nine years as a Manichee member, Augustine became disenchanted. Augustine eventually was conflicted about their teachings and his own spiritual state. He prayed, "Lord, give me chastity and continence: but not now." He enjoyed his sexual promiscuity and even had a son with his first concubine. When finally he had a conversation with a Manichean bishop, Faustus, he realized that that religion was not his answer.[4] Subsequently he studied skepticism, then Neoplatonism, and still later when he met Bishop Ambrose of Milan, he converted to Christianity.[5]

Augustine had a superb memory and was a true genius.[6] Given his own less-than-stellar education in North Africa (his early education consisted of rote memorization of Latin authors), the sparse access he had to Greek philosophers (he had not read Aristotle),[7] and his lack of biblical languages (he knew neither Greek nor Hebrew), it is simply amazing how prodigious a theologian he became. All that he wrote and wrought he did so with a pastor's heart; it is likely he preached more than 8,000 sermons,

---

2. It was a Mediterranean-wide phenomenon to practice strict ascetic renunciation in the pursuit of reason. Wills, *Saint Augustine*, 48.

3. Brown, *Augustine of Hippo*, 50–1. Cf. *Catholic Encyclopedia*, "Manichaeism."

4. Brown, *Augustine of Hippo*, 46–59.

5. Scholars dispute whether his initial conversion to Christianity was to Christ or Neoplatonic versions of Christianized philosophy. There is no question he eventually and decidedly understood himself to be a Christ-follower, though his resulting theology was framed in and for a Neoplatonic context. Rist sums it well, saying "Augustine's work is framed [but] not constituted by social conditions." *Augustine*, 11.

6. Jenson, *The Triune Identity*, 116: "His personal, spiritual and intellectual experience impressed themselves on Western theology in a way unparalleled in Christian history."

7. Rist: "In the late twentieth century we know more about the thought of Plato, Aristotle and Plotinus and the Stoics than [Augustine] did." *Augustine*, 1.

Augustine of Hippo (c. 354–430)

only 546 of which we possess.[8] Later Christians will love him for his piercing introspective bent, one that moves deeply into the devotional life. Across the centuries many theologians, especially in the Reformed tradition, will follow variously Augustine's theology on God's immutability and sovereignty, his psychologizing trinitarian model, his emphasis on grace across the Christian life, and his understandings about salvific election.[9] His brilliant mind coupled with his burning heart for Christ served to make him the most influential theologian in Christian history. McGinn pictured Augustine's influence thus: "Alfred North Whitehead once described the history of Western philosophy as a series of footnotes to Plato. It would be no less true an exaggeration to say that the history of Western Christian theology is a series of footnotes to Augustine."[10] Because he is so influential we will examine Augustine on ascetic views, creation, music, the beautification of the human soul, and God as beauty.

AUGUSTINE'S CHRISTIANITY VIS-À-VIS GREEK PHILOSOPHIC ASCETIC VIEWS

We should be accurate: it is not that all non-Christian ancient Greek asceticism was opposed to beauty, per se. We noted this before, but each ascetic or ascetic philosophy would define beauty differently. Still, what was rather constant was asceticism's opposition to physicality in general, and sensuality (i.e., the enjoyment of sensory experience and sexuality) in particular, as noted in our chapter on the Nyssan. The logic is not difficult; if physicality and sensuality are problematic then so will earthly and physical beauty be problematic, if not openly disdained. And frankly, if there are little to no beautiful physical forms by which to establish perspectives on

---

8. Ibid., 4.

9. Truly remarkable are just some of the Christian traditions and teachings that stem from Augustine: the wisdom of praying before preaching, the performative role of Scripture, Eden as a place of original perfection, the notion of hell as a perverted society, the belief that faithful Christian believers fill the void in heaven caused by the angelic fall, the (*massa damnata*) belief that the entire human race is now outside of Christ destined for hell and that before any personal sins occur, the church as the kingdom of God, the church as a mixture of both sincere and nominal believers, intercourse in marriage reserved for child-bearing alone, a federal understanding of Adam and the fall, theology about predestination, sacramental theological formation, an emphasis that love is God's great commandment, the necessity of God's revelation for knowledge about God, and that all people have a God-shaped hole in their hearts.

10. McGinn, *The Doctors of the Church*, 66.

beauty one will be hard pressed to suggest or describe just what is beauty. In other words, one could argue that love or justice or egalitarian community, because those include ennobling and dignifying aims, are beautiful theoretical categories. But one would still yearn to know how love, justice, or egalitarianism actually manifest in life. What does a loving act look like? If it cannot be beheld, what does justice mean? Egalitarian as modeled by whom, in what ways? This is not to denigrate the theoretical or merely intellectual, both of which, as will be shown, Augustine prized. It is to emphasize that we human beings are embodied selves. And that takes us to Augustine's theology.

Earlier we saw that Gregory of Nyssa in contrast to Neoplatonism believed that God created *ex nihilo*. Augustine averred similarly. Creation was neither an accident nor a Neoplatonic emanation of matter through *Nous* or World Spirit. Creation was God's intentional action, and it was an action that designed matter to be good. There is little in Augustine, writing in and for a Neoplatonic context as he did,[11] to suggest that matter is immediately evil. Indeed, Augustine once famously echoed The Wisdom of Solomon 11:24, "for He hates none of the things that He has made."[12] That God created matter is an affirmation of matter. Seven times God saw that his creation was "good" (Gen 1:4, 10, 12, 18, 21, 25, 31), indeed "very good" (1:31). Seven is the Hebrew number for perfection, completion, and maturity. Hence, creation was not merely sufficient or acceptable; God didn't finish and say, "well, that'll do." Good in Hebrew meant beneficial, pleasing, morally honorable, and beautiful. Hence, creation was thoroughly and completely good. Even more it was, God said, beautiful.

Many Evangelicals today narrowly understand Genesis's creation narratives as a counterargument to the doctrine of evolution. Whereas they read in Genesis that creation was intentionally designed, those same Christians frequently miss that matter and physicality were part of God's good plan. Unwittingly imbibing from centuries of ascetic evaluation, these believers can fail to see that physicality is not just a means to something better (e.g., relationship or eternal life), but that it is a very part of God's good design. In their sermonizing, contemporary Christian pastors and priests still fall prey to the Platonic understanding of flesh, as though it were itself

---

11. Brown, *Augustine*, 95, reasons that Augustine had so mastered Porphyry and Plotinus that Neoplatonic thought was "grafted almost imperceptibly into his writings as the ever present basis of his thought."

12. *Questions for Simplicianus*, I, 2:18, *The Essential Augustine*, 44–45.

physicality. Understood biblically, our bodies are not the problem even though we know that our bodies are beset with all kinds of problems! The Apostle Paul used "flesh," a pre-existing Greek philosophic category, to clarify by metaphor the struggles we Christians abidingly endure against the sinful appetite and the existential orientation that is opposed to God and godliness. For his part, Augustine knew that "flesh" is not a one-for-one with matter. He believed "flesh" was a result of a "prior sin of pride . . . a disorder brought on the mind by itself in its revolt against God"; it is thus both "a legacy and a choice."[13] (Sin is, Augustine believed in Platonic fashion, a negation of being, an ontological nothing that is nevertheless a powerful something; evil is a parasite that can only exist where there is being and goodness.)[14] For neither Paul nor Augustine was flesh synonymous with body. Yes, creation is infected, but it remains an expression of God's craftsmanship and goodness.

In a flourish of emotionally charged exclamation, Augustine attested to the beauty of God's good craftsmanship:

> How can I tell of the rest of creation, with all its beauty and utility, which the divine goodness has given to man to please his eye and serve his purposes, condemned though he is, and hurled into these labours and miseries? Shall I speak of the manifold and various loveliness of sky, and earth, and sea; of the plentiful supply and wonderful qualities of the light; of sun, moon, and stars; of the shade of trees; of the coulors and perfume of flowers; of the multitude of birds, all differing in plumage and in song; of the variety of animals, of which the smallest in size are often the most wonderful—the works of ants and bees astonishing us more than the bodies of whales? Shall I speak of the sea, which itself is so grand a spectacle, when it arrays itself as it were in vestures of various colours, now running through every shade of green, and again becoming purple or blue? It is not delightful to took at it in storm, and experience the soothing complacency which it inspires, by suggesting that we ourselves are not tossed and shipwrecked?[15]

He was well aware that God made these good things for us to enjoy and appreciate, and yet, true to his the-spiritual-is-greater-than-the-physical

---

13. Duffy, "Anthropology," 30.

14. Wills, *Saint Augustine*, 116. Bourke, *The Essential Augustine*, 43–4, summarized Augustine on evil as like unto a hole that is not made of something but which can be filled.

15. Augustine, *The City of God*, 854.

form, Augustine knew these things were but a foreshadowing of the things we will enjoy after the resurrection. Jeremy Begbie summed up Augustine hereon. There are

> suggestions that beauty is not so much something the world embodies as something toward which the world only directs us. Physical beauty is the lowest grade of beauty, being mixed up with many imperfections. We are urged to seek the beauty of the soul and the bodiless beauty that gives form to the mind and through which we judge actions to be beautiful. And above all we are directed toward the supreme beauty, that of God himself.[16]

In that perspective we see, compared to Greek philosophic-ascetic views, that Augustine's belief in creation *begins to open a view* whereby beauty can be perceived as radiating through the physical and material. He moves us down a path toward physical affirmation, but it is a struggle for him to do so.[17] A committed intellectual, Augustine preferred the intelligent and the spiritual over the physical and material. And yet he could enjoy the beauty of physicality for its own sake. In his last section of the *City of God*, Augustine expresses frequent delight and joy in the surprises of nature.[18] He knew that although a mother carries a fetus in her womb, it is God who brings the baby through gestation. It is God who fashioned the human person with both corporeal boundaries and spiritual qualities. Even a tiny insect, averred Augustine, "cannot be considered attentively without astonishment and without praising the creator."[19] In such instances nature's order pointed to God, the divine craftsman. Indeed, making a theological point that would be developed over the next two millennia, Augustine believed that creation was itself a book written without ink, a book that bore witness to God.[20]

---

16. Begbie, *Resounding Truth*, 86, where he references Gunton, "Creation and Re-creation," 1–19.

17. For example see his *Confessions*, 2.10, and 11.6 where he discusses the beauty of physical things like gold and silver that, being attractive though inferior, also can lead away from God's law.

18. Wills, *Saint Augustine*, 138.

19. Augustine, *The City of God*, book 23.24, p. 851.

20. Harrison, *Beauty and Revelation*, 120. Cf. Bourke, *The Essential Augustine*, 123–27. Augustine, however, was not studying things in any kind of scientific manner. Like the Greek philosophical milieu in which he lived and thought, Augustine tended to see all being as itself a testimony of God's existence, goodness, truth, and beauty. Cf. Eco, *Thomas Aquinas*, 137–44.

Augustine of Hippo (c. 354–430)

To relate everything in life to God is to do theology. I teach my own budding theology students to ask themselves, "how does God's existence and revelation bear upon the matter at hand?" Himself perceiving in theological ways, Augustine believed that physicality pointed to a more real ultimate reality: God himself. The secular-sacred dichotomy that has come to characterize how millions of Western Christians perceive everyday life was largely foreign to Augustine.[21] Because God was Creator, everything owed its existence to God and therefore was a sign of God's existence. The physical suggested the spiritual. Those two are not the same, but they are not dissected from one another either. Augustine immediately linked the body and soul:

> Moreover, even in the body, though it dies like that of the beasts, and is in many ways weaker than theirs, what goodness of God, what providence of the great Creator, is apparent! The organs of sense and the rest of the members, are not they so placed, the appearance, and form, and stature of the body as a whole, is it not so fashioned, as to indicate that it was made for the service of a reasonable soul? ... Assuredly no part of the body has been created for the sake of utility which does not also contribute something to its beauty.[22]

For Augustine, the spiritual shines through the material, even engracing the material in the doing. The material, for its part, is a locus, a pipeline for the spiritual.

Linking the physical to divine causation were, in Augustine's perspective, abstractions. These abstractions are dynamics and presences that exist but that must be perceived. More directly, all things have measure, weight, and number; indeed, it is those three that give physical things their constituent reality. "Measure assigns to all things their limit (*modus*), and number gives them form (*species*), and weight brings them to rest and stability (*ordo*)."[23] And yet, before the beginning of time (oxymoronic though that is) all there was was God. This meant for Augustine that these abstrac-

---

21. Though this did not make him unique for his day. Not only had Neoplatonists similarly construed reality along a varying spectrum of the spiritual pouring through the physical, so were the growing masses of everyday fourth-century Christian believers. Miles reveals that fourth-century Christian (churchly) paintings were already depicting the spiritual shining through everyday physical things and experiences. Miles, *Image as Insight*, 59–62.

22. Augustine, *City of God*, book 22.24, 853.

23. Harrison, *Beauty and Revelation*, 103.

tions—measure, weight, and number—all must have existed in the mind of God himself.[24] Indeed, measure points us to the measure without measure, number to that which cannot be numbered, weight to that which cannot be weighed: God.[25] Begbie noted, "In his commentary on the Genesis account of creation, Augustine repeatedly quotes the text from Wisdom of Solomon 11:20, 'But you have arranged all things by measure and number.'"[26] Following classical Greek philosophy in all of this, Augustine held that beauty was comprised of symmetry. Even more, numbers both reflected and participated in the wisdom of God, for Augustine.[27] At the mathematical level, beauty is thus a symmetry of well-proportioned numbers. Each physical entity, each being has its own series of numbers. Hence, the entire universe is characterized by a certain rationality. God, intellect itself, imbued the universe with reason. Reason and mathematics both sustain and reside beneath the beauty of everything. This brief mathematical overview of Augustine's theology not only shows us how piercing his own thought on creation was, it shows us that in fascinating ways he was foreshadowing later centuries and their theories of physics which similarly hold that the universe is a concert of numbers, beautifully aligned numbers within beautifully aligned formulae. Still more, Augustine, and those like him in Neoplatonic fashion, who argued that God's own ideas became physical things and beings, lay a foundation for the eventual birth of science itself. Scientists had to believe, and indeed must believe today, that the universe can be understood by the human mind if they are to spend any time or energy trying to understand it. The rational interconnectedness, if not the numeric interconnectedness, of the entire universe is itself a beautiful and staggering proposition.

While Augustine perceived the universe numerically he similarly understood it to be a great musical song. Indeed, Augustine held that music "derived from the eternal numbers which proceed from God himself."[28]

---

24. This numbers theme stems from Pythagoras (570–495 BC) who believed that a kind of mystical number system pervaded and sustained the universe. This understanding of numbers helped shape the world view into which Augustine was plunged. Later in church history churches and cathedrals will be built following very precise numeric patterns as a way to mirror the universe itself.

25. Harrison, *Beauty and Revelation*, 103. The threeness of measure, number and weight mirrored the Trinity, for Augustine. Cf. ibid., 101–10.

26. Begbie, *Resounding Truth*, 84.

27. Harrison, *Beauty and Revelation*, 106.

28. God was, for Augustine, "supreme measure, number, relation, harmony, unity and equality, and all manifestations and embodiments of music in the world are from

This is interesting not least because songs in Augustine's day were fairly simple. Except a doublet at the octave, the songs Augustine heard had only one melodic line; there were no mixed pitches or harmonies as we hear them today.[29] Even more, the use of instruments was not yet in use during Christian worship. In fact, instrumental music—because used in brothels, theaters, and pagan worship ceremonies—was frequently opposed by Christian leaders as a pagan and overly sensual form. And yet Augustine recognized something of the evocative and mysterious qualities of music. Music could lift us to God and suggest the eternal music that characterizes God himself. Conversely, deeply colored by his Greek ascetic pre-commitments, Augustine was wary that the five senses could "distract and weaken the soul."[30] *Music is therefore dangerous*; it so powerfully touches our auditory sense that it can deter us from the more important spiritual realities. Begbie clarifies that Augustine wrote about music used in worship "as a concession to weakness: words help the 'weaker mind rise up toward the devotion of worship.'" Anticipating future Christian pastoral concerns, Augustine "becomes adamant that music must serve texts: we sing so that 'the meaning of the words' can penetrate more deeply, and it is a 'sin-deserving punishment' if 'the music moves me more than the subject of the song.'"[31] The tussle is captured keenly when he writes, "I fluctuate between the danger of pleasure and the experience of the beneficent effect [of music]."[32] Augustine also knew the worshipper could be caught up in the worship music "without reference to its religious function." Music was thus a double-edged blade: it aided the worshipper and enhanced the worship experience, but could easily be a distraction.[33]

Whereas the doctrine of God's good creative act is foundational theology for our understandings of beauty, so also are Augustine's doctrines of the incarnation and the resurrection. As we noted above, physicality is not sinful per se. Instead, for Augustine sin causes human beings to become attached to our physical senses and our body, "rather than to the soul and

---

him." Begbie, *Resounding Truth*, 84.

29. Begbie further notes that in Augustine's day there was far more theorizing about music as a kind of mathematical consideration, and thus it was a technical rather than practical subject. *Resounding Truth*, 84.

30. Ibid., 83, 85.

31. Augustine, *Confessions*, 10.33.50, 53.

32. Begbie, *Resounding Truth*, 85.

33. Eco, *Thomas Aquinas*, 134.

reason." Balthasar wrote that Augustine exhibited a "personal nervousness" concerning "all sensible entities."[34] Sin perverts our interpretive ability: because we can only see from a limited and fallen perspective we mistake the parts for the whole. Augustine believed we too easily love things rather than that to which they point: God. Into this fallen, fractured, and infected existence God sent his Son. Some two centuries prior to Augustine, Irenaeus (c. 130–202) had developed a theology of recapitulation: God takes on fallen, broken, fractured, and diseased things specifically to redeem them. So, for instance, whereas a tree (of forbidden fruit) was the locus for our sinful fall, a tree (Golgotha's cross) was the locus for our salvation; or, if a woman (Eve) was culpable for original sin, then God recapitulated the order of things by involving a woman (Mary) in our salvation. Augustine echoed some of that recapitulationist theology when he held that in the incarnation, "Christ specifically assumed a disfigured human body in order to reform and heal it and restore the beauty which rightly belongs to it."[35] This gift of salvation—"the incarnation of the unchangeable Son of God"—is superior to the wisdom of the Neoplatonist philosophers. Those same philosophers, men who for philosophical reasons would have mocked the Christian doctrines of incarnation and resurrection,[36] assumed that only a few gifted intellectuals could attain salvation, but Augustine critiqued them for failing to see the incarnation as the "brightest example of grace!"[37]

It was not only creation *ex nihilo* that grounded Augustine's aesthetic. Harrison asserts that it was particularly the resurrection the prevented Augustine from embracing a Platonic dualism.[38] Plato hoped that we would one day escape our body, a prison for our soul. We human (from *humus*, dirt) beings will, Plato believed, after a 10,000-year cycle, get back our wings, wings that we lost when first we were entombed in physical bodies. Our souls, Plato averred, need to be reawakened to their spiritual state, and this reawakening can occur through philosophical study and contemplating beauty.[39] By way of contrast, Augustine knew that the resurrection,

---

34. Balthasar, *Clerical Styles*, 121.

35. Harrison, *Beauty and Revelation*, 43.

36. Brown, *Augustine*, 102. Brown, 98, reasons that Plotinus would have been comfortable with "In the beginning was the Word, and the Word was with God, and the Word was God." He could not have accepted "And the word became flesh."

37. *The City of God*, book 10.29, 335.

38. Harrison, *Beauty and Revelation*, 158–59.

39. McGinn, *The Foundations of Mysticism*, 28. This Platonic image remains staggeringly powerful today. I come across greeting cards and media posts about deceased

Augustine of Hippo (c. 354–430)

rather than implying escape from physicality, ultimately connotes the redemption of the entire human person, including one's body. In short, the resurrection is an astoundingly beautiful doctrine. Of all the world's religions only Christianity asserts that our ultimate hope is the eternal life of our physical bodies made new. In his *City of God* Augustine muses about all kinds of issues pertaining to the resurrection: it variously will involve both the righteous and the unrighteous, the redemption of our sexuality, and our age in the eschaton. Augustine even muses whether aborted babies and babies who die in infancy will be raised up, whether we still will have physical scars or deformities, and whether we will lose our unique personalities/individualities. Augustine is clear, the whole self will be resurrected, even our hair and fingernails. Even if the body is ground to powder in the grave God can resurrect it. Those who fail to comprehend this, he argues, fail to consider the omnipotence of God.[40] After the resurrection the human body will become a beautiful servant to the human spirit and all the body parts will glorify God.[41]

Augustine's theology on creation, incarnation, and resurrection shows a perspective that views physicality as frequently good, if troubled by sin. While Augustine admires the marvelous craftsmanship and oft mysterious inner workings of the human body, he prescribed asceticism for Christians.[42] So for instance, sex in marriage is good for procreation but not to satisfy sexual desire; this all the while he had not one but two concubines across the sweep of his life.[43] He believed that although the righteous are not trying to escape or be delivered from their bodies (indeed, the elect in heaven long for their own bodies)[44] they were to "make war upon their vices," enduring labors in the contest against temptation, the flesh, evil, and darkness.[45] Hence, we note again the marked sense that Augustine was conflicted about the physical realm in general, and the human body in

---

persons finally receiving their wings. When it comes to the afterlife, I fear Plato's constructs hold more sway on the popular Christian imagination than does resurrection doctrine.

40. *The City of God*, book 22.12–21, 835–850.
41. Harrison, *Beauty and Revelation*, 161.
42. Rist, *Augustine*, 205–6.
43. Bauerschmidt, "Adultery," 11, and Clark, "Asceticism," 68, in *Augustine Through the Ages*. Augustine especially loved his first concubine, with whom he had a son.
44. Bussanich, "Happiness, *Eudaimonism*," 421.
45. Augustine, *The City of God*, book 23.23, 849. See also Duffy, "Anthropology," 24–26.

particular. He believed that fallen humanity's aesthetic (heartfelt, sensory) sense leads us astray and causes us to focus on the material rather than the spiritual, the carnal rather than the eternal; all that even though the soul needs and uses the God-created bodily senses in order to perceive. The *imago dei* that is the human self is not completely erased, even though it is defaced, and so sensual things, even good things, can obscure our vision of God.[46] How do we make sense of this conflict? Augustine—committed to the doctrines of creation, incarnation, and resurrection—was nevertheless influenced by his own historic Neoplatonic context. Rather than baldly disdaining physicality, Augustine's focus was inward and fixed on the beautiful soul.

IMAGE OF GOD: THE BEAUTIFUL SOUL

If we directly asked him, "Augustine, in this life where especially is beauty?" he might well answer "in the soul itself." The soul is more beautiful than the body; the hierarchy is very clear in Augustine. The soul, not the body, "has a direct, privileged intuition and knowledge of the Truth or the Wisdom of God (identified with the Son), and owing to God's presence to it, Augustine concludes that it is, like these truths, immortal." Therefore one appropriately turns inward to the soul—that more rational and more sublime dimension of human nature—through contemplation to ascend toward God, truth, and beauty. Indeed, the human achievements of reason, imagination, art, literature, poetry, painting, sculpture, building, and the sciences testify to the soul's ability to touch on goodness and beauty.[47] In his ontological hierarchy, he held that God was at the top, angels and the human soul were in the middle, and all physical bodies held the lowest level.[48] More than the body, the soul is the image of God. Again, establishing a perspective that will inform centuries' worth of Christian asceticism and piety, Augustine taught that the soul is both superior to all corporeal things and capable of being beautified in this life. To that beautifying end, early in his Christian experience, Augustine turned inward and he intentionally did so to find

---

46. Harrison, *Beauty and Revelation*, 17, 20, 162–79.

47. Ibid., 15–16. "Not in the body, but in the mind was man made in the image of God," Augustine, *On John's Gospel*, 23.10, in Harrison, *Beauty and Revelation*, 142.

48. Bourke, *The Essential Augustine*, 43–44. Indeed, Augustine believed that in Eden's pristine garden Adam had a spiritual body, one that through the fall became more fleshly than it originally was. Rist, *Augustine*, 95–99.

Augustine of Hippo (c. 354–430)

God therein. The soul was the most Godlike, the most Godward, dimension of human nature.[49]

Informed by decades of creational theology, many contemporary Christians today may be uncomfortable with Augustine's "physicality tends to the problematic" position. And yet, again, we must see him in his context. Unlike Plato, Augustine did not hold that the human soul is eternal; only God is eternal and immutable. In contrast to Plotinus, who held that moral evil's origin is somehow connected to materiality, Augustine held that the soul, not merely the body, chose against God in the garden.[50] While the Neoplatonist Porphyry had reasoned "all body must be escaped," Augustine believed that the incarnation was a beautiful mystery, that God created human bodies to be good, and that the soul experiences reality in and through bodies. Against Greek philosophy, Augustine once wrote, "anyone who wants to separate the body from human nature is a fool."[51] Indeed, while Augustine did not understand the precise relationship between soul and body, he espoused a position wherein man is a "soul managing a body."[52] Again, we see the preestablished constraints, the conflicts, Augustine navigated for his own historic-philosophic context. The soul, created by God, nonetheless exists in a tension between divinity and corporeality, and as such may turn upward toward God or downward toward *cupiditas*,

> sinful love, disordered love that is fearful and covetous of things that can be lost and gives rise to "desires of the flesh," not to be restricted to unbridled sensual passions but including, e.g., lust for power, jealousy, hatred, greed, scandalmongering, selfishness. *Cupiditas* is not just blind lust, but human love seeking fulfillment in a transitory sphere that cannot deliver it. Under the sway of *cupiditas*, the ego is god and all else must serve its vain quest for happiness.[53]

---

49. Wills, *Saint Augustine*, 88. Rist, *Augustine*, 13, argues that for Augustine the soul was "our real self," or "our true humanity." Later, in the sixteenth century, Protestants will heighten this inward turn. Many, in their practice of iconoclasm, will emphasize the interior life of the Christian over against physicality and images.

50. Rist, *Augustine*, 103.

51. Ibid., 111, quoting Augustine, *The Soul and its Origin*, 4.2.3.

52. Ibid., quotes on 93 and 94. Further nuanced, Augustine did not believe the soul is merely the harmony/attunement of the body. He also rejected Aristotle's argument that the soul is the "form" of the body.

53. Duffy, "Anthropology," 43, 121.

One can either look upward to God or downward toward creation, corporeality, and sinfulness. Turning upward (*conversio*), seeking both God and the things of God, will involve the intelligence and the will. The Greek philosophers and ascetics had focused on the intelligence and exhorted people to master their passions through self-control. Augustine knew that that approach did not and would not work; it failed as an ascetic method precisely because it misunderstood human nature and it failed philosophically because it was devoid of God's revelation. Reason alone, Bussanich summarized Augustine, "is insufficient to insure the proper functioning of the will."[54] We require God's grace, Augustine taught. The human plight is far less our ability to reason aright than it is our ability to choose aright. Centuries earlier Aristotle had taught that we are what we love. In his own anthropology, Augustine averred the same.

The common human cycle of behavior, the pattern of soul-shaping, observed by Augustine is that first we experience pleasure and desire in our heart (*aesthesis*). Next we consent to that heartfelt pleasure. Following, we act on that pleasure-desire. Then, over time, our repeated actions become habits such that we shape our very souls. All of this, over time, does violence to the will and eventually becomes, Fitzgerald put it succinctly, "a chain which, strengthened by a person's failure to turn to God, is rooted in a prior choice; only with God's help can such habits be turned into good habits." "Bad habits are a weight on the soul" and "good habits are seen as virtue."[55] Not only do we see latent within this schema the foundations for later Roman Catholic spiritualities concerning the centrality of habits for moral formation,[56] we also see that Augustine believed the self can indeed become more Godlike and therefore more beautiful.[57] And yet, because our wills are fallen and darkened we cannot choose the good except by God's grace. Can the soul become beautiful? Yes, by the grace of God acting with the human will. With still more nuance, the individual choices are less important than the "basic inclination" to both love God and one's neighbor;

---

54. Bussanich, "Happiness, *Eudaimonism*," 414.

55. Fitzgerald, "Habit (*Consuetudo*)," 409–10.

56. In the heated rhetoric of the sixteenth-century Reformation sadly too much of this wisdom will be cast out as belonging to a kind of works-righteousness spirituality; Augustine was not implying that by rectifying our habits we save ourselves, but rather that we become more virtuous, more Christlike.

57. Augustine's insight here is prescient of contemporary neuroscience. Increasingly, psychiatrists and neuroscientists are proving that we program the very firing of our brain's neural networks through repeated actions, behaviors, and linguistic exercise.

Augustine of Hippo (c. 354–430)

As such, God's beauty can never be distorted or pass away. And though we are mutable and temporal, we can understand truth about God because he has created our intelligent souls to correspond with his own rational, beautiful self.[63] We see this love of God's immutability and eternity in the *Confessions*:

> "O God of hosts, turn us and show us your face, and we shall be safe," (Ps 79:8). For wherever the human soul turns itself, other than to you, it is fixed in sorrows, even if it is fixed upon beautiful things external to you and external to itself, which would nevertheless be nothing if they did not have their being from you. Things rise and set: in their emerging they begin as it were to be, and grow to perfection; having reached perfection, they grow old and die.... So when things rise and emerge into existence, the faster they grow to be, the quicker they rush towards non-being.... But in these things there is no point of rest: they lack permanence.... Entrust to the truth whatever has come to you from the truth. You will lose nothing.... Remain in the presence of God who stands fast and abides. (Ps 101:13, 27; 1 Pet 1:23)[64]

The Lord is transcendent, but God has created in such a way that he also shines through his creation. God is a paradox, both transcendent and immanent, utterly beyond and mysteriously within. Augustine thus holds that God's beauty is both beautiful in God's self and in what God has made. Previously we noted that creation served, to Augustine's mind, as a kind of book of knowledge; we can know that God is intelligent, orderly, beneficent, and causative by observing nature. God's glory radiates within and shines through his creation. Creation's beauty is thus like an ephemeral sign, it points to something enduring beyond itself: God.[65]

But this radiating and shining of God is not merely static within nature as something to be observed. Creation's beauty is not just wondrous, or even a cause for wondering about God, though it is indeed both of those. Building on the foundations of historically prior Greek philosophers, and anticipating the constructs of later Christian monastic and mystical theology, Augustine believed that the things of this life can impel toward, lift up toward, the eternal things and ways of God, especially for those with the desire and intelligence to both want and see that. Viladesau clarifies that

---

63. Cf. Augustine, *The True Religion*, 3.3 as noted in Harrison, *Beauty and Revelation*, 48.

64. Augustine, *Confessions*, 4.15–16, 61–63.

65. Harrison, *Beauty and Revelation*, 138–39.

for Augustine beauty (*pulchritude*) is something that necessarily requires perception by the "higher" and "more cognitive" realm of sensation (i.e., vision), while other kinds of sweetnesses (*suavitas*) can be perceived by the lower senses (e.g., hearing).[66] (I would apply this for today to note that *seeing* beauty and *appreciating* beauty is the difference between the experience of a mere observer and that of an aesthete.) The beauty of God lifts us up. *The beauty of God beautifies.* God's beauty is active and transformative. In classical philosophy this ascendant intellectual movement is known as *anagogy*: to lift up or move toward mystical or religious elevation.

We should clarify yet again, Augustine's desire for and appreciation of anagogy was not a means of self-help or works-righteousness. More accurately framed, it was the pursuit of God. Augustine was one of the founders of the doctrine of salvation by grace—indeed he will be called doctor *gratiae* by subsequent churchmen and theologians—so he was not promoting some self-help means of enlightenment or salvation. Let us remember, Augustine emphasized mankind's fallenness and depravity. In significant ways Christians, because of Augustine, believe that only God can save. But the bishop of Hippo also knew that Jesus and his disciples taught that we should pursue righteousness, godliness, and God himself.[67] To that end reading and studying Scripture certainly promotes anagogy, but so too does the appreciation of beauty as something shining forth from God through creation. In a now famous passage Augustine waxed both anagogic and poetic:

> What is it that I love when I love you? Not the beauty of any bodily thing, nor the order of the seasons, not the brightness of light that rejoices the eye, nor the sweet fragrance of the flowers and ointments and spices; not manna nor honey, not the limbs that carnal love embraces. None of these things do I love in loving my God. Yet in a sense I do love light and melody and fragrance and food and embrace when I love my God—the light and the voice and the fragrance and the food and embrace in the soul, when the light shines upon my soul which no place can contain, that voice sounds which no time can take from me, I breathe that fragrance which no wind scatters, I eat the food which is not lessened by eating, and I lie in the embrace which satiety never comes to sunder. That it is that I love, when I love my God.[68]

66. Viladesau, *Theological Aesthetics*, 107.
67. Matt 6:33; 7:7–8; 11:12; 19:29; Phil 4:8; 1 Tim 6:11; Heb 11:6.
68. Augustine, *Confessions* 10.6.8.

Augustine of Hippo (c. 354–430)

Yet again Augustine's hierarchical perspective comes to the fore: natural-external beauty is at the bottom, intelligence and the soul are in the middle, and God is at the top. In all of that beauty involves our perception and engagement. Between nature's beauty and God's beauty is the human person, created by God to enjoy God. And with still further nuance, it is not a naked intelligence, but one inflamed by the grace of God, that perceives God's beauty. Again hear Augustine:

> Surely this beauty should be self-evident to all who are of sound mind. Then why does it not speak to everyone in the same way? Animals both small and large see it, but they cannot put a question about it. In them reason does not sit in judgement upon the deliverance of the senses. But human beings can put a question so that "the invisible things of God are understood and seen through the things which are made" (Rom 1:20). Yet by love of created things they are subdued by them, and being thus made subject become incapable of exercising judgement. . . . If one person sees while another sees and questions, it is not that they appear one way to the first and another to the second. It is rather that the created order speaks to all, but is understood by those who hear its outward voice and compare it with the truth within themselves. . . . In that respect, my soul, I tell you that you are already superior. For you animate the mass of your body and provide it with life, since no body is capable of doing that for another body. But your God is for you the life of your life.[69]

God wants relationship with us his creation, and he gave us the capacity for that relationship, a soul that was breathed by the beautiful God himself.

WRAP-UP

With Augustine, the influential giant that he was, we wish we had more. He affirmed the beauty of God's good creation, but could not do so in ways that broke cleanly from his own Greek milieu. Nature's beauty and the human body's beauty were all relegated to a second-tier status; that configuration will both shape and typify the attitude of Christians toward beauty for centuries right through today. Unfortunately, however, that second-tier status also meant that beauty is tainted, obfuscated, and twisted by matter and physicality itself. Perhaps that was the case for Augustine because of his

---

69. Ibid. 10.10.

milieu wherein physicality was consistently understood as problematic, or perhaps it was due to his always wanting to put God first, which for him meant that things must always be understood hierarchically. Alas, even while he observed and joyously commented on earthly beauty, it was difficult for Augustine to allow beauty to be beautiful in and for its own sake.[70] Moreover he "demonstrated little interest in the visual arts."[71] Augustine failed to recognize that the goodness and beauty of creation and physicality need not in fact detract from God, or lessen God, or lessen a theological focus on God. With God there is always enough, always room for more and room for the other, as Gregory of Nyssa constructed it with his doctrine of *epektasis*.

Still, Augustine represents a significant biblical step beyond Greek philosophic and ascetic categories that were consistently disdainful of material beauty. If we were to imagine that when the Roman Empire chose Christianity in the fourth century that it did so in either pristine fashion, wholeheartedly and whole cloth, in a way that obliterated the former qualities of the empire, we would be grossly inaccurate. The kingdom is like a seed, Jesus taught (Matt 13:31; Mark 4:26; Luke 13:18), that is planted, grows, and eventually produces harvest. But, that seed always takes root in the given soil. Put differently, God does not ask us as persons to change before he makes us to become his living temples, he asks us to repent. That act of repentance is one made by sinners toward God. Then, having repented, God's Spirit moves into our hearts and lives and initiates transformation. Again, God comes to us where we are and although he loves us unconditionally, he does not intend to leave us in that condition. Similarly, at the macro level, societies do not sanctify themselves, eradicate their traditions and beliefs, and throw all in with Christ. The transformation of societies, and with it the transformation of world views, is, whether we like it or not, consistently gradual. We have theologians like Augustine to thank for being part of that gradual and perceptible transformation.

WHAT AUGUSTINE TEACHES US TO SEE:

- asceticism tends to denigrate beauty

---

70. This interpretation is affirmed by Sherry. Augustine "seems to have had a divided mind on the importance of beauty." *Spirit and Beauty*, 8.

71. Spier, ed., *Picturing the Bible*, 18.

Augustine of Hippo (c. 354–430)

- creation is good and can radiate God's beauty
- arranged by divine reason, the physical realm points to the spiritual realm
- even though music is dangerous, the universe is a song
- the resurrection redeems the human body
- the human soul is particularly beautiful
- we are shaped by what we love
- God never changes but he dynamically shines through creation
- the beauty of God beautifies

4

Pseudo-Dionysius the Areopagite (5th–6th Centuries)

The Porous Nature of God's Beauty

HISTORY FASCINATES ME. IT'S an adventure to wonder about, wandering about and exploring some historic site, imagining what it was like to live "back then" when daily life was profoundly different from that of my own era. Two thousand years ago, what did Romans think about when they looked into the eyes of their own children? Fifteen hundred years ago, when Syrians peered up toward Orion, what did they feel? And, I muse, in order to somehow understand them, how do we get inside the hearts and minds of those who lived in the past? Even with the aid of computer-generated–imagery laden, musically accompanied, multimedia presentations it is very difficult to get our imaginations inside that of persons from a foreign culture, let alone times-gone-by foreign cultures. Even Christians, though they are both committed to and united by the biblical narratives, have a formidable time understanding other Christians who are very different from themselves. For instance, Catholics don't "get" Protestants and Protestants don't "get" Catholics, and that is true even though they are both variations of Western Christianity. What then of Eastern Christians, the Orthodox? Some wonder, aren't the Orthodox just the twin sister of Roman Catholics? Because they are so admittedly mystical, the Orthodox can represent even more of a quandary to Western Christians. How do the Orthodox envision beauty? How do they process and frame a Christian understanding

Pseudo-Dionysius the Areopagite (5th–6th Centuries)

of beauty? This chapter invites us to open our imaginations to an Eastern Christian framing of beauty.

One of the most truly influential Eastern Orthodox theologians—indeed perhaps the most influential theologian in Christian history on beauty[1]—is a man known by the unusual title the Areopagite. His theo-aesthetic influence is particularly fascinating given he paid no attention to painting or art.[2] When his writings appeared first in the sixth century some Christian leaders erringly believed that Pseudo-Dionysius, as he is more commonly known, was the man referenced in Acts 17:34,[3] an Athenian disciple of Paul the apostle. Much later in Christian history, other scholars thought the Areopagite was a Monophysite bishop from either Egypt or Syria because his writings first appeared in history among Monophysite Christians arguing with other Christians who affirmed the Council of Chalcedon (AD 451).[4] The fact is historians and theologians do not know Psuedo-Dionysius's true identity. He was a mystic now shrouded in mystery. Perhaps that is fitting: Christian mystics point not to themselves but the source of their vision.

Fascinating is Charles Stang's theory about Dionysius' identity. Against regular, if also more cynical, notions that the Areopagite assumed that (biblical) name to spuriously establish his own authority, Stang believes that a Christian man took the name Dionysius precisely to model the "*rapprochement* between the wisdom of pagan Athens and the revelation of God in Christ."[5] Later Christians, especially Protestants, would chafe at mixing together Greek philosophy (or philosophy of any kind) and biblical teaching. Such a method, those espousing biblical purism aver, is syncretistic and unfaithful. Even Tertullian once irritatedly wrote, "What does Jerusalem have to do with Athens?" By that he meant, what does God's biblical revelation have to do with mere pagan thought? To reiterate, Stang believes that our theologian took the name Dionysius to model the melding and welding

---

1. Dionysius was archetypal for all medieval Catholic theologians on beauty and aesthetics. Barasch, *Icon*, 158–59. Cf. Eco, *Thomas Aquinas*, 44–45. Regarding medieval theologians and aesthetics Eco writes, "Dionysius may not have been fully understood, but his authority was unquestioned" (ibid., 23).

2. Barasch, *Icon*, 159.

3. "But some of them joined [Paul] and became believers, including Dionysius the Areopagite and a woman named Damaris, and others with them."

4. Pelikan notes that it was Joseph Stiglmayr (1851–1934) who first posited this theory. "Introduction," in *Pseudo-Dionysius*, 13. Monophysites (those who purport one nature) emphasize the divinity over against the humanity of Jesus Christ.

5 "Dionysius," 12.

together of the good, true, and beautiful about Greek philosophy with the same from Christian theology. The Apostle Paul himself both quotes the then-ancient Greek poet, Epimenides, and builds on the (minimal) truth of pagan Greek religion to argue for the preeminency of Jesus as eschatological judge and resurrected Lord, "What therefore you unknowingly [or ignorantly] worship, this I proclaim to you" (Acts 17:23). Similarly, Stang argues, a patristic Christian theologian intentionally used the name Dionysius the Areopagite to affirm a Christian-Greek philosophy amalgam. Just as the original Areopagite was from Athens, so this Dionysius will affirm correlation with the thought of Athens, so that the "incipient faith" of some Greek philosophers will be "baptized" into Christian theology and enfolded "into the new order and dispensation in Christ."[6]

Still further, and mesmerizing because it seizes upon the dynamics of the Areopagite's thought itself, is Stang's continued theory, one following D. S. Russell,[7] regarding the pseudonymous use of Dionysius. The latter believed the past can be present and at work in the now. Truly, if one carefully reads the New Testament one will be struck by the oddity of some similar first-century beliefs: long dead prophets, or their spirits (whatever that meant), can enter the present to visit and/or attend contemporary people (Luke 1:17); one man could in fact be another man (Mark 8:27–28); or that Christ Jesus can live inside believers (Gal 2:20). Continuing that ancient reading of the past and its interplay with the present, a dynamic that Stang describes as being *porous*, Dionysius writes about theology, life, and beauty as though the past and its effects are present and alive now; it is a belief or method whereby pseudonymity collapses the distance between the past and present such that the ancient authorities "come to inhabit [present authorities] and speak in their stead." Thus, the contemporary author (in this case Dionysius), especially by studying the apostolic writings, was an "extension" of the ancient authority (the Apostle Paul).[8]

Evangelicals might ask, the present is porous with regard to the past? Honestly this is all quite mystical. As we will see more carefully below, this perspective was not merely as though Dionysius was exercising his vivid

---

6. Stang, "Dionysius," 11, 14–15.

7. Russell, *Jewish Apocalyptic*.

8. Stang, "Dionysius," 19–21. Stang, 21, notes that Pseudo-Dionysius also wrote such that he knew the Apostles Peter, James, and Timothy, and that he himself was both present at Mary's dormition and with John on the Isle of Patmos, both of which are logically impossible given Dionysius's existence in the late fifth or early sixth century. Cf. Riordan, *Divine Light*, 29–30.

imagination about the past and its effects on the present, or the eternal and its effects on the now, or the spiritual and its effects upon the physical. Dionysius truly believed the theology he described and espoused. He truly believed the past erupts into the present and that God is both within and shining through physical reality; indeed, it is all intensely mystical.[9] More, it is insistently Eastern. The Eastern Christian mind does not play by the rules that the post-Enlightenment Western Christian mind does; for the former, categories overlap, inform one another, are enmeshed together, and indeed are porous.

Surely Stang's read is more interpretive than it is directly historical. Yet again, what seems fitting about it is its own enfolding with mystical theology. Per Stang and others,[10] we have in the Areopagite a theologian being mystical in his very self-chosen appellation. Dionysius, the theologian of "unknowing" par excellence, writes pseudonymously as a devotional practice: he writes to effect change more than he does to impress. Writing pseudonymously, Stang clarified, also enables the self both to be oneself and someone else, or more precisely in a Dionysian manner, both neither entirely oneself nor entirely someone else.[11]

This chapter will unpack Dionysius, "the most aesthetic of all Christian theologians,"[12] and his perspectives on beauty. However, this is a good time to pause and consider my own interpretive filter so that the reader may understand how this author processes the variety of Christian perspectives, philosophies, and histories in and for our own pluralizing era.

A FRAMING FORAY: PRISTINE OR PLASTICINE?

Christian history is dotted with all manner of restorationist movements. There have always been believers who either wanted more out of their own Christian experience or who were frustrated with the then-current

---

9. The word *mystical* has myriad definitions. Briefly, what it is *not* herein: a blurring of the categories of the divine and created, a means of salvation outside of Christ, or a form of the occult. What is intended herein: layers of existence and being that transcend rationality and discourse, intuitive and relational knowledge of the divine that defies logic, an openness to the mystery of God's self.

10. Balthasar, *Clerical Styles*, 148–49. Riordan, *Divine Light*, 33, describes Dionysius's "trans-temporal" method as involving both ecstasy (leaving oneself) and enstasy (entering into one's truest identity).

11. Stang, "Dionysius," 22.

12. Balthasar, *Clerical Styles*, 168.

packaged assembly that was the church, or both. In the late second century, ascetics, those who disciplined themselves for the sake of union with Christ, were already growing frustrated with the institutionalization and moral shiftings of the church. Indeed, monastic movements and communal orders throughout church history have constantly been driven by a yearning for more, for a better, truer, crisper, more engaging, and authentic Christian life; they sought purity and vibrancy by trying to echo Christ Jesus' own austere lifestyle. Similarly, the sixteenth-century Reformation was itself a vast restorationist movement: Reformers across Europe wanted to restore the church to apostolic truth, to return to the perceived purity and simplicity of the apostolic era; those Reformers sought new life and certitude through a doctrinal return to the Scriptures, but the cumulative force of such a return eventually meant schism for the church. Much later, the twentieth century witnessed the explosion of the Pentecostal-Charismatic movement: these renewal-minded people want to live in the daily presence and power of Holy Spirit as experienced by the apostolic community, especially as that is portrayed in the book of Acts. In each of those instances—monastic, Protestant, and Renewal—the goal was repristination. Each group wanted a return to the pure way of life that Jesus and his apostles enjoyed. Each group, in their varied ways, thought "if only we could get back to what it was originally like!" In aching for more, and desiring a more pristine version of Christianity, each of those groups were right; we should be ever salting and transforming our social environs for God's glory, ever conforming to the image of Jesus Christ, ever panting after more of God himself, all of that mirroring what the apostolic community in Acts modeled. And yet, each of those repristinizing groups was also wrong. Allow me to explain.

The apostles themselves didn't get "it," or didn't get Jesus, until the day of Pentecost (and even thereafter the struggles continued). Really, Jesus appears to them, having been resurrected from the grave, and like bubbleheads they ask him, "Lord, is this the time when you will restore the kingdom to Israel?" (Acts 1:6). They were still beleaguered by their former persistent Jewish belief that the messiah would be a political deliverer! (It was a belief that Jesus rebuffed, openly or covertly, in every single instance.) Truly, the New Testament is scandalous for how it portrays the disciples and the apostolic communities: foibles, character flaws, idiosyncrasies, sins, misunderstandings, and apostasies all dot the biblical narratives about the people involved in Jesus' coming. Who tells the "you just gotta hear this!"

story in ways that display such common shortcomings? (Truth tellers, that's who.) Who establishes a new covenant with such common, simple, self-directed, and problematic people? (The master potter, that's who.) After the Gospels themselves, most every Epistle was written to deal with problems, often deep and heretical and brutal problems, besetting local Christian communities. All of that means that the original apostolic churches (and there were multiples springing up from the onset) were themselves very human. Those Christian communities were comprised of folks whose own feet were made of clay. They were like Plasticine.

Plasticine is a British modeling clay. It is not a pure anything. Instead, it is a mixture of petroleum jelly, aliphatic acids, and calcium salts. The earliest Christian churches were comprised of men and women, young and old, Jews and Gentiles, slaves and free people—in short, sinners—being saved by grace. The Holy Spirit deigned to make those Plasticine people his very temple on earth. There *never was* a sinless, pure, perfect, or ideal apostolic church. All the restorationist Christian groups were thus wrong in their historical interpretation. And yet, the apostles are part of the foundation for the entire church.[13] One New Testament author said of these admixtured, Plasticine, mud-caked people, that (because of his own work) God's Son "is not ashamed to call them brethren" (Heb 2:11). My point for this book? God comes to us *where* we are. For myself as an eleven-year-old boy I heard the good news about Jesus Christ in the English language. God did not require me to learn *koiné* in Greek in order to have relationship with him. Furthermore, God comes to us as *who* we are. He does not wait to come to us after we are finally transformed into his image. He invites the foolish, silly, unlearned, and the plain to be his children,[14] and to pour his Spirit into them. He did that with the apostles and their kin, and God does that today around the world. Jesus said the kingdom is like yeast: it penetrates towns, regions, cultures, families and persons—right where and who they are—and draws all of those toward forgiveness and grace, renewal, godly righteousness, Christ-centered truth, and beauty. I am the same Eddie that I was when I was eleven years old, and yet I am an entirely different Eddie by the work of Christ's gospel and Spirit.

What does the awareness of life's Plasticine nature mean regarding beauty? Firstly, we simply must be willing to see beauty shining through a myriad of forms. Beauty does not only appear within the ideal, the sublime,

---

13. Matt 10:1–15; Acts 15; 1 Cor 12:28; Eph 2:20; 2 Pet 3:2.
14. 1 Cor 12:17–31.

or the unblemished. For example, beauty often shimmers within, or pulses through, people who are themselves bodily disfigured or even homely. Or, to take another example from a historical-political perspective, the crucifixion of God was just one more ugly Roman murder—ugly variously for its physical aesthetic, for its intentional violation of human dignity, and for the lies which motivated it—and yet from a theological vantage point it is arguably the most beautiful thing God ever did and ever allowed for the benefit of his creation. Hence, Christian aesthetes should be on the lookout for beauty's residence in both subtle and surprising places. Embracing that interpretive perspective is not remotely the same as saying all suffering, homeliness, or indignity is beautiful. It is, however, an approach, an interpretive lens that allows for beauty to freely appear where it is and as it is.

Secondarily, though related to the first point, and to the crux of this chapter, we need to allow that people who knew and loved Christ did so from their respective historical, geographical, linguistic, and temporal situations. That means that those world views and situations were and are frequently messy, conflated, and layered; those perspectival vistas were and are informed by commitments, traditions, and practices that are interwoven and difficult to discern. Further, those same perspectival vistas can themselves be thoroughly integrated with biblical revelation to form their own unique pastiche of Christian reflection and thought. Today, some Christians believe that if something—a perspective on beauty, for instance—isn't pristinely filtered through (their own) biblical-theological sieve then it is not worth their consideration. As noted earlier, Tertullian rather exemplifies such a position. Continuing to the point, for those of a more biblical-purist mind-set, if any philosophy is involved in an understanding of beauty then said understanding or perspective must be rejected because it is not immediately God-directed or God-filtered.

More specifically, some Protestants tend to reject the study of and appreciation of patristic authors like the Areopagite because they were so colored by Neoplatonism.[15] (The orthodoxy and/or heretical nature of Dionysius is debated at length by the best of scholars.)[16] Neoplatonism,

15. Though it is intriguing that these same Protestants don't much struggle with Augustine, the father of the Reformed tradition who so profoundly influenced the Protestant Reformers, despite his having been thoroughly engaged with, and thinking within, Neoplatonism.

16. Dionysius is frequently critiqued for not focusing enough on either Christ or the Trinity. To clarify, Copleston once wrote, "Personally I consider that [Dionysius's] writings are orthodox in regard to the rejection of monism; but that on the question of the

such critics argue, was too colored by pagan philosophy; and so they ask, "just what would Christians learn from pagans?" Those who reject any interplay between Christianity and Neoplatonism also may think, "disciples of Christ should only study and be obedient to God's word, the Holy Bible, not philosophy." They continue, "Why obscure God's revelation with Greek philosophy?"[17] This is particularly interesting because these same folks would have no problem dialoguing with and learning from non-Christian medical doctors, lab technicians, or engineers. The irony is that these well-intentioned Bible-affirming conservatives end up promoting a secular-sacred split, an epistemological dualism that bifurcates knowledge into domains "about God" and other domains "about the rest of life." That dualism is variously harmful to faith, witness, and lifestyle. I wonder, is Christianity about faith alone or is it about everything in life?

Again, for many believers, any Neoplatonic views of beauty are summarily ruled out because they are not singularly biblical.[18] I respect that commitment to biblical authority, but I fear it too commonly insists there is only one cultural way to understand biblical authority and/or process life. Ancient Christians can show us things about our walk in Christ that we may overlook, or even be entirely unaware about, today. Considering our life in Christ in general, or beauty specifically, the patristic Christian way is not the only way to filter and process, but then neither is ours. I am willing to learn from God's Spirit through any sibling in Christ who speaks truth, be that person an ancient Syrian or a contemporary farmer.

Blessed Trinity is highly questionable at least if they can be reconciled with orthodox Christian dogma. Whatever the intentions of the author may have been, his words, besides being obscure, as Aquinas admitted, are scarcely compatible, as they stand, with the trinitarian teaching of Augustine and Thomas Aquinas. It may be objected that insufficient attention is paid to the dogma of the Incarnation, which is essential to Christianity, but the author clearly maintains this doctrine, and in any case to say little about one particular doctrine, even a central one, is not the same as to deny it. Taking the relevant passages of the Pseudo-Dionysius in the large, it does not seem possible to reject them as definitely unorthodox on this point." *Medieval Philosophy*, 92.

17. Manent, "Athens and Jerusalem," 35–39 provides a succinct overview of this perennial dichotomy.

18. It bears noting, too, that we today are this side of some 300 long years of philosophies that intentionally sought to undermine both Christ and his church. Thus, among twenty-first–century biblically based Christians, philosophy *in toto* is frequently viewed as a kind of antithesis to God's revelation. And so it is easy to presume that it is "same as it ever was," when in fact many bright minds in the ancient church happily engaged philosophers and philosophy because they were sincerely interested in truth.

Moreover, as we traverse this framing foray, I insist that beauty does not much play by rules. Famous are the tales of beauty appearing to Jews looking across the sunsetted horizons of Nazi extermination camps. Beauty is elusive and hard to pin down, arduous to box up, difficult to define either quickly or exhaustively.[19] Put differently, *it is really hard to dogmatize beauty.* In my class on theology and beauty students are frequently frustrated that I only briefly define beauty. That is because when studying beauty—that itself is a rather clunky phrase; beauty is first to be marveled at, contemplated, appreciated, delighted in, and articulated with gratitude—I do not limit my aesthetic reflection and education to biblical exegetes, theologians, priests, or pastors; that, even though I believe the Bible provides us with God-given and Spirit-inspired categories, categories formed by the wisdom of those who deeply and sacrificially loved God. More expansively, we do well to learn from anyone willing to seriously consider and show us beauty. Delicious are the discussions I have with artists who experience, make, and see beauty in ways that are different from my own theologically trained ways. Beauty is not the property of Christians (least while not contemporary Christians), even while Christians have a unique, indeed *the* unique, perspective on beauty!

Dionysius is remarkable for being the first theologian to call God by the name beauty. Other patristic theologians knew that God is beautiful, or intimated that beauty flows from God, or averred that God's attributes can be understood as beautiful; the Bible itself ascribed beauty to God. Dionysius prods theological aesthetics by arguing that God is beauty itself. Both Greek philosophy and Christian theology prior to Dionysius had touched upon God being beauty itself, but Dionysius openly asserts it.[20] It

---

19. Plato himself had argued that "all that is beautiful is difficult." Sammon touched upon Plato's thought: "Beauty is a phenomenon in excess of definition and discursive thought. At the same time, because it appears in real, concrete things, beauty continually and attractively offers itself as an object of inquiry. It therefore somehow appeals to the discursive impulse within reason." Sammon concludes on this point that beauty carries us beyond reason and beyond rational understanding so that our failure to understand it is nevertheless a success. Sammon, *The God Who Is Beauty*, 21–22. More simply, O'Donohue writes, "Beauty is an endless and elusive theme. What beauty is can never be finally said." *Beauty*, 9.

20. Gregory of Nyssa previously called God by many names, but not by the name beauty. Cf. Sammon, *The God Who Is Beauty*, 109–110, 119, 194; and, Putnam, *Beauty in the Pseudo-Denis*, 89. More particularly, Sammon, 105, argues that Dionysius names God beauty precisely by following the Scriptures and not Neoplatonic philosophers.

is furthermore remarkable that he *named God beauty*[21] without simultaneously depersonalizing God, as do billions around the globe do today. We will survey the Areopagite regarding his vision of God and beauty, the hierarchical and theophanic nature of creation, and beauty's role in our union with God. Dionysius is astounding not only for how thoroughly he envisioned God and his beauty, but for how he believed God wants creatures to share that same beauty.

THE DIONYSIAN VISION OF GOD AND BEAUTY

Why do we love beauty? Aristotle answered, "That is a blind man's question." With irony Aristotle meant that our delight in beauty is self-evident. Beauty is not to be systematized, but enjoyed.[22] Undoubtedly Dionysius would agree on that point. And yet Dionysius knew there are many reasons to love beauty. Chief among those reasons is that *beauty reveals God*. Following Saint Paul, Dionysius believed that all of creation reveals the transcendent God: "Ever since the creation of the world his eternal power and divine nature, invisible though they are, have been understood and seen through the things he has made" (Rom 1:20). As he is in himself, God is unknowable to finite creatures. Nevertheless, God has made himself known. The Bible shows God making himself known through words, deeds, theophanies, and preeminently through his incarnate son, Jesus of Nazareth.

In what was a novel shift, Dionysius held that God less directly reveals himself through the beauty of creation. That is, God makes himself known in everyday life by lovingly shining within the things he has made. With God, beauty and *eros* love are thus intertwined, and in turn he shares those with his creation. The Areopagite put it thus:

> And the divine Eros also brings rapture, not allowing them that are touched by it to belong to themselves, but only to the objects of their love. . . . And hence the great Paul, constrained by the divine Eros, and having received a share in its ecstatic power, says, with

---

21. This is not simply a matter of enlisting an attribute of God as a new name for God; so that, for instance, one could name God "good" or "truth" (though no theologian does). Sammon establishes that a divine name is "a communication of God's very self into the created order." Names convey something of the person or subject's very being and essence. That Dionysius called God beauty was indicative of a bold and daring development; it represents a fundamentally novel step in theological reflection. Sammon, *The God Who Is Beauty*, 7. Cf. 95–120.

22. Ibid., 54.

inspired utterance: "I live, and yet no longer I, but Christ lives in me." These are words of the true lover, of one who (as he himself states) was beside himself (out of his senses!) and unto God (2 Cor 5:13), not possessing a life of his own (2 Cor 5:15) but the life of his Beloved, a life surrounded on all sides by an ardent love. And we must dare to affirm (for this is the truth) that the Creator of the Universe himself, in his beautiful and good Eros towards the Universe, is, through his excessive erotic Goodness, transported outside of himself, in his providential activities towards all things that have being, and is overcome by the sweet spell of Goodness, Love, and Eros. In this manner, he is drawn from his transcendent throne above all things to dwell within the heart of all things in accordance with his super-essential and ecstatic power whereby he nonetheless does not leave himself behind. This is why those who know about God call him "zealous," because he is vehement in his manifold and beneficent Eros towards all beings, and he spurs them on to search for him zealously with a yearning eros, thus showing himself zealous for love inasmuch as the things that are desired are considered worthy of zeal and inasmuch as he allows himself to be affected by the zeal of all beings for which he cares. In short, both to possess eros and to love erotically belong to everything Good and Beautiful, and eros has its primal roots in the Beautiful and the Good: eros exists and comes into being only through the Beautiful and the Good.[23]

In recent decades Evangelical theologians and pastors have argued that Christian love is distinctly motivated by *agapé*: love that is selfless, sacrificial, serving, and other-directed. Common is the belief that by loving the other the Christian denies the self. Devotionals on this theme are commonly interwoven with Bible verses like John the Baptist's "He must increase, but I must decrease" (John 3:30), and Jesus' "If anyone wishes to come after me, let him deny himself, and take up his cross and follow me," (Matt 16:24; Luke 9:23). The thinking herein is that God loves selflessly and so should we. As a pastoral lesson that devotional framework has merit—indeed, we should look out for the interests of others—but theologically there are problems therein. For starters, it ignores the biblical teaching that God is a jealous God (Exod 34:14; Deut 6:15). He believes he exclusively deserves our allegiance and praise (e.g., Luke 14:25–33). In short, God cares passionately that we love him exclusively above all others.

23. Balthasar, *Seeing the Form*, 119, quoting Pseudo-Dionysius, *The Divine Names*, IV, 13, 105–6.

Pseudo-Dionysius the Areopagite (5th–6th Centuries)

In similar fashion, God loves loving us! The Scriptures do not portray the Judeo-Christian God as a Greek god who is stoically removed from his creation, dispassionately sitting on his heavenly throne watching as his eternal plan unfolds, all the time disinterested in the minute particulars while he awaits his foretold end. Jesus, following the Old Testament on God's emotional responses, shows that God variously gets excited when even one person repents (Luke 15:1–10), pays attention even to the birds of the field (Matt 6:26), knows the precise number of hairs on our head (Luke 12:7), and watches what we do regarding the sick, hungry, and imprisoned (Matt 25:31–46). In his archetypal-of-the-kingdom parable of the Prodigal Son, Jesus tells a story wherein the Father passionately loves his unfaithful but repentant son (Luke 15:11–32). In short, we see in all of those that *God is involved in his own love for us*. God sacrificially and selfishly loves us, but he is involved in his own loving. (Would it really be loving if his self wasn't involved?) In the best sense, that is what *eros* is: love that involves the self, love that burns in oneself for the other self, love that loves the other as the other.

Theologians, philosophers, and biblical exegetes have tussled with one another for decades, centuries even, over whether *eros* has any place in the Christian life. For many *eros* conveys erotic love and eroticism. Just pronouncing the word *eros* can evoke images of the indiscreet, lewd, or pornographic. However, the Christian mystical tradition not only is not embarrassed by God's *eros*, it celebrates it. It holds that God exuberantly loves! God does not wait to be loved. He rushes toward his creation to love it, to lavish himself, his goodness, his Spirit, his joy and delight upon his creation. What does any of this mean for beauty? Dionysius believed it beautiful that *God is like an explosion of love*. In his loving, God even yearns to love and be loved. Again, God is happy to love and be loved.[24]

In this dynamic of love and being loved God is ecstatic. Ecstasy is from the Greek *ekstasis*: to stand outside of, to move outside of, or to be carried out of oneself. Indeed, in this ancient sense ecstasy is a love that moves out to the other, but it involves the loving self. Hence God's love is directed to the other subject(s) thought it nevertheless involves God.[25] Mc-

---

24. Coakley, "Introduction," in *Re-Thinking Dionysius*, 2, avers that Dionysius presents "an unspeakable union with the divine," and "an ecstatic intermingling of the divine and human eros."

25. Balthasar reasons that for Pseudo-Dionysius this God-to-creation erotic love links the vertical to the horizontal in reality. Love and beauty are not idealized, nor are they chained within the forms. Love and beauty are rather manifested in and through the

Ginn writes that "Dionysius took the daring step of affirming ecstasy first of God himself, both in terms of *creating ecstasy*, whereby he stands outside himself in the eros that constitutes the world, and of what we might call the transcending ecstasy by which he always remains perfectly in himself and outside all things." In his ninth Letter, Dionysius describes this as "divine inebriation in which God like a drunken lover stands outside of all good things, being the superfullness of all these things." Astoundingly, the goal of this love is to cause the beloved (the human person) to become like God himself. McGinn notes that ecstatic love, for Dionysius, is so resplendent and so transformative that it moves the beloved subject beyond "both affirmation and negation," such that the self passes "beyond the human condition and become[s] divinized."[26] Because this is a chunk to chew on, a thick slab of theological data, let's digest this more carefully.

God's love is not, for Dionysius, meant only to affirm us or reassure us; this is no mere sentimental love for the Areopagite. God's love has its aim our transformation, our deification or divinization. The Eastern Orthodox call this deifying process of transforming love *theosis*: our being made into the image of God himself. Western Christians often write and speak devotionally about *sanctification*: our becoming holy like Jesus Christ. Usually by that Protestants and Catholics imply a kind of moral transformation that makes us sin less. The Orthodox, following Dionysius and others, do affirm that our transformation involves our moral formation, but it more profoundly involves our very ontology: in our being, indeed in our bodies, we will—through loving union—become like God. Not like God as little gods. Not like God as separate gods. Not like God as new gods. But like God in the sense of being permeated by God's very identity and love, lifted up into God's self in a mutual penetration of being that can barely even be described with words.[27] There is in all of this a porosity between God and his creation.[28]

---

forms. Balthasar, *Seeing the Form*, 121.

26. McGinn, *The Foundations of Mysticism*, 179.

27. See Rybarczyk, *Beyond Salvation* for a lengthy exposition of *theosis*.

28. Eastern Orthodox Bishop Ware calls this panentheism: God in his creation. Ware, *The Orthodox Way*, 46, 118. We must clarify. Protestant Process Theologians (e.g., Whitehead, Hartshorne, Cobb) believe that the universe is a body for God the soul. Process Theology has God inextricably bound to his own creation and working out his own being and identity in and through creation. The Eastern Orthodox would shudder at such a notion. Ware maintains that God freely, voluntarily, and lovingly commits himself to his creation, but that in the end God towers transcendently over his creation. Differently

From whence did Dionysius gather this idea of erotic love? The Bible or his own Neoplatonic context?[29] Many centuries earlier Plato had written that the goal of the *eros* of the One (God) was not mere possession, "but for generous begetting," an "engendering and begetting upon the beautiful." The *eros* of the One sought to both "love the Good" and "beget the good."[30] Hence, Dionysius certainly embraced Platonic thought hereon as he developed his own mystical vision of God. And yet Dionysius's theology on God's love was also informed by the Apostle Paul's writings. More than any other ancient writer, more than the four Gospels combined or the entire Johannine corpus, Dionysius quoted from and alluded to the Apostle Paul. Indeed, it is quite likely that Paul himself occasionally was baptizing ancient wisdom in and through Christ.[31] In all of this we are confronted with the kingdom-as-yeast dynamic, a transformation by God's revelation of existing philosophic thought and forms, in Dionysius's theology.

THE HIERARCHICAL AND REVELATORY NATURE OF CREATION

In Neoplatonic philosophy beauty passes from the absolute One through hierarchies of being; each emanation is thus directly dependent upon the preceding level in the hierarchy of being. Concomitantly, in Neoplatonism the One was thus both protected from change and physicality, and beauty (and with it goodness and being) was always mediated. In Dionysian theology beauty comes from God, not through emanations or lesser beings but from God himself. Each creature directly depends upon God for its immediate existence.[32] And, without becoming his creation (so that transcendence is maintained), God pours through his creation, pours being, goodness, and beauty through each creature (so that immanence is also

---

stated, building upon God's own self-revelation we can truthfully say volumes about God, but we do so knowing that God ultimately and infinitely transcends all of our linguistic and mental categories.

29. The Areopagite is ambiguous and complex. Cf. Sammon, *The God Who Is Beauty*, 187–88.

30. McGinn, *The Foundations of Mysticism*, 26.

31. Stang, "Dionysius," 12–13.

32. Putnam, *Beauty in the Pseudo-Denis*, 24.

operative). Thus, in Dionysius's theology of beauty God's transcendence and immanence are neither severed nor equated.[33] Dionysius wrote

> That, beautiful beyond being, is said to be Beauty—for
> it gives beauty from itself in a manner appropriate to each,
> it causes the consonance and splendor of all,
> it flashes forth upon all, after the manner of light, the
>   beauty producing gifts of its flowing ray,
> it calls all to itself,
>   when it is called beauty.[34]

Every creature and being thus becomes a theophanic—a God-revealing—locus. Each to its own extent, each in its own capacity shines forth the beauty of God. Lower creatures project something about God, but higher creatures do so even more. Dionysius's belief is that the human mind can discern the qualities of each in ascending fashion up to God himself.[35] "Each material entity communicates beauty precisely in and through its own ontological constitution." Sammon continued delineating Dionysius's perspective, "But the material entities are never merely pointers with no significance of their own."[36] For instance, consider the analogy of light.

    The Bible is full of passages using the metaphor of light. Throughout sacred Scripture we learn variously that light denotes God's revelation, is an instrument for God's purposes, was God's first creation, is a source for life and salvation, and is identified with God's own goodness.[37] Knowing all that, Dionysius used the sun to convey theological meaning. The "great, shining, ever-lighting sun" is "a distant echo of the Good." As such the sun is itself also a mirror of God:

> It illuminates whatever is capable of receiving its light and yet it
> never loses the utter fullness of its light. It sends it shining beams all

---

33. Compared to Deism, the Christian God is thus actively and lovingly involved with his creation; indeed he has unwaveringly committed himself to his creation. Conversely, compared to all manner of pantheisms, the Christian God is not one with his creation. Hence, Christian theism, a world view driven by biblical teachings, is more sophisticated, more abstract, and more difficult to understand and embrace than either Deism or pantheism. What the Bible actually teaches and/or with subtlety implies is often both difficult to understand and emotionally problematic to accept.

34. Dionysius, *The Divine Names*, IV, 7, [page not given], in Eco, *Thomas Aquinas*, 24.

35. Viladesau, *Theological Aesthetics*, 113.

36. Sammon, *The God Who Is Beauty*, 151.

37. Ibid., 108.

around the visible world, and if anything fails to receive them the fault lies not in the weakness or defect of the spreading light but in the unsuitability of whatever is unable to have a share in light. For of course light passes over many such substances and illuminates others beyond them. Actually there is nothing in the visible world to which the light does not reach in all its abundance.[38]

Admittedly, this is all very paradoxical: God shines through his creation without being or becoming it.[39] And yet, even though God sustains and beautifully shines through each thing or creature that does not mean that all things, all creatures, or all beings are equal. Dionysius maintains that there is a hierarchical quality to life. Indeed, the Psuedo-Areopagite invented the term hierarchy.[40]

In Dionysius's hierarchy higher beings both participate in the life of lower beings and benefit the lower beings; there is a harmony within the hierarchy. Summarizing Dionysius hereon Putnam wrote, "Everything is linked together according to the universal law that a higher order of nature in its lowest members joins a lower grade in its highest manifestations. But the hierarchic strands are not so tightly knit as to leave no scope for interplay among them or no room for the blunders implied in human freedom."[41] Further nuanced, Dionysius believed that creatures (angels and humans) with capacity for wisdom of and knowledge about God are thereby closer to God than those that are not, just as creatures that have life (animals, insects, plants) are closer to God than are things (rocks, water) that do not have life. He wrote, "the Good which is above all light . . . crams with its light every mind which is above and beyond the world, or around it or within it. It renews the powers of their minds."[42] Dionysius is often difficult to understand,[43] but here the logic is simple: wisdom, knowledge, and life facilitate sharing of God's love. All of this is an intended order, one given by God.[44]

So, again, in Dionysius's theological vision, true is the repeated biblical assertion that "no one has ever seen God" (Exod 33:20; John 1:18;

---

38. Pseudo-Dionysius, *The Divine Names*, 697D and 700A, in *Pseudo-Dionysius*, 74.
39. Barasch, *Icon*, 158–163, notes that Dionysius's theology is replete with paradoxes.
40. Sammon, *The God Who Is Beauty*, 164, 176.
41. Putnam, *Beauty in the Pseudo-Denis*, 26–7.
42. Pseudo-Dionysius, *The Divine Names*, 701A, in *Pseudo-Dionysius*, 76.
43. Barasch, *Icon* 159.
44. Putnam, *Beauty in the Pseudo-Denis*, 28–31, 74–6.

1 John 4:12), and yet God makes himself known through his creation, a creation shining with beauty. At the same time, Dionysius is clear, creation is not therefore God. McGinn posited that for Dionysius, "All things both reveal and conceal God." Continued McGinn, "Therefore the universe is both necessary as an image and impossible as a representation of God for whom there is no adequate representation."[45] Creation displays God's glory and beauty all the while God himself transcends what he has made. Beauty is thus an evidence, a sign, a scent even of the existence and presence of God. Dionysius put it thus:

> Hence, any thinking person realizes that the appearances of beauty are signs of an invisible loveliness. The beautiful odors which strike the senses are representations of a conceptual diffusion. Material lights are images of the outpouring of an immaterial gift of light. The thoroughness of sacred discipleship indicates the immense contemplative capacity of the mind. Order and rank here below are a sign of the harmonious ordering toward the divine realm. The reception of the most divine Eucharist is a symbol of participation in Jesus. And so it goes for all the gifts transcendently received by the beings of heaven, gifts which are granted to us in a symbolic mode.[46]

Centuries before Dionysius, Aristotle had reasoned that both mathematics and beauty represents a *metaxu*, a middleness, between the sensible and the super-sensible, between physical existence and super-physical (intelligence and the immaterial) realms of existence. So, for instance, mathematical objects (e.g., numbers, equations) "exist neither entirely in sensible entities nor entirely separate from them."[47] Following that ancient line of thought, Dionysius similarly perceived that beauty moves between the material and immaterial, between the physical and the spiritual realms.[48] Beauty is porous, it elusively moves in and through creatures, objects, and persons. We intuit beauty's presence. We perceive its residence in the world around us, and yet it is tremendously difficult to chain down. Like God himself, beauty can be discussed and intellectually appreciated, but the doing of those does not exhaust beauty. Indeed, with Dionysius theology that is apophatic (the

---

45. McGinn, *The Foundations of Mysticism*, 174.

46. Pseudo-Dionysius, *The Celestial Hierarchy*, 121D–124A, in *Pseudo-Dionysius*, 146.

47. Quoted in Sammon, *The God Who Is Beauty*, 50.

48. Sammon, *The God Who Is Beauty*, 50.

Pseudo-Dionysius the Areopagite (5th–6th Centuries)

way of unknowing) finally trumps theology that is cataphatic (the way of knowing), God's transcendence is emphasized over his immanence, and God's darkness (mystery) is to be elevated over God's light (revelation). More needs clarifying hereon.

God makes himself known in the beauty of creation; as the above illustrates, Dionysius rejoices in that. However, God's self-revelation in no way exhausts God. That we indeed can know much about God does not mean we can know everything about God. (Certainly, the Bible was not given to us to provide an encyclopedic knowledge of God, but to facilitate our relational encounter with the living God.) An Eastern Christian, Dionysius was comfortable with the fact that God, in his irreducible essence and in his profoundly transcendent personhood, is beyond our capacity to fully understand. Even that we may know God and experience him in our lives does not scratch the surface of God's eternally deep self. Moses saw and/or experienced something of the transcendence of God in Exodus chapters 19–20. Lightning flashes and thunder, trumpet blasts, earthquakes, fire and smoke, and a thick cloud of darkness accompanied God's presence. That Mosaic image characterized Dionysius's apophatic theology: God is present yet he cannot be reduced to phenomenon; he is there but he is not there.[49]

For itself, human nature, in Dionysian theology, is mysterious and irreducible, consisting of layers that transcend neat and tidy description. How much more then the ineffable God? For Dionysius God,

> Transcends everything by virtue of his power. He is the substantive Cause and maker of being, subsistence, of existence, of substance, and of nature. He is the Source and measure of the ages. He is the reality beneath time and the eternity behind being. He is the time within which things happen. He is being for whatever is. He is coming-to-be amid whatever happens. From him who is come eternity, essence and being, come time, genesis and becoming. He is the being immanent in and underlying things which are, however they are. For God is not some kind of being. No. But in a way that is simple and indefinable he gathers into himself and anticipates every existence. So he is simply called "King of the ages," for in him and around him all being is and subsists. He was not. He will not be. He did not come to be. He is not in the midst of becoming. He will not come to be. No. He is not. Not only things that are but also the essence of what they are come from him who

---

49. McGinn comments that the "mysticism of darkness is not found among pagan philosophers." This apophatic bent, this particular emphasis on God's transcendence, stems back to Gregory of Nyssa. *The Foundations of Mysticism*, 175.

precedes the ages. For he is the age of ages, the "precedessor of the ages." ... All eternity and time are from him.[50]

Such an emphasis upon God's *not* being strikes the Westerner's thinking as unusual, if not heterodox. But Dionysius wants us to be clear that God transcends our intellectual constructions; even saying "God is eternal" can cause us to believe we have somehow put a definitional boundary or discursive claim upon our knowledge of God. God is beyond all words; the Eastern Orthodox constantly assert thus. In humility we do well to quiet ourselves before the infinitely transcendent source of life, time, and being. And so, in the doing of theology perhaps better than articulation is song. After all, the angels in heaven are not talking about God but singing about and to him![51] Theology, the Areopagite asserted, is best done on our knees,[52] bowing our bodies and souls before the Ancient of Days, the one who created time itself, the being who transcends all being. Later theologians, building upon both the writing and the worshipful spirit of Dionysius will suggest that "theology is exhausted in the act of *wondering adoration* before the unsearchable beauty in every manifestation," and so our highest and most accurate mode of speech is praise.[53]

BEAUTY'S ROLE IN OUR UNION WITH GOD

Most Christians believe that corporate worship enjoins a thicker kind of relationship, a deeper form of embrace, between the church and Christ than that done by individuals. The Bible teaches, "God inhabits the praises of his people" (Ps 22:3). We see that assertion illustratively borne out in Acts when Paul and Silas were in jail in Philippi praying, "and singing hymns of praise to God. . . . and suddenly there came a great earthquake . . . and all the doors were opened, and everyone's chains unfastened" (16:25–27). Many churchly leaders teach that the Lord is particularly present when the church gathers in his name (Matt 18:20). The Areopagite also believed the worshipping community has a unique capacity to lift up the soul to God.

---

50. Pseudo-Dionysius, *The Divine Names*, 817C–820A, in *Pseudo-Dionysius*, 98.

51. Balthasar, *Clerical Styles*, 160, draws this correlation between human theology echoing angelic theology in Dionysius's own theology.

52. Riordan, *Divine Light*, 35.

53. Balthasar, *Clerical Styles*, 170. My italics.

Pseudo-Dionysius the Areopagite (5th–6th Centuries)

But Dionysius ups the ante. He asserts that beauty itself inculcates a kind of sharing between God, ourselves, and his creation.[54]

Following the lead of Aristotle, Dionysius held that beauty is causative. Beauty, because it is ultimately God, is a principle of determination. When God creates, Sammon reflected on Dionysius's theology, "He gives every existing thing a unique and particular shape in his hyper-determinancy, a share in the excess of his divine being."[55] (Again, we see that God's love is ecstatic: outgoing, outward oriented.) Frequently, theologians describe creation as an act of God's power or wisdom. By orienting it with and to beauty Dionysius contrastingly envisions creation as an act of abundance, overspilling, joy, and love. However, creation was not a one-time event. We saw earlier that Dionysius believed God sustained every living creature and every bit of existence in an immediate, ongoing, and immanent manner. This sustaining, this life-giving, stems from the surplus of God's own beauty. Rather than a one-and-done creator, God is the one who "calls all creatures into the beauty of its own divine being simply for the sake of those creatures themselves and their enjoyment of divine beauty."[56] God's beauty, in the Dionysian understanding, is thus clearly not static. God, by extending beauty to creation and creatures, in some intelligible sense variously gives those their purpose and end. Each particular creation and creature,

---

54. Later Roman Catholic theologians like Thomas Aquinas in the thirteenth century and Erich Pryzwara and Henri de Lubac in the twentieth century will develop this relationship, this correlation, between God and ourselves using the category *analogia entis*, the analogy of being. The *analogia entis* position maintains that there is some correlation between God and his creation; God has established this correlation, we humans do not enjoy that owing to our own effort, brilliance, or goodness; the divine-human correspondence can be rooted in the doctrine of *imago dei*: we were created as spiritual beings with for capacity for God. Balthasar describes salvation and the *analogia entis*, the belief that God first imprints creation with his own nature and then saves it through Jesus Christ, as God crowning his own gift. It is grace upon a God-created nature. Balthasar, *Clerical Styles*, 172.

With great passion and verve theologians have disputed the validity of this theory. Karl Barth called *analogia entis* "the invention of the anti-Christ" because it threatened the preeminence of Christ as the only mediator between God and man. Other Protestant theologians disdain *analogia entis* because it seems to posit a relationship between God and humankind based on being rather than on faith. This topic correlates to the issue of whether we can know anything about God by virtue of creation (the doctrine of general revelation), or whether we can only know about God through his self-revelation (the doctrine of special revelation).

55. Sammon, *The God Who Is Beauty*, 182.

56. Ibid., 184.

in keeping with its own varied capacity, therefore exists in the harmony of God's beauty.[57]

Earlier we noted that life is porous in the Dionysian perception of life. The past can move into and affect the present, time is not as fixed as Westerners generally envision it. There is an in-betweenedness (to make up a word that is nevertheless appropriate) about beauty that crosses boundaries and opens up new perspectives. To convey this porosity, this in-betweenedness, some 185 times Dionysius used the term *metexo*: sharing, participating in.[58] The conclusion to be drawn is that Dionysius was not merely suggesting an imitation of or copying of God's own beauteous nature but a creaturely sharing in the attribute of beauty. Beauty is real, is shared, and belongs to the things in themselves as a gift from God. Indeed, the archetypal beauty, for Dionysius, is Christ himself. Jesus is God's beautiful gift who bountifully shines the love and beauty of God upon humankind. Clearly alluding to the story of the Prodigal Son (Luke 16) the Areopagite put it thus:

> But, while in silence welcoming the beneficent rays of the really good and super-good Christ, by them let us be lighted on our path, to His divine works of goodness. For assuredly is it not of a goodness inexpressible and beyond conception, that He makes all things existing to be, and brought all things themselves to being, and wishes all things ever to become near to Himself, and participants of Himself, according to the aptitude of each? And why? Because He clings lovingly to those who even depart from Him, and strives and beseeches not to be disowned by those beloved who are themselves coy; and He bears with those who heedlessly reproach Him, and Himself makes excuse for them, and further promises to serve them, and runs towards and meets even those who hold themselves aloof, immediately that they approach; and when His entire self has embraced their entire selves, He kisses them, and does not reproach them for former things, but rejoices over the present, and holds a feast, and calls together friends, that is to say, the good, in order that the household may be altogether rejoicing.[59]

Beauty is thus tethered to God's love for his creatures. Again, we do well to observe that for Dionysius beauty initiates and facilitates sharing and union with God.

57. Putnam, *Beauty in the Pseudo-Denis*, 47–51.
58. Ibid., 28.
59. Dionysius, *Epistle* 8.1, 1085D–1088A, in Sammon, *The God Who Is Beauty*, 167.

Finally, for Dionysius beauty is less something to be defined[60] and more something that is given to define us. Beauty is therefore anagogical: its aim is to lift us up to God. We observed this formulation in our previous chapter on Augustine and like him Dionysius follows ancient Greek philosophers on the belief that beauty has a transformative effect upon us. Dionysius echoes them through a Christian sieve: without diminishing the inexhaustible source himself, beauty lifts the onlooker toward God's immaterial divine beauty. As a kind of silent call, beauty *summons* the beholder to move toward beauty's end: God himself. Beauty calls us to the good, who is the living God.

WRAP-UP

Regarding beauty and theology several new strides were made with Dionysius. He named God beauty. We do not merely have attributes about God; rather, every attribute is itself beautiful because God is irreducibly beautiful. Archetypal for later Eastern Orthodox spirituality and mysticism, we are not surprised to know that the preeminent experience for Orthodox mystics is the vision of God. Protestants generally want to hear God's word, to know what information God has for them, and to understand what God says about himself; the preferred Protestant human organ is the ear. The Orthodox prefer instead the eye: they want to see both the beauty of God and the beautiful God himself. Small wonder that he who in the twentieth century said "beauty will save the world" was himself Russian Orthodox. Fyodor Dostoyevsky knew that beauty, like God himself, cannot be tamed, over-defined, or exhausted. Beauty is a transcendent category that can transform reality.

Like Gregory of Nyssa before him, Dionysius took pre-existing Neoplatonic philosophy and tweaked it to his own theological ends. Yes, God was absolute and transcendent, but he was also dynamic and immanent. God himself both loves to create and loves to lavish himself upon his creation in and through beauty. Those do not contribute to God's self, yet they express something of God's bounty. Dionysius does not present us with a modern view of beauty, one wherein nature, objects, and people are in and of themselves deserving of careful and scrutinizing study for being

---

60. Dionysius does, in a few instances, define beauty as harmony, clarity, light, the good, and God himself. Obviously, those terms do not exhaust the extent to which Dionysius employs beauty in his theology.

beautiful. No, Dionysius was, like all human beings, a man of his own age. Accordingly he was more interested in how things echoed, imaged, projected, and symbolized God. Umberto Eco calls this aesthetic perspective a "metaphysical symbolism," one whereby "all things are like so many mirrors, which reflect in their beauty the unique visage of God." Continuing, Eco said, "The Middle Ages never forgot that all things would be absurd, if their meaning were exhausted in their function and their place in the phenomenal world, if by their essence they did not reach into a world beyond this."[61] It would take several centuries for the West to undo this profound theologically integrated view of both beauty and reality. Not until the rise of Roman Catholic Scholasticism, in general, and philosophical positivism in particular, would things begin to be studied in and for themselves, as themselves, and not for how they pointed to, or harkened unto, God. Today we post-Enlightenment Westerners would find it tremendously difficult to get our hearts, heads, and imaginations back into a world view where God was everywhere to be found.

Finally, Dionysius is unique for suggesting that beauty is a means of our union with God. Evangelical Protestants would likely view such a perspective as dangerous: does that not imply pantheism? Or, does that not imply universalism? For his part Dionysius did not trespass those categories. He knew that God loves what he has created but that that same creation must volitionally accept God on God's own terms. Beauty is a gift that must be received if it is to wed us to God. Yet, when it is received it holds the potential to shape us after our own maker, the Beautiful one himself.

WHAT DIONYSIUS TEACHES US TO SEE:

- God's name is beautiful
- beauty reveals God
- God is involved in his love for us
- God's love is other-directed
- God porously shares his beauty with and through creation
- the universe is a divinely organized hierarchy of beauty
- beauty is a porous gift

61. Eco, *Thomas Aquinas*, 139. With the second quotation Eco was echoing Huizinga, *Waning of the Middle Ages*, 194.

Pseudo-Dionysius the Areopagite (5th–6th Centuries)

- theology is chiefly a matter of wonder
- beauty is causative
- beauty summons us to beauty

5

The Medieval Era and Thomas Aquinas (1225–1274)

Beauty in Our Eyes and Minds

Does beauty really exist or do we merely experience things as beautiful? Would everyone agree that something, say for instance Vincent Van Gogh's painting *Purple Irises*, is beautiful, or is it true that beauty merely exists in the eye of the beholder? Especially in our populist era, where everyone gets a vote, is it the case that beauty is only a matter of opinion? After all, my favorite color is green and yours is red; doesn't that prove beauty is entirely subjective? The relegation of certain questions to a subjective interpretation owes greatly to the influence of Immanuel Kant, a philosopher to whom we will turn later. We should know, however, that perspectives on subjectivity and the importance therewith for approaching and framing beauty were developing centuries ago in the medieval era. Let us be nuanced: since philosophy's advent ancient philosophers knew that human persons are sensing and perceiving beings. Plato himself famously defined beauty as "that which pleases, when seen." And yet, the ancients believed they were observing instantiations of objective beauty.

That the sensing and perceiving subject is *necessary* for beauty's realization is a development that finds its dawning in the medieval era. We will say more below. Suffice it to say here that relevant for our own understanding, philosophers have been aware of the notion of subjectivity and its centrality in the experience of beauty for at least some 800 years. Seen from this philosophic vantage point, we are, in more ways than can be measured, the product of those who not only went before us but those who *thought* before us.

Because we today are indeed so profoundly shaped by the practices, ideas, traditions, and values of the past, it behooves us to examine a couple of significant historic seasons as seasons. Heretofore we have been looking exclusively at theologians and their positions on beauty and aesthetics. However, as influential as great thinkers were and are, our own contemporary vistas are also the result of huge and significant historic epochs. In our next chapter we will examine the Reformation and three seminal theologians therein. In this chapter we will consider the medieval era and Thomas Aquinas as indicative of the subtle, and not so subtle, shifts that were occurring concerning beauty and aesthetics.

THE MEDIEVAL ERA: SEEING IMAGES, GRASPING BEAUTY

It is part of the human condition to suppose that everyone does life the way we do. Then, when we find out that they—whoever *they* are—do things differently, or look at things differently, we become resentful. If global human history, permeated as it is by millennia of ethnic discrimination, racism, and genocide is any indicator, we quickly mistrust those who perceive life in ways divergent from our own. "How can they be so dull?!" The generations coming out of Western antiquity and the generations of folks who lived in and through the medieval era did not remotely view beauty, aesthetics, or images the way we twenty-first–century Westerners do.

Medieval Europeans, living on the vestiges of antiquity, perceived much of life as an enormous metaphysical force field. In their world everything had hidden qualities, imperceptible attributes, and invisible powers. For medieval Christians, physical things pointed to spiritual things; this anticipated life both intersected with and foreshadowed the next life. Christianity had, for the most part, triumphed over the world view of Greco-Roman religious ideas. For instance, most people believed that one God created the world, holds it together, grants Christ's grace to the repentant, and judges the actions, words, and thoughts of everyone. Furthermore, they believed that same God was involved, or could be involved, in everyday life. The biblical story was replete with miraculous events, angelic visitations, the actions of God's Spirit, and the providence of God in and over history.

For Him Who Has Eyes to See

We may accurately summarize this medieval perspective as envisioning an open universe. For instance, the later eighteenth-century Deists, or twenty-first-century atheists, believed in a closed universe. God had, for the Deists, created the world and established the laws of nature to thereafter guide and govern the world, but God himself did not truly intervene in the affairs of nations or the daily needs of everyday people. For the atheists, the universe is merely an amalgam of energized matter (variously understood by differing philosophers) interacting with energized matter. For both the Deists and the atheists, the universe is a closed entity. The popular astronomer Carl Sagan (1934–1996) aptly summarized the attitude of those espousing a closed universe: "The cosmos is all that is or ever will be." Again, medieval folks lived centuries prior to those espousing a closed universe. Indeed, so alive and so metaphysical was everyday life that many Christian lay people were wary of the existence of witches, continued to believe in magic, and practiced astrology. Chesterton reasoned that Christianity had overcome pagan antiquity, but only to a certain measure.[1] The old pagan ways clung tenaciously to the European imagination.

That brief overview in mind, we won't be surprised to know that theories about optics at work in the medieval era were also metaphysically charged. In the fourth century before Christ both Euclid and Ptolemy taught that human eyes emit invisible rays toward objects, and that those rays enable the eyes to visually seize the objects. An alternate theory, espoused by both Aristotle and a Muslim philosopher named Alhazen (AD 965–1040), was that objects emit rays that touch upon our eyes so that vision occurs. In both of those optical theories, there is an exchange, an actual metaphysical contact that occurs between objects and peoples' eyes. And, the historic record shows, these exchanges frequently had a profound effect upon the viewer. Let's put this in perspective.

Concerning the five senses, the world of Evangelical Protestantism is today primarily aural: we favor hearing. Worship music and sermons are the two primary components of an Evangelical church service. Millions choose a church on the basis of either how much they like the sound and style of the worship band or on the preacher's ability to touch their hearts. Especially in Pentecostal piety, pastors encourage their parishioners to listen for the voice of God's Spirit amid life's routine circumstances. Hand in hand with that is the belief that people can come to faith in Christ through hearing, even as Paul taught in Romans (10:17). We must not press this

---

1. Chesterton, *St. Francis of Assisi*, 27–31.

The Medieval Era and Thomas Aquinas (1225–1274)

too hard, but by way of contrast, the medieval world, at least as it concerned Christian experience, favored seeing.[2] Much of the Catholic mass was whispered by the serving priest, so the worshipping congregants had little to hear.[3] In the petite hill town of Assisi, while gazing at the San Damiano crucifix, Saint Francis (1181–1226) heard Jesus say to him, "Francis, repair my church." That audiovisual experience was seminal in Francis's lifelong turn to Christ. Catherine of Siena (1347–1380) became a nun after she saw a vision of Saint Dominic. Staring at a crucifix, Lady Julian of Norwich (1342–1416) was profoundly touched and resolutely transformed. In sum, vision was truly powerful in the medieval period. Common people expected that religious images could communicate to them, enrapt them, and even effect religious ecstasy.[4] We would also do well to realize that they did not view images in the kind of neutral manner that we (supposedly) do today.[5] They were not at all viewing religious art *as art*, but rather did so as part and parcel of what it meant to be Christian. Viewing Christian art was a practice of common piety; it was a way to share in a perception of reality that was widespread.[6]

Even in the Catholic mass, "the sight of the host, the *touching* of the body of Christ by the visual ray of the worshipper," Miles noted, "was thought to have a salvific effect."[7] In the medieval era the images and the paintings inside churches were intended to profoundly impact the viewing congregants. Priests learned to make very stylized and dramatic gestures to

---

2. Dyrness, *Reformed Theology*, clarifies that medieval seeing was very much processed by what was known through hearing, especially through hearing the mass. Medievals gave the eye, he notes, "a privileged though not exclusive role." Ibid., 29.

3. Miles, *Image as Insight*, 97. She adds, "the service of the word, except for the sermon, was conducted in Latin, a language that had become unintelligible to laypeople and even to most priests." Ibid.

4. Ibid., 67.

5. Today's viewer sees an advertisement and is suspicious about its truthfulness; she knows that products rarely make us as happy as the advertisement suggests. Similarly, when a contemporary person sees a news photograph he expects that the picture is conveying pertinent information. Contrastingly, "the historical viewer," Miles notes, "expected images to present a world in which reality and values were organized in an absolute, harmonized, and permanent configuration. The historical viewer expected to contemplate the image and be formed by it; he or she did not expect to receive information from it or to evaluate it critically." Ibid., 128.

6. Dyrness, *Reformed Theology*, 36–44.

7. Miles, *Image as Insight*, 96. Original italics. Sometimes when the laity could not see the priest holding up the Eucharistic host they would shout, "Lift it higher." Dyrness, *Reformed Theology*, 29.

draw the visual attention of the laity. There were even costumes and theatrical portrayals employed to bless, benefit, and draw in the worshippers.[8]

It may help us to grasp their imagination if we realize that there were very few images present in everyday medieval life. We moderns are bombarded with images. Television, movies, and the Internet on both computers and cell phones have us awash in a ubiquitous sea of electronic images. It is difficult to drive down an urban freeway without being inundated with billboard ads. Many magazines have more full-page ads in them than written content. We block out, or think we do, layers of images that daily confront our eyes. In the medieval era there were no advertising houses, no printing presses, no electronic media to mass produce images. Businessmen did not promote their companies with eye-catching signs. The only images that the average peasant would see in her life were the ones at a prominent church; knowing that, some priests would get a donkey or mule and go on parish tours carrying images so the rural folk indeed could have opportunity to view the sacred objects and paintings and thereby be blessed. Images' minimal presence alone made paintings and statues significant. If we mix in to this dynamic that medievals believed that images were locales for/of experience, we can begin to imagine how wondrous they were perceived to be. "In the Medieval era vision was," Miles clarified, "the strongest possible access to an object of devotion."[9]

Catholic Church leaders knew these things, too. Priests taught the laity that contemplating a religious image was a means to possible beatitude. Images were sacramental vehicles, not officially so but practically so. In the thirteenth century John of Genoa wrote an influential textbook entitled *Catholicon*. Therein he taught that there are three good reasons for the church to use images:

> First, for the instruction of simple people, because they are instructed by them as if by books. Second, so that the mystery of the incarnation and the examples of the saints may be the more active in our memory through being presented daily to our lives. Third, to excite feelings of devotion, these being aroused more effectively by things seen than by things heard.[10]

---

8. Miles, *Image as Insight*, 68, 73, 98.

9. Ibid., 96. And this visual emphasis was ancient. In the patristic era unbaptized catachumens, made to sit in alcoves off the nave, were only allowed to hear but not see the liturgy. Miles, 180, cites Moeller, "Piety in Germany Around 1500," 50–75.

10. Baxandall, *Painting and Experience in Fifteenth Century Italy*, 41.

The Medieval Era and Thomas Aquinas (1225–1274)

Common in my own undergraduate church history classes is a student's question, "Why would they admire images, or consult church tradition, when they could just read the Bible?" My students do not realize that Bibles had to be hand copied and so were quite expensive; only monasteries, churches, and the aristocracy could afford Bibles. Equally important, most medievals could not read at all. For centuries into the Middle Ages even many priests were illiterate; their ecclesial training consisted of memorizing church rites and rituals. Truly, until long after the Gutenberg printing press was built in 1439 most people were illiterate. Keith Moxey notes that by the year 1500 only 5 percent of the population, at most, could read.[11] As in Jesus' day, folks would pay rhetoricians or lawyers to read aloud and/or draft letters or important documents. That situation, it is not hard to infer, made images all the more important and powerful. They stood out precisely for being so sparse. Indeed, religious images were prized. When the Black Death swept Europe in the fourteenth century a sudden rush of extraordinary fiscal gifts, as appeals for prayers and blessing, were given to churches that in turn used that new wealth to foster new paintings and frescoes. Architectural design accommodatingly shifted so that greater light shone into the churches to better display the artwork.[12] Formerly grey and dark churches began increasingly to favor more light and vivid colors.

Within this metaphysically charged environment medieval theologians embraced and taught the older Greek philosophical belief that images both contained and conveyed the prototype, the original subject or person. In other words, a wooden crucifix not only symbolized Jesus' death to the viewer, it actually touched upon the crucifixion at Golgotha itself. Or, as we will see later in a chapter specifically on iconographic theology, an icon of Jesus' mother Mary was believed to be a window through which one could view Mary herself. Plato had taught anamnesis: calling to mind an event or reality as though it were present in this moment. (Jesus exhorted this mimetic practice regarding the celebration of his Last Supper; Luke 22:19; 1 Cor 11:24–25.) We saw in our earlier chapter on Pseudo-Dionysius that there was a patristic belief in the porous nature of time and the supernatural: miracles and the past could erupt in and through the present, and the future could poke into one's current time. Anamnesis—remembering again in a participatory manner—was practiced while viewing Catholic images. Pictures and beauty were not so static as we view them today. Indeed,

11. Moxey, *Popular Imagery in the Reformation*, 24.
12. Miles, *Image as Insight*, 65–66.

miracles and healings took place at the feet of such Christian paintings and symbols. The French abbot Suger of St. Denis (1081–1151) described his own ecstatic state, the result of gazing at the precious stones within the altar and its sacred vessels:

> When—out of my delight in the beauty of the house of God—the loveliness of the many-colored gems has called me away from external cares, and worthy meditation has induced me to reflect, transferring that which is material to that which is immaterial, on the diversity of the sacred virtues: then it seems to me that I see myself dwelling, as it were, in some strange region of the universe which neither exists entirely in the slime of the earth nor entirely in the purity of Heaven; and that, by the grace of God, I can be transported from this inferior to that higher world in an anagogical manner.[13]

Moreover, Miles asserts that frescoes and paintings were understood by medieval Christians as being like the single frame of a movie: they enabled the viewer to see an actual moment of the historic event. "To see these frescoes," Miles clarified, "was to see actions momentarily suspended so that each detail could be savored."[14]

Beholding religious images was not just a way to be introspective or pious, to pose it in a more psychologizing and contemporary way. Aesthetic contemplation was a means to blessing, a way to experience something of the other world, and an instrument for the shaping of one's own heart and affections by God's grace and goodness. Contemplating images was a way to make people better. Miles notes that this was not a practice reserved for the holy, for monks or nuns alone.

> People expected to experience visions, and they did experience them. Even the ordinary worshipper without aspirations to mystical experience could expect that this contemplation of the images surrounding him in his local church would erase the distance between his personal existence and the sacred events and figures of scripture, thus placing his life in the context of the divine scheme of creation, redemption, and eschatology. Images encouraged the identification of the life of the worshipper with past and future sacred events by revealing a visually present universe. The medieval

---

13. Ibid., 67, quoting *De Administratione*, in Panofsky, *Abbot Suger on the Abbey Church of St.-Denis*, 21.

14. Ibid., 72.

worshipper became, through concentrated vision, present at the nativity, the crucifixion, the resurrection, and Last Judgment.[15]

Having been to Ukraine, Serbia, Romania, Bulgaria, and Greece, I know that this understanding of vision's invisible power abides even today. Many Eastern Europeans shun eye contact with strangers not only as a formal social norm but also to avoid entangling bad luck or an omen, or even catching a curse, from such seeing. Belief in the "evil eye" remains alive today. Conversely, that same disposition toward seeing motivates many Eastern Orthodox Christians to prayerfully contemplate icons in their "red corner," the beautiful corner, that devotional assembly of objects that characterizes the homes of millions. Seeing beauty, especially as it shines through Christian forms and symbols, is understood to be an avenue for peace, felicity, and God's blessing.

Admittedly, the medieval belief in metaphysics and the effects of that on seeing is quite foreign, and indeed scientifically passé, to most Westerners, particularly most Evangelical believers, today. Without suggesting a one-for-one appropriation of medieval theories of optics, I do believe it worth pausing to note that we continue to be shaped by what we see. Negatively, one only need to think of the effects of pornography on the hearts and minds of men (and increasingly women), or about the devastating influence of women's fashion magazines on women's self-perceptions. Every semester I have young men and women in my campus office processing the destructive effects of their seeing. Positively, we tend to become like, or emulate the values of, our physical vision's focus. For example, athletes repeatedly watch video of themselves, or others, who perform the play, move, or action with efficiency and excellence as a way to help their own brains more readily perform said play, move, or action.

Evangelical and Pentecostal church leaders who believe that no aesthetic is better than a religious aesthetic are fooling themselves. People necessarily will be aesthetically involved one way or another, so if it is not sacred it will undoubtedly be secular. Why not foster aesthetic engagement in our worship? We human beings not only *live in* space and time, we *embody* space and time. Alternately stated, it is in our bone marrow to make things that delight our vision, to foster experiences of beauty that allow for peaceful contemplation, and to appreciate excellent design. If we do not foster Christian or Christianized opportunities for our very human visual longings, we will satisfy those with other-than-Christian or Christianized

15. Ibid., 67.

symbols and images. I believe that trade-off is having devastating consequences on today's believers.

Having offered a broad but brief societal perspective on how medievals practiced and understood what it meant to see form and religious beauty, let us now to turn to a theologian to see what innovations or changes that may have been at work within that broader matrix.

THOMAS AQUINAS: NUANCING THE TOPIC

Whereas Augustine is the most influential Western theologian of all time, Thomas Aquinas is undoubtedly the most influential Roman Catholic theologian ever. Born at Aquino, near Naples, Italy, into a family of some nobility, as a young boy Thomas was sent first to an abbey for elementary education and then to the University of Naples. His family wanted Thomas to serve in the Benedictine order, but at the university he joined the Dominican order, a wandering monastic group given to the disciplines of studying, teaching, and preaching. He was a quiet pupil. Accordingly, targeting his quiet demeanor his fellow students called him a "dumb ox." His teacher, Albert the Great, saw much potential in Thomas and famously retorted, "You call him a Dumb Ox: I tell you this Dumb Ox shall bellow so loud that his bellowings will fill the world." Eventually Thomas became a university professor in Paris and taught there until the last two years of his life, during which he taught at yet another university in Naples. At the age of forty-nine, while riding a donkey to the Council of Lyons, he hit his head on a tree branch, fell ill, and died not long thereafter at a monastery near Rome.

Thomas is famous for his delineations concerning faith and reason; reason is a gift of God that works and teaches in the service of faith. And for all the medieval emphasis upon reason, Aquinas held that in the end that clinging to God in union through faith is better than mere human knowledge. Thomas wrote, "For we are conjoined through faith to things higher than those to which the natural reason pertains and we inhere in them more certainly, to the extent that divine revelation is more certain than human cognition."[16] Among philosophers, Thomas is famous for having woven Aristotle's ideas into a "new synthesis of science and theology,"[17]

---

16. Aquinas, *The Divine Names*, 1.1., quoted in Sammon, *The God Who Is Beauty*, 271–72.

17. McDermott, *The Great Theologians*, 67.

The Medieval Era and Thomas Aquinas (1225–1274)

though Thomas rejected Aristotle where he violated biblical teaching. On natural theology, that which can be known about God apart from biblical revelation, Aristotle was deemed an authority by Thomas. Of Aquinas's use of Aristotle Artz wrote that Thomas "always saw Aristotle through a Neo-Platonist haze."[18] Thus, that older idealizing, hierarchical, universalizing perspective was not abandoned by Thomas. We should also note that in contradistinction to Augustine, whom Thomas followed on many aspects, Aquinas much emphasized human free willing.

Thomas never wrote a specific document about beauty or the fine arts.[19] And yet, a committed philosopher, he was interested in goodness and truth and beauty—together with being, the transcendentals of philosophy. Thomas touched upon beauty across his writings. First, we must clarify that much of what Thomas wrote about aesthetics and beauty reiterated many previous philosophers and theologians. For instance, following Plato's adage, Thomas understood that *"beauty is that which, when seen, gives pleasure."* And in that light, like the ancients, Aquinas reasoned that too much pleasure could actually be harmful; thus, beauty could be dangerous.[20] Keeping with accepted tradition, Thomas held that *beauty has anagogical power* to transform us, especially in our intellect and soul, to higher realms of character and virtue, even toward God himself. This is because our being was created by God to have correspondence to and with God's own being. Our being and the beauty therein reflects God's being and beauty. And yet, preserving the ancient Christian apophatic emphasis, Thomas knew that our anagogical movement toward God in no way exhausts God. Aquinas was emphatic that God remains ever transcendent—"God's hiddenness is never overcome."[21] On this same point, that both our being and the beauty of creation correspond to God, Thomas believed that images can point us to God; it is no surprise, then, that he defended the use of Christian imagery for both theological and practical reasons: images can instruct in the faith and generate devotion.[22]

Also true to established categories, Aquinas held that *there was a God-designed hierarchical quality to life.* Some things and creatures had greater being than other things and creatures; some people were greater

18. Artz, *The Mind of the Middle Ages*, 265.
19. Eco, *Thomas Aquinas*, 115–16, 163, 181–83, 213.
20. Sammon, *The God Who is Beauty*, 266.
21. Ibid., 278.
22. Cf. Phillips, *Destruction of Art in England*, 14.

than others. Indeed, Aquinas was very much a man of his own era: he maintained and sustained that the aristocracy was superior to the common folk.[23] Like the entire Greek philosophic span, Thomas believed that *the good and the beautiful were inseparable.* While the good is sought by every creature through the appetite, beauty is recognized and sought after with the intellect; the older Platonic-Augustinian bifurcation of the human self into lower (appetite) and higher (intellect) realms remained present in Aquinas.[24] Indeed, Thomas highly esteemed both contemplation and the contemplative life because quietude fostered greater apprehension of the good and the beautiful.[25] Like Augustine and Pseudo-Dionysius before him, Aquinas believed that *creation was willed rather than emanated;*[26] creation's beauty, then, is planned, not accidental; God meant for beauty variously to be perceived, shared, and enjoyed.

Specifically, in his reflections on beauty and aesthetics, Aquinas was most reliant upon Dionysius; indeed, he wrote a commentary on Dionysius's *Divine Names*.[27] Like his Eastern forebearer, Thomas even made the bold step of calling God by the name beauty; though he did so committed to the belief that God's names, while they are self-revelatory, never fully explain God.[28] In his aesthetic reflections, Aquinas referenced Dionysius more than any other author; this even though Thomas is renowned for relying heavily upon Aristotle.[29] Some 1,700 times Aquinas cited Dionysius.[30] And yet, Aquinas was not merely regurgitating Dionysius. Instead he was contextualizing Dionysius for his own milieu and concerns. On that point, to understand Thomas in his milieu, it is important to note that medieval theology was broadly characterized by organization and codification more so than novelty and creativity.[31] Still, this does not render Thomas irrelevant for our own consideration. He is today viewed by many theologians

---

23. Eco, *Thomas Aquinas*, 182, 213.

24. Viladesau, *Theological Aesthetics*, 107.

25. Eco, *Thomas Aquinas*, 87.

26. Sammon, *The God Who is Beauty*, 7.

27. *The Divine Names* was the only non-biblical book about which Thomas wrote a commentary. Cf. Sammon, *The God Who is Beauty*, 262.

28. Ibid., 266–76.

29. Ibid., 261.

30. Ibid., 262.

31. Artz: "Even the most radical and the most original of medieval thinkers never ceased to maintain vestiges of their own time and they were never wholly modern." *The Mind of the Middle Ages*, ix.

The Medieval Era and Thomas Aquinas (1225–1274)

as an enormous giant in the annals of theology. We will unpack the positions that make Thomas unique: his beliefs about beauty as it concerns *the concretization of forms* and *the role of the viewer*.

THE CONCRETIZATION OF THE FORM

Following earlier philosophers and theologians Thomas maintained that there are objective (i.e., ontologically existing categories independent of human causation) and necessary categories for beauty's existence. These categories—clarity, proportion, and integrity—had long been established by tradition, but Thomas took and modified them in subtle but significant ways. Clarity is brightness or brilliance, or even effulgence of color. To the medieval mind more color indicated more beauty; medieval folks loved bright primary colors and used them extensively in their church decoration and apparel.[32] Similarly, we twenty-first-century denizens, chiefly because of our harnessing of electricity, are regularly surrounded by brightness and shimmering spectacle. We enjoy pictures of the earth at night that show how entire continents are dotted by and enswathed in light. A medieval person could barely imagine such a possibility. If we remember that prior to the twentieth century there was no electricity, we can imagine why brightness and brilliance were so esteemed in aesthetic formulation.

Proportion, the most widely accepted formal aesthetic category in antiquity,[33] touches upon the harmony of a body, design, or thing. If someone's right ear was sizably larger than their left ear, the ancients and medievals would not view said person as being beautiful. They insisted on symmetry and balance in their aesthetic. Eco notes the Greek theory of *kairos*, "fitness or measure," for the given circumstance, is apt for describing the attribute of proportion. There is a relationship both between the whole and the parts and all the parts to the other parts. Aquinas especially touched upon proportion in his reflections on music theory and music.[34] It is, Eco asserts, with the last of the three categories—integrity—that Thomas makes a subtle but significant shift for the history of aesthetics. Hence we will probe a bit deeper from hereon.

Integrity involves the completion of the form. A thing, person, or instantiation of beauty is what it is by virtue of its own irreducible *form*: the

---

32. Eco, *Thomas Aquinas*, 105–6.
33. Ibid., 71.
34. Ibid., 77. The quote is from page 74.

idea in God's mind now become manifest; the dynamic that gives reality to matter; the that-ness (*quidditas*, in Latin) that makes the thing, person, or instantiation to belong to the category or species that it does. Once again, this is a metaphysical way to frame reality: there are invisible somethings—forms—that give rise and shape to visible somethings. And lest this seem antiquated, let us wonder, just what indeed makes a hummingbird different from a pelican? Our answer today would be, "Their respective DNA." A medieval philosopher would wryly then answer, "Yes, but what makes their respective DNA different?" Put thus, we can see some of the genius of the notion of forms: it is a heuristic, a broadly accepted educated guess that, while not exhausting the question, helps us frame the issue in a way that goes beyond merely positing "it's entirely a mystery" or "it is itself a god." Hummingbirds don't mate and produce pelicans. Why? It is not their form.

Eco says about Thomas on integrity—sometimes translated by later scholars as perfection—there is neither too much nor too little of a quality, color, or element; the thing, the object viewed is primarily a matter of being just right.[35] The form is not, Eco argues, an invisible or nonphysical "pure structure or pattern, which can be abstracted by the mind from a complete object and imposed upon shapeless stuff, but [is] rather a structure or pattern which is materially at one with the object." For Aquinas, full integrity occurs only *in* a being. In the being "substance truly exists, lives, and enfolds." Eco continues, "The beings . . . which populate Aquinas' universe are *not pure symbolical manifestations of the divine creativity*. They are concrete realities, and as such they can be understood as 'forms.'" Later Eco encapsulated Thomas: "aesthetic value is rooted in the concreteness of things."[36] Again, there is in Thomas a *concretization* of the form that is significant for our understanding the nuance at work in Aquinas's theo-aesthetic thought.

There is then, Eco emphasizes, a *subtle but important shift* at work in and through Thomas: the thing itself embodies the form. Previously, across philosophy's history, the emphasis had been upon the invisible, preexistent, divinely caused and therefore objective cause: the form. With Thomas the thing-as-such is taken more seriously as embodying the form. Let's apply this.

When Thomas looked at something he was less envisioning the appearance of a divine, or quasi-divine, invisible idea now materialized; that was more in keeping with how Augustine and Pseudo-Dionysius practiced

---

35. Eco, *Thomas Aquinas*, 99–100, 206.

36. The first two quotes are from ibid., 71, the last one is on 193. My italics.

their aesthetic. Thomas was more intently looking at the thing itself as beautiful. Thomas was not trying to see an invisible form, he was enjoying the form in front of him. He was not, Eco argues, divorcing the form from the sensible.[37] Whereas the older classical vantage point accentuated the ideal, Thomas was opening the door toward a perspective that would focus on the there-ness—the actual presence in the thing—of beauty.[38] Is this discussion about form and concretization concerning beauty becoming too abstract and therefore of little consequence? Let me suggest why this matters.

A FORMING FORAY: CONTEMPORARY EVANGELICAL SPIRITUALITY AND AESTHETICS

As I have said before, I have the privilege of teaching theology at a private Christian university. That means I am regularly surrounded by Evangelical piety. In chapel services, dorm devotionals, and classroom prayers, regularly I hear student leaders pray like, "We welcome you here, Lord Jesus. Come have your way with us. Help us to just get out of the way so you can accomplish your purposes. We know, Lord, that this is not about us, it is only about you." Not even by a skosh do I question the heartfelt sincerity of such prayers. Because students have learned to pray by hearing the entreaties of their parents and pastors I know these prayers are part and parcel of a socialized world view. And yet it is a world view that tends toward the Gnostic: it scorns the physical for the spiritual, and it broadly holds that the miraculous is greater than the mundane. Unwittingly, it is a holdover world view from both antiquity and the sixteenth century Reformation: the invisible form is greater than, and therefore more desirous than, the physical thing-as-such.[39]

---

37. Ibid., 193.

38. Ibid., 70–1, 86–88, 95–96, 141, 185–86, 193–203, 212.

39. Unquestionably, besides antiquity and the Reformation, there are other contributors and ideals from history involved within Evangelical piety. For instance, we could add both the Kierkegaardian introspective turn and the Schleiermacharian subjectivizing turn toward experience. With those philosophical and theological impulses we should also mix in a simple "be ye thou separate" from the world attitude, continually interpreted as "be separate from physicality," an abiding attitude in Evangelicalism. Each of those, in their own varied ways, frustrates an understanding of God working in and through the here and now.

For Him Who Has Eyes to See

Never in those devotional settings, but indeed in my classes, I suggest to my students that not only is such a spiritual world view not immediately biblical, it is unhealthy. I tell the leaders, "The Lord has given you the gifts of leadership and musicianship precisely so *you can be in the way*. He delights in working *through you*. By your service, you have the opportunity for the Holy Spirit *to shine through you* for the benefit of others and the glory of God. The amazing thing about our life in Christ is that he invites us to share in his own work." Evangelicals fondly and routinely teach "Christianity is not a religion, it is a relationship." And then they inadvertently limit the extent of that relationship by suggesting that abiding goodness or transformative interaction occurs exclusively when God himself descends and supernaturally touches a person's heart, body, or circumstance. No, I insist, with God there is always more, always room for relationship, always a delight for sharing! God is a jealous God: he wants his people to be his exclusive people. But God is not a stingy God: he's not trying to keep people *out* of his working. Rather, he is earnestly seeking more workers *to join* in the sowing, watering, and reaping. Jesus' Spirit gives gifts not just to bless the gift-receivers themselves, but so that an exchange, a co-working, a dance, a shared endeavor, a mutual delight can occur in the offing. We are given gifts and opportunities so that we can be involved in sharing those with others. The focus of trinitarian mutuality is not just that somebody was edified in the churchly service (or the cooked meal, blanket donated, the sick given medicine, or the homeless given an abode), but also that we ourselves, and we corporately, were allowed to be present variously to foster, enhance, be involved in, and flourish together in and with God himself. *God enjoys our being involved in the doing.* Why instruct us to lay hands on one another for prayer if the "real" emphasis is the supernatural thing God does *despite* that touching? Again, *either-or* constructions are regularly and commonly embraced by Evangelicals when Scripture shows it is a *both-and* dynamic both to serve God and to serve with God.

Aesthetically, this *either-or* Evangelical framing of piety too easily neglects the blessing right in front of us for the supposedly greater supernatural blessing that we seek. Over coffee, I once discussed salvation with my formerly agnostic but now converted Eastern Orthodox mother. After I talked about heaven she said to me, "Ed, I wonder if you miss the salvation right in front of you?" Puzzled, I responded, "what do you mean?" She returned, "A hug from one of your kids is salvation now. Enjoying a nice meal is salvation in the now. Or a good cup of coffee. Those are to enjoy the

The Medieval Era and Thomas Aquinas (1225–1274)

blessings of God in the here and now." I have pondered that conversation many times in the years since. Indeed, what is salvation? Dying and going to heaven? I'm all for that! And yet the biblical portrayal is that salvation is enjoying God now, the people he's surrounded us with now, and the goodness and beauty of his own creativity now and on into eternity.

Regarding an aesthetic perspective, Evangelical piety too easily misses the joy and goodness of the physical realm. God loves what he created. He did not create the universe simply so people could be born, die, and then go to live with him in heaven. That is not the biblical witness. In Genesis God called his creation good. That is breathtakingly profound for our own perception of beauty. But if God's pronouncement of creation's goodness does not suffice, note that later in history *he became his creation*. Summarizing biblical teaching, Anglicanism's *Westminster Shorter Catechism* has it right: "Man's chief end is to glorify God and enjoy him forever." Do we think that "enjoy him" means only in heaven?

I will not develop further the implications of the Evangelical nascent Gnosticism[40] except to say that I believe it also causes Evangelicals to overlook the beauty and goodness that daily surrounds them. My boyhood pastor was theologically in error to teach us that we ought not enjoy the beauty of physical life. True, it ought not be worshipped, but creation is good. We can sit on the deck of a house and soak in a gorgeous mountain view for its own sake. God does. "The universe, Aquinas tells us, is always beautiful in the eyes of God."[41]

SUBJECTIVE PROCESSING: THE ROLE OF THE VIEWER

Whereas a subtle philosophic shift was at work with Thomas on the concretization of the form he also gave new attention to the role of the viewer. And, as with the embedded nature of the form, he did so not by introducing a position that was *de novo*, but one that modified earlier understandings. Like the world of antiquity that preceded him, Aquinas was aware that beauty was something that needed to be recognized: "beauty is that

---

40. Particularly, my reflections hereon were stimulated by Ewing, "The Hidden Pentecostal Doctrine: A Modern Gnosticism." To sample some of my own aesthetic formulation see Rybarczyk, "Pentecostalism, Human Nature, and Aesthetics: 21st Century Engagement."

41. Eco, *Thomas Aquinas*, 191.

which pleases when it is perceived." Thomas was clearly aware that there were both objective and subjective components to beauty.[42] This, however, was no mere appeal to subjectivity. Rather, for Aquinas, it had to do with the process of intellection: how and when we perceive.

It's an interesting question. Observing a scene, or hearing a musical piece, when do we realize that we are apprehending beauty? Or, when does beauty "hit" us? Some twenty-first-century museum curators and aesthetes today believe our awareness of beauty happens at a precritical level.[43] Building on a couple centuries of Romantic philosophy, these types of aesthetes believe that beauty touches our soul or heart *before* it does our brain. We "feel" some kind of kinetic energy, we become aware of the presence of something extraordinary, and then we remark to ourselves, "ahh, isn't that fantastic?!" In fact, if we get too critically minded, for these Romanticist aesthetes, we can criticize the beauty right out of something. So, for them, beauty is discerned *before* we turn on our prefrontal cortex; beauty touches our senses before we begin to consciously consider it in a critical, scrutinizing, conscious, and analyzing manner. In short, for many Romantics beauty is intuited. Eco argues repeatedly that is not at all what Aquinas believed to be true about human intellection and apprehension of beauty.[44]

Against more contemporary and Romanticist notions, Thomas believed that we begin to apprehend beauty when we are critically processing its presence. The beautiful thing may be present in life but it waits, as it were, to be beholden. And if "this judgment is to actually take place, it is necessary that a seeing or looking should be focused upon the thing." Furthermore, remarked Eco, "it is therefore necessary that there should be a new and essential type of proportion, this time between the knowing subject and the object." Until the object is seen it cannot declare itself. But when a viewer, observer, perceiver, comes upon it then it is that the thing expresses and "declares itself." Again, beauty only becomes beautiful when

---

42. Bourke, *The Pocket Aquinas*, 261. Thomas follows Plato's above-quoted definition in *Summa Theologiae*, 1a v. 4 ad 1.

43. Gladwell, *Blink*, 253, relates the story about how Thomas Hoving, former director of New York's Metropolitan Museum of Art, used to have his employees cover or hide pieces of art so that when he "discovered" them he would process them spontaneously and determine how he felt about them on the spot. Famed American philosopher John Dewey called this "the original innocence of the eye," or the "pre-analytic phase." *Art as Experience*, 260 and 151 on the respective quotes.

44. Eco, *Thomas Aquinas*, 60, 63, 192–93.

The Medieval Era and Thomas Aquinas (1225–1274)

a knowing subject is present to perceive.[45] True, our senses are involved in perceiving and apprehending the beautiful, but it is our reason, our brain, that realizes its presence. The intellect is critical for Thomas. With even more precision Eco said, "beauty has to do with cognition."[46] Animals, though they participate in nature, do not enjoy its beauty because they are not intellectually processing the appearance of beauty. Thomas's own teacher, Albert the Great, made no reference to the knowing subject, so this is a marked shift, even if to us it seems marginal.[47]

So, if we were to go to the Vatican Museum in Rome with Aquinas, to choose a locale closer to his own home, he would urge us to learn something first about the genres, eras, artists, and their patrons before we walked inside the doors. "It is necessary, in short, to have a very profound knowledge of the object. Looking at an object aesthetically means looking at its structure, physical and metaphysical, as exhaustively as possible, in all its meanings and implications, and in its proportionate relations to its own nature and to its accidental circumstances." Eco continued his summary of Thomas on aesthetic judgment, "It means, that is, a kind of reasoning about the object, scrutinizing it in detail and in depth. Only then can it be appreciated in its harmony and structure."[48] True aesthetic appreciation, true grasping of beauty, happens in the process of judging and assessing. Whereas our Romanticist friends would want to enjoy the "aha" moment of being surprised by the artwork inside the Vatican, Thomas believed there is greater aesthetic pleasure to be had for thoroughly squeezing the lemons, for going into depth about the possibilities, variations, and subtleties of the juice, the beauty, itself. In fact, Thomas was resolute on this: "The human intellect does not immediately, in first apprehending a thing, have complete knowledge."[49] We do better, in terms of recognizing and appreciating beauty, to understand that which we are observing.

---

45. Eco, *Thomas Aquinas*, 119.

46. Ibid., 118.

47. Ibid. notes that it was fairly marginal for Thomas himself. Even though it was a new perspective, a small metamorphosis, Thomas did not muse for long thereon as "it was of no specific interest to him." Eco's remarks about Albert are on 58. Sammon, *The God Who is Beauty*, 258, makes the same point on the divergence between Albert and Thomas.

48. Eco, *Thomas Aquinas*, 196. Eco continues on this theme, 196–203.

49. Thomas Aquinas, *Summa Theologiae*, 1, 85, 5c, in Eco, 197.

For Him Who Has Eyes to See

WRAP-UP

In observing Thomas's emphasis upon the necessary role of the viewer we would be incorrect to suppose that he was somehow beginning to argue that beauty is in the eye of the beholder; that development would take many subsequent generations to unfold. Nevertheless, he is remarkable for having tilted the discussion, if even subtly, away from the standard idealizing and metaphysical view of beauty that he inherited from antiquity. Did he, by teaching these views, have an influence on subsequent generations of churchmen or artists? Scholars believe it difficult to assess.[50] Do artists influence the broader culture or is it that they are influenced by the broader culture? Undoubtedly, it is some of both. And so it is with Christian philosophers and theologians. Indeed, philosophy and theology are enjoined to be ever diligent in pondering society's new, or newly framed, questions, and seeking answers that are both true to the biblical witness and culturally relevant. Furthermore, Thomas was not the only one beginning to tweak the older inheritances about beauty and form.

Duns Scotus (1266–1308), the whipping boy for later philosophers and schoolmen (he gets called "Dunce"), posited philosophical considerations that would help to permeate and change later, future understandings when he argued that particulars are superior to essences.[51] That is, the thing-as-such is superior to the category to which it belongs. For instance, James the man is greater and more real than the category of human nature. Or to put it still differently, Scotus believed that we don't have universals in our minds, universals that we inherit at birth and then apply to particulars; rather the existence of particulars causes our mind(s) to group them into categories that organize and therefore universalize them.

More radical than Scotus's emphases upon the particulars were the views of the Nominalists. Founded by William of Ockham (1288–1347), who reacted to the ideas of Scotus, the Nominalists believed that names, alternately understood as universals, are more accurately understood as our arbitrary articulations. Names may exist in our minds as concepts but they are better understood as a way for us to agree together about what it is that we are speaking and thinking. For Ockham, "the universal concept arises simply because there are varying degrees of similarity between individual

---

50. Artz, *The Mind of the Middle Ages*, 401, 413. Eco, *Thomas Aquinas*, 211, reveals that the historic context, both philosophical and artistic per se, was changing around Aquinas even while he was writing.

51. Eco, *Thomas Aquinas*, 206.

things. Socrates and Plato are more similar to one another than either is to an ass; and this fact of experience is reflected in the formation of the specific concept of man."[52] Names have no metaphysical existence, as Plato had thought, and do not exist prior to their becoming realized or actualized within matter. "Only individual things exist; and by the very fact that a thing exists it is individual."[53]

These are subtle philosophic shifts, but they will help pave the way for views that fit our own increasingly postmodern way of perceiving aesthetic, beauty, and truth. For instance, are we looking a unique instantiation of beauty? Or, is the thing we observe better understood as the manifestation of an eternal though invisible category known to God as beauty? Philosophers would continue to press the meanings of categories, wrench them for new definitions, and continually redefine what reality, and beauty with it, truly was.

Surpassing the importance of philosophy was the rise of humanistic artwork, an artistic flourish known today as the Renaissance. From the mid-fourteenth to the mid-sixteenth century, painters, sculptors, architects, and writers increasingly moved away from the older idealized, ultra-metaphysical, and classical Greco-Roman stylized forms to newer forms and expressions that intentionally employed and even capitalized on human emotions. With churchly art the focus went from communicating God's transcendence in classical forms to the expression of biblical themes in ways that facilitated an emotional point of contact for the viewers in the Renaissance. The result of this on aesthetics were tremendous. The effect that artwork had on the viewer, more than ever, was present in the mind of artists. Artwork itself increasingly involved earthly themes, even if the earthly was still used to move viewers toward the heavenly. This too, like the concretization of the form in Aquinas, was a realization that particulars could be beautiful in themselves, even while they pointed to the eternal.

WHAT THOMAS TEACHES US TO SEE:

- beauty is dangerous

---

52. Copleston, *Ockham to Suarez*, 57.

53. Ibid., 56. To nuance this, Thomas Aquinas believed that there is a metaphysical explanation for the similarity of natures, precisely because God creates individuals as members of species. Cf. Copleston, *Ockham to Suarez*, 58.

For Him Who Has Eyes to See

- beauty can transform
- the good and the beautiful are inseparable
- beauty involves proportion
- beauty resides in concrete forms
- the subject is involved in the experience of beauty
- we more astutely appreciate beauty when we are critically minded about it

6

Post-Patristic Interlude
An Explosion of Christian Art and Aesthetic

THE PATRISTIC ERA (AD 100–800) was a season of tremendous Christian theological development.[1] Studying the biblical books on the one hand, and engaging Greek philosophy on the other hand, the church learned how to make her theological and world view claims to Hellenistic culture. It was a season rich with theological maturation.

As we saw earlier, however, theologians did not pay much attention to the topic of beauty. The pressing concerns were Christology and trinitarian doctrine. In other words, theologians wanted to present the unique person, work, and nature of Jesus Christ and concomitantly his relation to God, and as God, to Gentile God-fearers and the philosophically minded. Besought with practical pastoral and organizational concerns, church leaders may have enjoyed the blossoming of Christian architecture and a Christian usage of beauty, but they only rarely incorporated beauty into their theologizing. When they did do so they followed the lead of earlier Greek philosophers. This made sense to the patristic Christian theologians. They knew that Greek philosophers were interested in truth and so these theologians were willing to study Greek lines of thought, reject what was

---

1. The dating of eras is largely arbitrary. Charlemagne was crowned emperor at St. Peter's Cathedral in Rome on Christmas Day, AD 800. His coronation began the Holy Roman Empire, a loosely affiliated of Christian fiefdoms. Many scholars place this date as the beginning of the medieval era.

not biblical,[2] and appropriate them where they saw fittingness with biblical truth claims. And what the Christian theologians inherited from the Greek philosophers was a rather idealized understanding of beauty.

Plato, as is widely known, believed in the existence of forms: ideas that resided in god's mind. Those ideas were the archetypal patterns, blueprints, and sources for all the particularities in physical life. Particular things, alternately put, were instantiations and realizations of the ideal forms. This understanding of the forms, one that was not universally embraced but one that was almost universally engaged, easily and logically led to the belief that beauty was itself an ideal. Beauty, in Platonic thought, existed out there, somewhere in the invisible transcendence, and then intermittently manifested itself in physical reality. The *idea* of beauty was more enthralling for these ancient thinkers than was apparent, in front of one's eyes, beauty. Plato's aesthetic scheme, and in its wake, the majority of antiquity on aesthetics and beauty, was indeed profound.[3]

Patristic Christian theologians zealously embraced this idealizing template. Christians knew that there was/is a reality that is more perfect than this earthly existence; both life in God's heavenly presence and the resurrected life to come will be more real, more pure, more fully and more sensory exhilarating and uninhibited than this obfuscated, cloyed, sin-filled, and difficult existence. Christians believed that God, himself the uncaused cause of all existence, was more real than the transient and ever-changing form of earthly existence. We see this dualistic vantage point on life present in the New Testament. The book of Hebrews, for instance, across its thirteen chapters steadily portrays a contrast between lesser and better, good and great, typifier and the typified, shadow and reality, the expectation and the fulfillment thereof. Moreover, the Revelation is equally dramatic in painting a portrait of another, alternate existence in the presence of God in the heavenlies, the other-life that exists alongside, above, or following our present perverse, toilsome, and evil-inflicted realm of

---

2. For instance, Gregory of Nyssa and Pseudo-Dionysius both rejected the Aristotelian belief that the universe was eternal. For these two, God created *ex nihilo*. Or, to take another example, theologians of the patristic era constantly had to do battle with and critique a multitude of notions wherein Jesus was ontologically subordinate to God the Father.

3. Plato stated, in his *Republic*, as Viladesau summarized it, "that if a poet talented in evoking all kinds of emotions were to visit [Plato's] ideal [political] state, the citizens would honor him, but for the good of their souls would send him away to another city." Better to encourage virtue than emotions. Viladesau, *Theological Aesthetics*, 186.

existence. Scholars dispute the level to which the New Testament authors as a whole were influenced by the categories and thought patterns of Greek philosophy. The point is that the interface between the Christian faith and a Greek Neoplatonic philosophic template was not hard to develop. Indeed, that such an interface was pregnant and ready for birthing is, many scholars have argued for centuries, an important reason that Christianity eventually and swiftly overtook Hellenistic culture.

This beauty-as-ideal perspective was a ready-made fit for patristic Christian categories of thought. Unfortunately, from a twenty-first–century perspective, this rather caused theologians to look past the thing-as-such. These theologians were excited to describe where God himself was shining in and through an object, scene, or person but they were not as acute in seeing the object, scene, or person as itself/herself beautiful. Their universe was enchanted, dripping with the fingerprints of God himself. Fully convinced of God's existence, Christian theologians were eager to observe and point out that and where the ideas of God's mind manifested themselves in nature. And yet, this idealizing perspective caused them to rather overlook the particular beauty immediately confronting them. For instance, they may have appreciated that a Bougainvillea bush (to choose a plant in my own backyard) produces flowers year-round and so testifies to God's constancy and fidelity, or believed that because a Bougainvillea has thorns it testifies to the Christ's passion, and yet they would have not focused on the flower's own glorious magenta hue, one dotted with a delicate pentaganol-star–shaped lily-white center—and the whole blast of color of which sits poignantly within a dark field of green—as a thing of complex beauty in itself.[4] This attitude was not limited to intellectuals. Frederick Artz, detailing Gothic church architecture and construction said, "Everything the artist saw in creation reflected God." And what the artist saw in nature was not the beauty of the thing per se, but "the beauty of the Lord's creation as in St. Francis' *Hymn to the Sun*."[5] In all my life I've never encountered either an Evangelical or Pentecostal who indwelled such a vivid creation theology as this:

---

4. Along this same idealizing aesthetic line, Boethius (AD c. 475–526?) maintained that musical theory was "more excellent than music itself." Eco, *Thomas Aquinas*, 87. Even medievals interested in scientific investigation were still captivated by notions of universal unity, truth, or truths that would finally tie all knowledge and understanding together in one single package. Artz, *The Mind of the Middle Ages*, 249, 253–55.

5 Ibid., 399–400. Among the less philosophically minded this idealizing, "spirit is greater than matter" world view spilled out into beliefs in magic, alchemy, and astrology.

For Him Who Has Eyes to See

Most High, all powerful, good Lord, Yours are the praises, the
glory, the honor, and all blessing.
To You alone, Most High, do they belong,
and no man is worthy to mention Your name.
Be praised, my Lord, through all your creatures,
especially through my lord Brother Sun,
who brings the day; and you give light through him.
And he is beautiful and radiant in all his splendor!
Of you, Most High, he bears the likeness.
Praise be You, my Lord, through Sister Moon
and the stars, in heaven you formed them clear
and precious and beautiful.
Praised be You, my Lord, through Brother Wind,
and through the air, cloudy and serene,
and every kind of weather through which
You give sustenance to Your creatures.
Praised be You, my Lord, through Sister Water,
which is very useful and humble and precious and chaste.
Praised be You, my Lord, through Brother Fire,
through whom you light the night
and he is beautiful and playful and robust and strong.
Praised be You, my Lord, through Sister Mother Earth, who
sustains us and governs us and who
produces varied fruits with colored flowers and herbs.
Praised be You, my Lord, through those who give pardon for
Your love, and bear infirmity and tribulation.
Blessed are those who endure in peace
for by You, Most High, they shall be crowned.
Praised be You, my Lord, through our Sister Bodily Death, from
whom no living man can escape.
Woe to those who die in mortal sin.
Blessed are those whom death will find
in Your most holy will,
for the second death shall do them no harm.
Praise and bless my Lord, and give Him thanks
and serve Him with great humility.
AMEN[6]

Who today sees the elements in God's creation as exploding with meaning and significance? In that poetic prayer about creation Francis typified the symbolizing and vivid way medieval people understood life.

---

6. St. Francis, "Canticle of Brother Sun."

Post-Patristic Interlude

Not all was benign, however. At the ecclesial level there were political benefits to teach and inculcate such a universalizing and idealizing perspective. Artz was not being cynical when he argued,

> The general theory that all parts are absorbed in a transcendent whole fitted the purposes of the church, first, because it was mystical in placing the source of truth outside this world and beyond the grasp of reason, alone, second, because it proved the necessity of the union of the church under the hierarchy of the clergy culminating in the pope, the representative of God on earth, and finally, because it implied the subordination of the individual to a divine authority.[7]

Perhaps another way of exhibiting the Patristic theological vantage point would be to say that, because they believed beauty caused individual beauties to exist,[8] they loved beauty but overlooked beauties. Or, they loved the painter more than the painting, the musician more than her music. O'Donohue wrote, "The Medieval world loved symbols. It often probed things so deeply to discover their supernatural reality that it ended up losing sign of the sensuous presence of the thing itself."[9] Not until philosophers like Thomas and Renaissance men like Leonardo da Vinci would people begin to take interest as things as they are, in life for its own here-on-earth complexities.[10] Looking back, who would criticize these patristics and medievals for glorifying God more than his creation? And yet, it is still worth our own observation, considering the historic development of beauty, to clarify that idealizing perspective. As it concerned beauty they were thinking more metaphysically and less concretely.[11] We notice these shortfalls less to judge the patristics than to clarify how the Western human perception of and involvement with beauty has changed over the centuries.

Again, the patristic theological emphasis when it came to beauty was on the there-ed-ness, the fix-ed-ness, of beauty. In an inversion of our own contemporary philosophic structures, beauty objectively existed for the ancients; beauty was the real category while beautiful things were less real. Greek philosophers, and later like them Christian theologians, were merely recognizing the existence of objective beauty. For his part, Aristotle

---

7. Artz, *The Mind of the Middle Ages*, 255.
8. Eco, *Thomas Aquinas*, 92.
9. O'Donohue, *Beauty*, 46, original caps.
10. Artz, *The Mind of the Middle Ages*, 238, 248–49.
11. Eco, *Thomas Aquinas*, 14, 118, 125, 137–44.

believed that color was an objective and steadfast quality in things; color was not an accident to form; and that attitude toward beauty existed well past the medieval era.[12] To reiterate, beauty existed in the mind of God, for theologians, or as an emanation of God, for philosophers that belief saw them emphasize the idea over the particularity. They did not much reflect upon the beholder's role in the experience of beauty.

The medieval period (AD 800–1400), alternately known as the Middle Ages, frequently gets a bad rap. And that is just unfair, not least of which is because of beauty. The Middle Ages saw the celebrative construction of thousands of European churches and cathedrals: often prominently placed and frequently impressive, these aesthetic constructions were a symbolic and vivid way to announce the denizens's allegiance to God. Approaching a town on foot or horseback and upon seeing the churchly edifice perched high above all other buildings, visitors would have had no doubt about the Christian presence inside the walls. For generations on end, not just architects and masons but entire communities would work annually to contribute to the growing specter of a towering building erected to glorify God in their midst. One website summarized it thus:

> The building of the cathedral was a community affair and a matter of civic pride. Cities competed with each other for which could have the tallest spire. When Notre Dame de Paris soared to 114 feet, Chartres built to 123 feet and Amiens followed with 138 feet. Beauvois tried for 157 feet, but the vault collapsed and the people ran out of money trying to build. Each church had its wealthy patrons, but ordinary citizens too contributed sheep, poultry, cheeses, animal skins and vegetables to the building of their cathedral. While the cathedral was under construction an entire village of workmen would be established at the site. Roads would be constructed to quarries, and even rivers were diverted to provide transportation for the heavy materials.[13]

---

12. O'Donohue, *Beauty*, 86.

13. Severance, "Magnificent Medieval Cathedrals." "Churches were usually slow in being built because only part of each year's income was set aside for building. On a large church a skeleton staff would be kept between building seasons." Artz, *The Mind of the Middle Ages*, 399. Coulton clarifies that such construction occurred in fits and starts over generations. Enthusiasm could be followed by seasons of weariness but on the whole "the building or rebuilding of a church was generally, and perhaps always, a matter of strong local interest." *The Fate of Medieval Art*, 365.

Post-Patristic Interlude

Today we contemporaries really do not know how to get our imaginations inside, or around, such an enduring enterprise. What must it have been like to be part of such a grand communal endeavor? What would it feel like to share the pride and excitement about a soaring civic, aesthetic, and religious venture? Furthermore, some cathedrals took 200 years to build, as different segments were completed and varied components were added. When we moderns want to go to the moon we expect to go there now! Many medievals, contrastingly, were happy to spend their entire lives contributing to just one portion of a colossal project.[14]

If in the United States society is moving away from an appreciation for both church (as a theological, spiritual, communal, humanitarian, and existential necessity) and church buildings (as physical places given specifically both to the community-wide worship of God and sources of civic pride), medieval folk took tremendous pride in making a church or cathedral the center of their collective lives.

> Not only the building of the cathedrals, but the cathedrals themselves became a focal point of community life. The market was usually near the cathedral and townspeople often conducted business inside the church. At Chartres, the labor exchange was in the transepts while the crypt sheltered pilgrims and the sick. Plays were often staged on the cathedral steps. Yet the primary purpose of the cathedral was worship. Historian Philip Schaff wrote that "The great cathedrals became a daily sermon, bearing testimony to the presence of God and the resurrection of Jesus Christ." It lifted the people's thoughts to spiritual things. The ample spaces filled with sunlight through the stained glass "reminded them of the glory of the life beyond. . . . The strong foundations and massive columns and buttresses typified the stability of God's throne, and that He hath made all things through the Word of His power."[15]

The true joy that characterized the Christians living then and their delight in Christianizing their local regions of Europe is often lost on us when we

---

14. Follett's *The Pillars of the Earth* provides a wonderfully rich fictional portrayal of what the building of medieval cathedrals was like.

15. Severance, "Magnificent Medieval Cathedrals." In many ways these churches served as the public space that pagan markets previously had. "Lawsuits and university disputations and degree-ceremonies were regularly carried on" inside church walls. The church building was rather like a home for townsmen. Coulton, *The Fate of Medieval Art*, 324–25. These churches could house fairs, markets, banquets, dancing, wild sport, and even merchants' booths. See Phillips, *Destruction of Art in England*, 19.

think about the Middle Ages. They were, we have been taught for centuries, "backwards and dark." Here's why.

Celebrating their newfound liberties, humanist writers and Protestant Reformers both referred to the medieval period as the Dark Ages. Wanting to slur the heritage that preceded them, these leaders and thinkers used the appellation "Dark Ages" as a way to distance themselves from the medieval past.[16] For the same reasons "Gothic," having nothing to do with the Goths of history, was a sixteenth-century pejorative term coined to denigrate architecture that had fallen out of fashion.[17] Likewise, the pejorative noun, "Dunce," was a reference to the (in)famous medieval Scholastic Catholic theologian, Duns Scotus (d. AD 1308), a Scottish professor whose pedantic style represented all that was bad in the estimation of the newly illuminated Renaissance Humanists. Renaissance people—most of them committed church-folk, if not avidly confessing Christian believers—reasoned that their own freshly enlightened era—one ironically drawing upon the patterns and aesthetic forms of classical Greco-Roman antiquity—clearly surpassed the clunky and toilsome world view of their dull and dim predecessors. (Into the eighteenth century, the phrase "The Enlightenment" would similarly serve as a means both to denigrate "ignorant" predecessors and elevate the status of the newly sophisticated.)[18] It is true that the Scholastics—those who studied and learned at schools, contrasted to monasteries—were tiresome in their interest and ability to address and answer a multitude of questions. Artz summed the Scholastics this way: "it is hard to find any important philosophical question that has ever occupied the mind of man that was not raised and subjected to a thoroughgoing analysis by the philosophic writers of the thirteenth and fourteenth centuries."[19] Yet, the notion that medieval philosophers sat in their universities and speculated as to "how many angels could dance on the head of a pin" is simply not true. (That that adage continues to abide today proves how abiding a stereotype

---

16. Latourette, *Beginnings to 1500*, 604. Garside Jr., *Zwingli and the Arts*, 30, clarifies that even in the medieval era this kind of judgment on the past was going on among reform-minded, "primitivist" Christian subgroups.

17. Artz, *The Mind of the Middle Ages*, 392.

18. The drive to intentionally mar the reputation of the entire previous era lurks deep in the human heart. Ancient Egyptian Pharaohs are known to have erased the inscriptions on pyramids and edifices of former Pharaohs and their architects and replace them with their own names, both to honor themselves and obliterate the memory, the existence even, of former leaders.

19. Artz, *The Mind of the Middle Ages*, 261.

Post-Patristic Interlude

can be.) Indeed, there was much that was beneficial that came from the medieval period. Here's a sample:

>*Technological advances like windmills, water-wheels, dams, compasses, wheeled farming plows, sawmills, construction cranes, agricultural crop-rotation, soap, cast-iron, horse collars, horse shoes, paper and the printing press were all invented. These developments increased production of food, furniture, textiles, housing construction, literature, and bettered living conditions. The design and building of clocks helped entire towns run more efficiently. Over generations these advances helped to lift masses of agrarian workers into the middle class, and similarly empowered the middle classes to become cultural-political brokers across Western Europe. In short, technological advance was tremendously significant both in ending feudalism and initiating the development of the nation-states of modernity.[20]

>*Slavery was ended. Priests, bishops, and aristocratic churchmen eventually, though sporadically, agreed that slaves deserved to be served the sacraments. That admission into the life of the Church over time led to the belief that slaves deserved their freedom. Sadly, widespread slave trading would reappear in the fifteenth century, but it was Medieval Christians who first brought that devilish system to an end.[21]

>*Aristotelian philosophy was rediscovered. Amalgamated with a Christian understanding of reality, the likes of which we noticed earlier regarding Aquinas, this paved the way for the burgeoning of science and medicine as they are known today.[22]

>*Universities were built and reason was emphasized. Reason was deemed to be a gift from God, a servant to and for faith. If education and knowledge are power for the betterment of human living conditions, we should know it was Roman Catholic universities

---

20. Ibid., 249–53. For more on medieval technology see "Technology in the Medieval Age." The printing press brought down the cost of books to one-eighth of the prior cost and so made book ownership possible for the common man; it also greatly enhanced teaching and learning. Artz, *The Mind of the Middle Ages*, 252.

21. Regarding technological development and slavery's end see Stark, *The Victory of Reason*, 28–31, 38–50, 131–59.

22. Just to clarify, yes, other civilizations had beneficial technological developments over the centuries. However, science, the disciplined process of hypothesizing, studying, critiquing earlier experiments and hypotheses, and proposing ever more accurate solutions and understandings, is a distinctly Western development. Cf. Pearcey and Thaxton, *The Soul of Science*, 21–28.

that, owing to a love for learning unto the glory of God, first imprinted on the Western collective consciousness the benefit of reason, research, learning, and the application of those for everyday life.[23]

Truly, the medieval era was profoundly different from today's post-Christian society. What must it have been like to live in a time when thousands of towns and cities were intentionally seeking to glorify God in their aesthetics? Surely we must not romanticize that era; of course there were exceptions, problems, and afflictions.[24] Indeed, the quicksand-like nature of the human condition is a constant that is only naïvely abandoned as we try to fashion a Christian perception of life. Yet still, for a theologian like myself, one who wants to see the whole earth freely (not forcibly) acknowledge, share, speak, and symbolize the love and glory of the living God, the medieval period is fascinating.

WHAT THE MEDIEVAL ERA TEACHES US TO SEE:

- creation is a source for theology
- symbols can convey beauty
- there are communal aesthetic ways to glorify God

---

23. Latourette, *Beginnings to 1500*, 546–552. By the year 1500, seventy-seven universities resided in Catholic Europe. Said universities were constantly working to rid themselves of control by both political magistrates and the church. Cf. Artz, *The Mind of the Middle Ages*, 316–17.

24. E.g., birthing children often resulted in the death of mother and/or child. Medicine was crude; treatment involved bloodlettings, astrological signification, superstition, and remedies that were often worse than the original malady. Pickpockets fancied a crowd gathered on the cathedral's steps.

7

The Reformation
Correcting and Overcorrecting Aesthetic Abuse

IN 2001 THE TALIBAN dynamited two twenty-foot-wide and over one hundred-foot-tall sixth-century Buddhist sandstone carvings in northern Afghanistan. That iconoclasm—shattering of images—was a crime against humanity. In the sixteenth century countless numbers of what would be now-priceless statues, carvings, woodworkings, stained glass, and paintings were destroyed in central and northern European churches. The difference between those two iconoclasms? The overwhelming bulk of Protestant iconoclasm was conducted by folks *within their own* places of worship. As someone who appreciates history and loves art, the Protestant iconoclasm grieves me. And yet, my grief is mitigated by some understanding of the context. There are indeed values and qualities far more important than images and art.

Why is it that so many Protestant churches today are aesthetically empty? Significantly, because the Reformation furrowed a rut that is now some 500 years plowed into our collective consciousness. Many Westerners in twenty-first-century churches are rootless. They do not think of themselves in light of their grandparents or their great-grandparents, let alone prior centuries' worth of belief and practice. Hence, more than ever it is invaluable to know from whence they came. As self-reflective persons we simply must know why we do things the way we do. In this chapter we will frame the iconoclastic actions of the sixteenth-century Christians, denote causes for the Protestant iconoclasms, and then note the varied aesthetic perspectives and motivations of three influential church leaders: Martin Luther, John Calvin, and Ulrich Zwingli.

MEDIEVAL ICONOCLASTIC PRECURSORS

Destruction of art and church buildings was not a sixteenth-century novelty. Across the centuries older churches were frequently razed in order that new churches could be built on the same location. One simple reason was that the buildings and their accoutrements would become dilapidated. Even in the first couple centuries congregations would outgrow the original gathering place and then either modify or level it altogether to build anew.[1] This process of demolition and rebuilding also occurred because churches from antiquity often had architectural components made of wood and so demolishing and rebuilding was a practical necessity. Stone foundations and tombstones from antiquity served as the repeated bedrocks for newer developments. Sometimes church stonework and/or pieces of the statues within their walls were thrown into the furnace because the charred remnants produced a wonderful lime coating that could be applied to existing church walls so as to wash them with a brilliant new white sheen.[2] More commonly, new styles and architectural forms arose because both church leaders and the common folk wanted to build to God's glory using recent innovation.[3] Sometimes patrons, for instance wealthy wool merchants, wanted to build a new church on the spot of an old church; by tearing down the old and erecting the new they were able to honor themselves and leave a beautiful edifice for posterity.[4] Often, then, reasons for destroying older Christian buildings and imagery was a matter of simple pragmatics. There were, however, also intellectual and theological reasons for iconoclasm.

Supposedly written by Emperor Charlemagne between 790 and 792, the *Caroline Books*, the *Libri Carolini*, argued that reality was comprised of inner and outer worlds. The inner world, the world of the soul, was more real than the outer world, the bodily and physical world. Following ancient Greek philosophical constructs, these documents reasoned that words and texts are more important than images. Words conform and touch upon the inner world more readily and abidingly than do images. The Second

---

1. Krautheimer, *Early Christian and Byzantine Architecture*, 2–32.
2. Coulton, *The Fate of Medieval Art*, 433, 437, 441.
3. Phillips, *Destruction of Art in England*, 3.
4. Coulton, *The Fate of Medieval Art*, 440.

The Reformation

Council of Nicea (787), a Byzantine church council, had ruled that sacred images were permitted and encouraged on the basis of the incarnation. The *Libri Carolini* argued against Nicea. Although they were not published until 1549, whereupon they influenced John Calvin's perspectives, these books make evident the existence of iconoclastic attitudes inside the Middle Ages.[5]

Certainly there were medieval churchmen who believed images were idolatrous. In Britannia John Wycliffe (1330–1384), himself protesting other abuses evident inside Roman Catholicism, was opposed to the emphasis that the people gave to images. Following his lead the Lollards, a fifteenth-century oppositional movement inside Britannia, echoed the older *Libri Carolini* philosophy: images, like all external signs, were less real than words. Consequently they taught that "Words, not visual images, are the most important way for men to come to religious truths." Moreover, the Lollards believed that because God is omnipresent, no place or image is more holy than others; this was a theological argument that interpreted Jesus' teaching, "God is spirit and those who worship him must worship in spirit and truth" (John 4:24), to mean physical space or location is insignificant. Persecuted as heretics by the Roman Catholics, the Lollards believed that the use of images in worship was idolatrous. Reflecting on the English history of iconoclasm Phillips noted that often at the root of iconoclasm is the "profound inclination of some men to see a sharp dichotomy between nature and spirit, to reject earthly life as a means to knowing the divine."[6]

There were concerns other than philosophical. For instance, in the twelfth century Cistercian and Carthusian monks began to protest the opulence of both churches and monastery chapels. Then as now, varied folks protested that the money spent on artwork would be better spent on caring for the poor.[7] On a different front, some fourteenth-century Catholics favored churchly art but not private art or book illustrations; the latter, these Roman Catholic leaders believed, were more easily misunderstood and so were dangerous.[8] Headed into the sixteenth-century folks grew increasingly anxious, and therefore resentful, by seeing a flourish of paintings of

---

5. Dyrness, *Reformed Theology*, 23.

6. Phillips, *Destruction of Art in England*, 33. Quotation from 5. The Lollards, emphasizing the power of words, emphasized reading the Scriptures in one's own vernacular and translated the Bible into English.

7. Ibid., 18, 33. Luther would later argue the same thing.

8. Dyrness, *Reformed Theology*, 31–34.

For Him Who Has Eyes to See

hell and dread judgment on church frescoes and paintings. That resentment eventually became a motive for iconoclasm.[9]

Theological and intellectual arguments aside, a lingering problem was abuse. So many churches housed an abundance of religious images. In medieval England, there was one church per 100 families, and that "without counting chapels or wayside shrines." One French Catholic critic said that churches were often built to house the relic of some saint, rather than to glorify God.[10] Churches originally might have been a public testimony to God's glory, but they could also be rendered spiritually and existentially vacuous for the surplus of their very numbers. In Zurich, an eventual hot spot for iconoclasm, "the commissioning of ecclesiastical art increased one hundredfold between 1500 and 1518."[11] Within church walls the relics, an important impetus for building churches, availed such a profound personal aesthetic because they put the observer into proximity with an item from Christian history. Relics thus became enormously popular, but the abundance of said objects increasingly strained folks' credulity; they could not all be legitimate. And the making of artifacts was legion. "Nearly every monastery," Phillips wrote, "owned a girdle of the Virgin or of the Magdalene to be worn by expectant mothers."[12] Not uncommonly, churches housed disturbing statues of the Trinity: one body with three heads.[13]

Erasmus (1466–1536) was a humanist scholar whose ideas proffered important cues for sixteenth-century reform-minded priests and leaders. He himself finally remained loyal to the Catholic Church (he hoped for renewal, not full-blown schism),[14] nevertheless Erasmus witnessed the overabundance of churches and their relics and argued that it was wrong to direct so much attention to artwork. With irony, Erasmus once remarked that there were so many pieces of Jesus' cross in churches that it would take a freighter to pull them all up a river.[15] It was inappropriate that images, he wrote, were "treated as if they were alive; that people . . . bow their heads,

---

9. Miles, *Image as Insight*, 103–4.
10. Coulton, *The Fate of Medieval Art*, 323.
11. Dyrness, *Reformed Theology*, 43.
12. Phillips, *Destruction of Art in England*, 23.
13. Coulton, *The Fate of Medieval Art*, 382.

14. Garside Jr., *Zwingli and the Arts*, 29, 34. He qualifies, Erasmus held a viewpoint that was "self-consciously apart from and outside the institutional forms and traditional [Catholic] content he was criticizing." Ibid., 35.

15. Phillips, *Destruction of Art in England*, 36.

fall on the ground, or crawl on their knees before them; and that worshippers . . . kiss or fondle the carvings."[16] In fact for Erasmus so many churches fostered avarice precisely because they were so full of jewels and gold and silver. Erasmus did not like what he believed were the nonessentials of Catholic piety: praying to saints, vain rituals, and pursuing relics.[17] The image that should be revered, in Erasmus's teaching, was Christ of the Gospels and not images made by human hands. Moreover, God is Spirit and so he ought be worshipped with spiritual sacrifices.[18] (Because Erasmus was profoundly influential for the Radical Reformation, we will note more about his ideas in our survey below of Ulrich Zwingli.)

Many medieval Catholic priests argued against idolatry, and still others reasoned carefully between using objects and worshipping them. For example, Nicolas of Cusa did not like how his parishioners in Tyrol worshipped the saints "for the prosperity of their crops and their herds." The act of calling upon saints, he maintained, was "a relic of paganism."[19] Still, hardly any parish priests suggested that the images should be destroyed. Subsequently, there were only isolated instances of Catholic iconoclasm in the sixteenth century.[20] And, if Protestant iconoclasm strikes us as lamentable, we should know that the Protestants were in fact building on and furthering the criticism and concerns that were already present during the medieval era.[21] Following decades of sixteenth-century protest and even revolt, however, the widespread position of the Roman Catholic Church followed the earlier lead of Pope Gregory the Great (r. 540–604) who argued that images served well as educational texts for the uneducated.[22] The Catholic Council of Trent (1563), responding to the empire-wide unrest, gave guidelines for the use of religious images and affirmed their usage. Moreover, the Catholic Counter-Reformation intentionally produced

---

16. Miles, *Image as Insight*, 99.

17. Phillips, *Destruction of Art in England*, 39.

18. Zachman, *Image and Word*, 14–15. Erasmus is thus a seminal influence on the Protestants who will turn Christian experience and practice toward the subjective. Cf. Garside Jr., *Zwingli and the Arts*, 36–37.

19. Coulton, *The Fate of Medieval Art*, 379.

20. Miles, *Image as Insight*, 109.

21. Dyrness, *Reformed Theology*, 7, 31, 45.

22. Christensen, *Art and the Reformation in Germany*, 15, 32.

paintings and sculptures that intensified feelings in their observers. Religious art, for the church, became a way to regain ground from the word-oriented Protestant Reformers.[23]

PROTESTANT ICONOCLASM

There were many reasons that Protestant[24] iconoclasm erupted in the sixteenth century and as our above survey indicates said iconoclasm was a continuation of earlier arguments and actions. Yet another reason was the convoluted and fractious historical context. Often low-church[25] Christians will today delineate the microcosmic factors the fueled the Reformation to the exclusion of the macrocosmic. Indeed, at the microcosmic (i.e., religious) level there were concerns about salvation, authority concerning truth claims, and the abuse of clerical office. However, too often neglected in contemporary thought about the Reformation are the larger, more abstract, macrocosmic (i.e., social) factors that both fueled and were fueled by the microcosmic. For instance, there was a growing rise in the use and promulgation of the local vernacular; in their varied geographical locales people decreasingly used Latin. Eventually, impelled by the printing press's ability to produce mass literature, these local vernaculars were foundational for the rise of Europe's nation-states as we know them today. Economically, fostered by increasing access to and production of capital, a middle class began to rise and gain prominence in governing their local municipalities. These middle-class towns and cities, erupting with more representative structures of government, formed treaties and trade agreements that also contributed to economic and political independence from Rome. Especially as one moved away geographically from Rome and the papacy, there was an increasing popular desire for change. It's not hard to imagine that people were frustrated with feudalism, a disorganized amalgam—orga-

---

23. Miles, *Image as Insight*, 118–21. The Council of Trent cursed those who opposed images.

24. The term Protestant first appeared in Germany in 1529. Most Reformers went by the appellation "evangelical." Cf. McGrath, *Reformation Thought*, 6. The Latin noun *Protestare* originally had two primary definitions: to bear witness to the truth; to protest abuse. Garside Jr. astutely warns against our viewing the Protestants as monolithic. The Reformation was "not simply Lutheran. It was Zwinglian, Calvinist, and Anglican as well. It was also Anabaptist and Socinian." *Zwingli and the Arts*, 3.

25. Those without priests, sacraments, a formalized liturgy, or a Christianized calendar.

The Reformation

nized chaos, really—of political alliances that promulgated the aristocracy's hold on Europe. Finally, there were enormous philosophic shifts occurring in Roman Catholic universities, shifts that eventually birthed humanism. Espoused first by professors in northern Italy but eventually by churchmen across Europe, humanism was no unified philosophy and had no single professor or champion. Rather, motivated by the slogan *ad fonts* (back to the ancient sources) humanism was a movement that sought to study the classical period in order to enhance spoken and written eloquence. (For the Reformers, *ad fonts* would be altered to mean back to the apostolic sources.) Phillips sums humanism as the perfection of human reality as "gauged by the standards of the classical past."[26] Simple as that seems, humanism began to represent a threat to the status quo of medieval Scholasticism and as such served as additional fuel to Reformation fires. The cumulative effect of the force of these macrocosmic factors ended the medieval era. For our part, we highlight these factors to recall that Protestant iconoclastic actions were driven by multiple motives: spirituality, economics, theology, social frustration and a desire for change, and politics.[27] There was no "pure" motive to end idolatry. Iconoclasm exploded among folks who may not themselves have understood all the issues at play in their own hearts.[28] Dyrness clarifies that whereas theology was influential for Reform-minded folks it was not always determinate.[29] There were still more causes of iconoclasm.

Many Roman Catholics who began to destroy church artwork, and they were then all Catholics, had grown weary and wary of the use of images. Truly, it is difficult for us to get our imaginations inside those of others, especially when they are centuries removed from us. But church tradition had been deeply ensconced into the minds, hearts, and imaginations of Western European Christianity. If we accept that Pope Gregory the Great laid a foundation for Catholic belief and practice,[30] that means 900 years had passed from his time to the sixteenth century. That was a long season

---

26. Phillips, *Destruction of Art in England*, 37.
27. See McGrath, *Reformation Thought*, 15–34.
28. Phillips, *Destruction of Art in England*, 4.
29. Dyrness, *Reformed Theology*, 10.

30. Gregory made the following beliefs and practices, among others, official Catholic teaching: that God's electing grace must be activated by repentance, sacrifice, denial of bodily pleasures, sacramental participation, and works of love; that the mass is an offering of Christ to God; that sex within marriage is exclusively for procreation; that purgatory exists; and that prayers for the dead in purgatory are efficacious. Pelikan, *The Emergence of the Catholic Tradition*, 354–56.

through which traditions concretized! To establish some contemporary comparison, we recall that the United States is only 240 years old. Accustomed to lightning-like generational change,[31] today we can barely imagine life being so constant as it had been for 900 years into the sixteenth century. Many people were tradition-fatigued.

Of course, those 900 years were not uniform, as earlier chapters herein have made evident. But for the practice and piety of the common people a lifelessness had accrued that became stultifying. Especially in non-Latinized countries,[32] churches were stuffed with images, relics, and artwork, but they no longer energized the people; in fact those implements dulled people's experience at church. Dyrness elucidates that art was not objectified then the way it is now. Twenty-first–century people look at art and ask many questions revolving around how it touches them, how it makes them feel. Churchly art that was *in situ*—sitting in its original designed-for position—was intended to express many ideals to the people, ideals that formed a complex of ecclesial, political, theological, spiritual, and pious aims. Again, living on this side of the French Revolution, the rise of Modernism, and the 1960s—all of which aggressively shoved religion to the society's peripheries—it is nearly impossible for we contemporaries to imagine life as such a thoroughly integrated complex.[33] But through the medieval era and into the sixteenth century the church was the single greatest influence on Europe. Hence, many people vented their anger against the Roman Church by destroying images. "The real significance of [art work] for their historical setting does not lie in the occasional beauty that these genres reached,

---

31. For instance, the electric radio was only in use for some twenty-five years before the television was available for public use in 1936. The radio had revolutionized the American way of life but then was transcended by the capacities of television. As of 2006, the average American home has more televisions than people. Cf. "Average home has more TVs than people."

32. Wherever Latin had penetrated deeply into a geographic region that region remained Catholic after the Reformation and Counter-Reformation. Wherever Latin had not penetrated deeply into a geographic region that region went to the Protestants. The predominant Catholic territories were Spain, Portugal, France, and Austria. Many countries were divided between the two pretty much along the lines of how far Latin had previously penetrated. Exceptions to this rule: Protestant Ireland (in opposition to England), Catholic Poland (in opposition to Germany), and Catholic Lithuania (with close ties to Poland). Latourette, *Beginnings to 1500*, 699.

33. O'Donohue laments our setting: "With the revelation of corruption in so many political and religious domains, our perception of ideals has become tinged with cynicism. Yet no society can endure without the sense of honor, dignity and transcendence enshrined it its set of ideals." *Beauty*, 191.

The Reformation

but in the social and devotional trends that they represent." As noted in our previous chapter, people very much expected that visible objects, especially church-sanctioned images and statues, would help them touch upon invisible reality. The church taught people how to think, feel, evaluate, and imagine. But by the dawn of the sixteenth century when people walked into image-laden and art-filled places of worship they were reminded of their deep frustration and malaise.[34] Even more, they were spiritually hungry.

When the Reformation detonated people entered their own churches and destroyed the sacred space where they had worshipped for years. We might envision out-of-control rage, but more accurately it was a righteous anger. More surprising, Dyrness says frequently those iconoclastic actions fulfilled corporate repentance. In acts of public contrition the people destroyed images in order to make visible their repentance before God. They wanted to assure their salvation and so did not want any idolatry to clutter the atmosphere, but they also were earnest in wanting to keep God first in their hearts, even if that meant that images had to be destroyed in the doing.[35]

Not all Protestant villages, towns, and cities were sites for iconoclastic violence. Indeed, "Iconoclastic attitudes and activities were one of the least agreed-upon aspects of the Protestant reformation in Germany and Switzerland,"[36] notes Miles. Civil magistrates commonly played a role in limiting destruction. In some towns and cities officials allowed patrons, those whose family's estates or those who themselves had paid for the artwork, to enter churches and remove precious pieces; indeed, in several cases the magistrates themselves were the patrons. Still other civil leaders did not want violence of any kind under their watch; it was their duty to keep the peace.[37] Sometimes the civil magistrates even punished those who defamed or ruined religious art. The situation in Protestant lands, then, varied from locality to locality and was sporadic from the 1520s through the 1560s. Many little towns and villages across central and northern Europe were iconoclastic locales. Cities renown for Protestant iconoclasm were Geneva and Zurich, Switzerland; Augsburg, Copenhagen, and Münster, Germany; La Rochelle, Rouen, and Saintes, France; as well as other towns in Belgium

---

34. Dyrness, *Reformed Theology*, 7–12, 46. Quotation, 12.
35. Ibid., 46–47.
36. Miles, *Image as Insight*, 100.
37. Christensen, *Art and the Reformation in Germany*, 71.

and the Netherlands; all locations many hundreds of miles away from Christendom's capital of Rome.

PROTESTANT THEOLOGIANS ON AESTHETICS

Summarily, it helps to know that everyone Martin Luther to John Calvin to Ulrich Zwingli can be placed on a grid that moves from literary critique to action, from lesser to greater levels of opposition concerning religious images. Luther hated that images were worshipped, but he did not order their destruction. Calvin took several decades to write, reedit, and reissue volumes of his pastoral *Institutes*, and only after decades of thinking did he address religious images therein. Zwingli was the most acerbic toward both Rome and religious images. Less destruction of Christian art occurred in the lands influenced by Luther than Zwingli, with Calvin somewhere in the middle. (Their respective opposition to religious images paralleled the degree of their critique of Rome, with Zwingli being the most uniformly emphatic.) The general Protestant opposition to religious images and an intentional churchly aesthetic was pragmatic: they were far more concerned with the resulting effect upon the people than with theological or intellectual constructions, though were we discussing their era over coffee with them they would likely disagree with that generalization. Nevertheless, because they remain to this day so influential we do well to survey the theological filtering of these three enormous Protestant leaders.

MARTIN LUTHER (1483–1546)

Initially opposed to the use of religious images, especially as he pastorally addressed the iconoclastic foment around him in Germany, Luther—the renown father of the Reformation—moderated his views as time progressed. Though he repeatedly opined about images in his writings, he never wrote a single treatise specifically on images and aesthetics. As early as 1522 (he wrote his 95 *Theses* in 1517), Luther was already writing more generously concerning use of religious images in churches and homes.[38] In part, Luther himself had not been vexed by the power of images. He felt no great affinity for them and so felt no personal anxiety or guilt about their use. If, however, they became a cause for idolatry then they should be destroyed.

---

38. Christensen, *Art and the Reformation in Germany*, 42–46.

The Reformation

More problematic to the German Reformer was the belief that patronage would garner merit with God; he attacked this sinful attitude, Christensen clarifies, "with all of his awesome strength."[39] Better that believers should give to aid the poor in their midst[40] than to donate a religious object to a church. Nevertheless, even the struggle with works-righteousness was not sufficient cause, Luther wrote, "to abolish, destroy, and burn all images."[41]

Then, making clear that images should be understood as a matter of conscience, Luther cited the eighth-century iconoclastic controversy: "the emperor held that he had the authority to banish the images, but the pope insisted that they should remain, and both were wrong. . . . They wished to make a 'must' out of that which is free. This God cannot tolerate." Many things in life may be abused, Luther continued, but it does not then follow that they should all be invalidated. Life constructed that way would be disastrous and utterly confused. To wit Luther noted, "wine and women bring many a man to misery and make a fool of him," but we do not for that reason "kill all the women and pour out the wine."[42] With pastoral wisdom Luther then counseled that if images be completely and violently eradicated the community may only cause those same images to be more dearly embraced by people's hearts. It would not suffice to destroy outward images while the heart remained filled with idols. Luther counseled that we allow God's word to do its convicting and cleansing work in human hearts.[43] It was far better to practice iconoclasm in one's heart than in the churches.

While his consistent focus was on justification by faith, images were clearly for Luther a matter of *adiaphora*: matters of opinion that are nonessential to the faith.[44] Sometimes Luther wrote approvingly of the destruction of images, but only when that was done by the approval of the civil authorities and not by mob violence; he did not want rebellion or anarchy.[45] Encouraging civic peace, Luther wrote, "The devil does not care about im-

---

39. Ibid., 46–47.

40. Luther wanted both to outlaw begging throughout Europe and require every city to care for their own poor. Janz, ed., *A Reformation Reader*, 97.

41. *Luther's Works*, 51:84, quoted in Christensen, *Art and the Reformation in Germany*, 47.

42. First quote from *Luther's Works*, 51:81–82. Second quote from *Luther's Works*, 51:85 quoted in Christensen, *Art and the Reformation in Germany*, 47.

43. Christensen, *Art and the Reformation in Germany*, 48.

44. Ibid., 74. The Apostle Paul discusses such matters in 1 Corinthians 8 and Romans 14.

45. Ibid., 49–50.

age breaking. He only wants to get his foot in the door so that he can cause shedding of blood and murder in the world."[46] Clearly, Luther was not altogether opposed to images; he himself published a German edition of the New Testament that contained illustrations. The first commandment, "you shall not make for yourself an idol," Luther interpreted to have been a ceremonial dimension of Jewish law, one that had been rendered null by Christ. Now we are free in Christ to choose, even though we may not violate our conscience in our choosing and acting.[47] If Christ and his gospel did not prohibit it, that is if the Word of God—a critical component in Luther's theological filter—did not openly prohibit an action, then Christians must then discern its value and worth. Once he wrote, "I do not hold that the Gospel should destroy all the arts, as certain superstitious folk believe. On the contrary, I would fain see all arts, and especially that of music, serving Him who hath created them and given them unto us.... The Law of Moses forbade only the image of God; the crucifix is not forbidden."[48] Luther was in favor of biblical scenes being painted on church walls and the walls of homes.

Frequently, Luther dealt with the question of Christian art and images in an ad hoc manner. However, it is helpful to see that Luther was processing the arts within a larger set of theological commitments. Although he rhetorically called reason a "whore" and detested philosophy[49]—something the Roman Catholic scholars valued—as an invention of the devil to confuse people, Luther nevertheless reasoned using inclusive theological categories; he was not only addressing the issue pragmatically but from a

46. Ibid., 50.

47. Christensen, *Art and the Reformation in Germany*, 50–51.

48. Coulton, *The Fate of Medieval Art*, 408. It is worth pausing to note a helpful overview of Protestant reflection on *adiaphora*. Even today the Protestant slogan *sola scriptura* is echoed; the Bible alone has authority on matters of life and faith. And yet, that slogan is not uniformly understood within the Protestant wing of Christianity. There are those who take a maximalist position, like Luther, and believe that we are free to do anything that the Bible does not expressly forbid. He once wrote, "The matter of Christian liberty is nothing to joke about. We want to keep it as pure and inviolate as our faith." Furthermore, "There is to be freedom of choice in everything that God has not clearly taught in the New Testament." The conscience must not be burdened. Cf. *Luther's Works*, 40:134; 40:127, quoted in Christensen, *Art and the Reformation in Germany*, 50–51. Then, there are those like Zwingli who, taking a minimalist position, maintain that practice must be restricted to that which is expressly allowed in Scripture.

49. Balthasar, *Seeing the Form*, 44–47, argued that Luther gutted a Christian and aesthetic vision of reality when he began to study the Bible more narrowly, particularly revolving around the doctrine of salvation.

The Reformation

broader theological perspective. Significant regarding artwork and images was Luther's theological understanding of sacraments. Classically stated by Augustine, a sacrament was an visible sign of invisible grace. Luther modified that by holding that "a sacrament consists in the combination of the word of promise with a sign, that is, it is a promise accompanied by a sign instituted by God and a sign accompanied by a promise." While it is true that every physical thing and visible act can point toward something beyond itself, or be understood as a picture of an invisible reality, every physical thing is not therefore a sacrament. A sacrament is an act instituted by God and combined with a promise. Important for Luther's theological construction is that sacraments are physical acts, done to our bodies, in which we participate through our bodies. These acts are appropriated by the senses and grasped with the heart (will). Sacraments, thus, are beneficial not only for our minds, hearts, and wills, but also for our bodies. In short, Luther had a theological outlook that recognized that God's coming to us involves our bodies. Or, to state it alternately, Luther viewed the physical creation as good. For Luther, unlike the ancient classical tradition, "Created things are not copies of eternal paradigms but full-blooded realities in their own right." The word is "an expression of God's generosity." Luther loved the finite creation.[50] That awareness of and appreciation for physicality is significant for understanding the use of Christian artwork and images.[51]

Second, Luther tethered his aesthetic thinking to human nature. People, Luther maintained, necessarily imagine pictures about what they are thinking. He believed it impossible for people to read or hear information without imagining that in their minds. Jesus, when he beheld Caesar's image on a coin, did not condemn or prohibit that symbolism. Further still, as portrayed in biblical revelation, God himself acted in ways that could be seen: the exodus and other signs in the Old Testament, and Jesus Christ himself in the New Testament.[52] Similarly, Luther averred, Christians are free to behold crucifixes and painted or illustrated biblical scenes.[53] Image-making was, Luther realized, inherent in human nature. He knew that "A person's picture of God determines his idea of worship. Indeed, the First Commandment is basic for Luther's idea of worship. Faith itself is the

---

50. Begbie, *Resounding Truth*, 98–101. Quote from page 100.
51. Vajta, *Luther on Worship*, 345–47. The quote is page 345.
52. Ibid., 3.
53. Christensen, *Art and the Reformation in Germany*, 52–54.

essence of worship; for faith is the fulfillment of the First Commandment, and idolatry is nothing but unbelief."[54]

Similarly, Luther understood that we are physical beings who inhabit space and time. He interpreted the Apostle Paul on Christian liberty and responsibility to mean we are free *for* others. As it concerned liturgical space, it follows that we need order, reverence, and dignity in our worship space because it is best for one another's worship experience. Yes, because Jesus taught "they must worship in spirit and truth" (John 4:24), believers can worship God almost anywhere. Yet, external things—church design and accoutrements—mattered because we indwell those during our worship. Because Christian worship is a corporate activity worship space is not simply a private matter for each believer to adjudicate for themselves.[55] Crucifixes, altars, and even images of the Virgin Mary were permitted by Luther. He knew both that the worship space impacted people's faith formation and that images, for all their potential problems, could nevertheless be pedagogically beneficial for believers.[56]

Of more concern to Luther than employing religious images was the empty repetition of the Mass. Into the sixteenth century many Europeans saw the Mass as having an almost magical, miraculous possibility. Many believed that the more the Mass was performed the better.[57] Luther was deeply disturbed by this practice. The medieval Roman Catholics believed Jesus' "do this in remembrance of me" was facilitated by regular, and as we noted above, most-frequent repetition. Not only did empty ritual provoke Luther's works-righteousness critique, it also mislocated the true purpose of worship: to encounter and glorify Christ. Luther believed that remembering Christ was not a (re)sacrifice of Christ to God, but a proclamation of Christ's work for sinners.[58] The word of God is an active and living dynamic that pierces human hearts.

In all of this Luther was less decidedly opposed to Christian tradition and liturgics than our other two Reformers. Importantly, Luther was

---

54. Vajta, *Luther on Worship*, 3.

55. Christensen, *Art and the Reformation in Germany*, 58–59.

56. Ibid., 54–65. Cf. Begbie, *Resounding Truth*, 98–99.

57. For instance, in Wittenberg, "the Castle Church had sixty-four clergy to attend to the divine office and perform some 9,000 commemorative Masses annually." Christensen, *Art and the Reformation in Germany*, 14. Hand in hand with repetition was the problem that masses were financially endowed. Luther despised people giving money so that masses would be performed. Janz, ed., *A Reformation Reader*, 97.

58. Vajta, *Luther on Worship*, 44, 57–62, 82.

The Reformation

trained more immediately in Scholastic, rather than humanist, philosophy; though we note that he sought, using biblical teaching and Augustine's writings, to critique and correct scholastic theology, not embrace or embody it.[59] We are not entirely surprised then to know that Luther envisioned a "spiritual reformation within the context of the then-prevailing ecclesiastical tradition."[60] Similarly, Luther highly esteemed the use of music in church worship. Himself a passionate music lover, he both sang and played the lute. Indeed, as it concerned worship and discipleship he placed music above the other arts. Among other reasons, he appreciated music because, like preaching the gospel, it was auditory and shaped people's feeling and thinking. Music could "make souls happy, because it drives away the devil, because it awakens innocent joy . . . because it rules in times of peace."[61]

JOHN CALVIN (1509–1564)

A generation after Luther, the famed father figure of sixteenth-century Reformed theology, John Calvin had studied law at the Universities of Orleans and Bourges and had studied both theology and Latin at University of Paris, where he was trained as a humanist. That humanist orientation inculcated in him a love and respect for studying the Bible and the church fathers in their original languages. As we will see, this humanist orientation also motivated him to elevate words over images. By 1536 when he arrived in Geneva, his eventual geographical hub of leadership and influence, the spiritual, theological, and aesthetic reforms were well underway. "The entire apparatus of medieval devotion had already been dismantled," Dyrness notes, "the monasteries had been closed, the images were gone, the Mass had been abolished."[62] At that time Calvin had not addressed religious images. Pressed variously by biblical study (he wrote a commentary on every book of the Bible), pastoral concerns (he preached an average of 170 sermons per year),[63] and political struggles (the city sometimes resisted and sometimes acquiesced to his desires to enforce godly living on the citizenry; it was a situation that kept Calvin emotionally drained), he would wait to carefully weigh in on religious images until 1550 and still later in

---

59. McGrath, *Reformation Thought*, 59–60.
60. Phillips, *Destruction of Art in England*, 108.
61. Begbie, *Resounding Truth*, 100, quoting *Luther's Works*, 30.2:696.
62. Dyrness, *Reformed Theology*, 62.
63. McDermott, *The Great Theologians*, 98.

1559, in subsequent editions of his systematic theology, the *Institutes of the Christian Religion*. (The first edition of 1536 contained only six chapters. The final edition of 1550 had eighty chapters.)

Influenced by Luther's earlier lead, Calvin believed deeper reform was necessary. Whereas Luther wanted to work with the historic Roman Catholic structures, Calvin believed it was necessary to make a clean break with the "superstitions of the papacy."[64] And indeed, looking back we can now see that among Evangelicals Calvin has produced more followers than Luther. Following an earlier path charted by Augustine, the patristic theologian whom Calvin called "the greatest authority" in antiquity,[65] Calvin's theological emphases were the glory of God, the providence of God in guiding the affairs of men,[66] God's sovereignty over creation, personal sanctification, and the special revelation of God. It is the latter especially that frames Calvin's understanding of Christian art and images.

In a manner surpassing Luther's own heightened accentuation, Calvin emphasized the word of God. Together with the right administration of the sacraments, the word of God was a mark of the true church. After all, the apostolic community in Acts made a central focus preaching and studying God's word (Acts 2:42) and the Apostle Paul made God's word central to churchly mission (1 Cor 1:23; Rom 10:17). Christ himself is present, Calvin taught, in the Christian community through rightly serving the sacraments and preaching the word. This word-over-image construal was by Calvin's time well-established. Indeed, Calvin used the *Libri Carolini* documents, with their word-over-image bent, to argue against Nicea (787) and that older sanctioning of images.[67]

Plato, as we noted in an earlier chapter, was wary of beauty precisely because it was elusive and dangerous; it can lead people astray. Throughout his career, Calvin read several of Plato's works and even described Plato as the "most religious of all philosophers and the most circumspect." Like Plato, Calvin believed both that beauty can awaken love in our souls and that the soul's highest good is likeness to God.[68] And we should note, like

64. McGrath, *Reformation Thought*, 198.

65. Bouwsma, *John Calvin*, 119.

66. Though Calvin is renown for teaching predestination he placed that doctrine at the end, and not the beginning or center, of his theological formulation. Predestination became more important for Calvin's followers than it was for Calvin. McGrath, *Reformation Thought*, 197–202.

67. Thiessen, ed., *Theological Aesthetics*, 141.

68. Zachman, *Image and Word*, 15–16.

Plato, Calvin preferred the invisible to the visible, the aural to the visual. We will see similar tendencies below regarding Zwingli, but it is important to clarify that the humanists (though the extent of that varied from scholar to scholar), educated as they were in philosophic categories, tended to work with and through the strong dualisms of Platonic thought, categories that Jeremy Begbie says inculcated perspectives of "superiors and inferiors, physical and non-physical, outer and inner, material and non-material, bodily and spiritual, ceremonial piety and inner devotion, flesh and spirit, and the like."[69] This does *not* mean that Calvin or the Reformers were committed humanists, but that they were influenced by humanism; they were borrowing and then nuancing bits and pieces of its overarching perspectives.[70]

That humanist-dualist education notwithstanding, Calvin, like Luther, believed that God's creation was good. For instance, he believed food was not only for our sustenance but our enjoyment. Wine, he reasoned, "is not only 'very healthy' but is given to us to make us 'merry.' He owned the biggest wine cellar in Geneva."[71] And yet, Calvin did not press out the interconnected implications of creation's goodness with regard to human artistic giftedness, aesthetics, or the use of the human imagination.[72] This is interesting particularly because Calvin believed that nature is a theater for God's glory. Calvin knew that God shines through all he has made. Cre-

---

69. Begbie, *Resounding Truth*, 116. This briefly established, it is not surprising that Calvin gave Christ's incarnation no role to play in his aesthetic reflections. Cf. Dyrness, *Reformed Theology*, 71 and 76, note 74.

70. McGrath offers a helpful five-point grid hereon. 1) Humanists and Reformers both disdained scholasticism, but for different reasons: humanists because they saw scholasticism as unintelligible, Reformers because scholasticism was theologically erroneous. 2) Concerning Scripture, the humanists loved it for its eloquence and antiquity, but the Reformers loved it because it embodied God's word and promises. 3) About the church fathers, humanists appreciated them for their eloquence and antiquity, while the Reformers loved some of the fathers because they rightly interpreted the New Testament. 4) Both groups supported education; the humanists promoted the liberal arts, the Reformers promoted religious ideas. 5) Rhetoric: humanists loved rhetoric where it promoted eloquence while the Reformers employed rhetoric for the sake of conveying, in preaching and writing, gospel truths. McGrath, *Reformation Thought*, 60–63.

71. Bouwsma, *John Calvin*, 52.

72. Dyrness, himself situated in the Reformed tradition, notes this about Calvin's lacunae concerning human imagination. "Whatever Calvin's good wishes might have been for those gifted in the arts," Dyrness added, "Calvin gives them no positive encouragement or guidance. As a result, artists and sculptors were mostly out of work in the Geneva of Calvin's time." *Reformed Theology*, 79.

ation's glory, Calvin maintained, is a "mirror in which we can contemplate God, who is otherwise invisible." He once waxed eloquent, "Has the Lord clothed the flowers with great beauty that greets our eyes, the sweetness of smell that is wafted upon our nostrils, and yet will it be unlawful for our eyes to be affected by that beauty, or our sense of smell by the sweetness of that odor? What? Did he not so distinguish colors as to make some more lovely than others?"[73]

We know that religion—a right heart's attitude—was critical in Calvin's thought.[74] Perhaps this is why he believed it acceptable and even laudatory for people to make images and statues that reflected nature and secular history, but was not equally accommodating regarding Christian images; for civil purposes believers could have images in their homes but not have them in the churches.[75] He refused to accept that images are a "way for the [human] spirit to reach God." In reality, images distracted worshippers from God. Calvin wrote, "Nor is it of any importance, whether they worship simply the idol, or God in the idol, it is always idolatry, when Divine honours are paid to an idol, under any pretense whatsoever."[76] Similarly, Calvin did not want there to be any blurring between the secular and the sacred. He even had the Genevan churches locked during hours of non-operation so that the purpose of the building could be maintained: corporate worship and preaching of the word.[77] Images and artwork about the secular realm—nature and history—did not tread as close to issues about the heart as did the overtly religious. To Calvin, observing artwork about nature and history was not the temptation to idolatry that religious art was.

More decidedly, however, Calvin's understanding of images went both to his understanding of God and reality. Implied within his afore-noted emphases on God's sovereignty, glory, and providence, Calvin believed that God is utterly transcendent and invisible. Accordingly, in our thoughts about God, nothing can be mixed together with God. He towers above

---

73. Dyrness, *Reformed Theology*, 72–73, quoting Calvin's *Institutes*, volume I, v, I and III, x, 2.

74. Begbie, *Resounding Truth*, 109.

75. Coulton, *The Fate of Medieval Art*, 178, 184.

76. Phillips, *Destruction of Art in England*, 83, quoting Calvin's *Institutes*, I, 106; Tracts I, 148–49.

77. Because he believed we meet with God in spirit and truth, Calvin taught that Christians can pray anywhere; the church was not a location to enter for superstitious (observing images or contemplating the Eucharistic host) reasons. Dyrness, *Reformed Theology*, 82.

all human conception. Because we are fallen we are prone to create false portrayals of God; we are blinded by ignorance and malice. Thus, any mixing of God and our ideas about God is idolatrous. Truly, the only way we know any truth about God is through God's own self-revelation.[78] Yes, even non-believers can see something of God's glory in creation (Rom 1) and even they have implanted in their hearts some knowledge of God, but God's special revelation, the Bible, helps us see it more clearly. So seminal, so influential is this line of thought for subsequent generations of theologians that we will elucidate this further.

Seeing our wretched fallen state, God decided nevertheless to come to us, to reveal himself to us. By creating us, God originally etched upon our hearts a knowledge of his own existence. However, we neither know that God is creator, savior, or judge, nor know that he yearns for relationship with us, by observing creation. We know those latter, more specific, things because of God's special revelation, the Scriptures. Or, to make another example, we know to exclaim the beauty of God in nature because we read about that in the Bible, not because creation directly teaches us there is a beautiful being—God—who created beauty. Calvin wrote that Scripture is the remedy that "not only makes those things plain which would otherwise escape our notice, but almost compels us to behold them; as if he had assisted our dull sight with spectacles."[79] Or put more simply, all people can see God's glory in creation, but Scripture helps us see it clearer. That manner of perception, in Calvin's theological formulation, maintains the sovereignty of God: he was first mover, not us; he towers over us and lives far beyond us; he graciously comes to us, opposed to God though we are in our fallen nature. Again, however, for our purposes herein, we can see why it relegates the realm of art and aesthetics to a subordinate position for Calvin. Art and images can indeed teach, but they are far short of God's special revelation, the Bible, God's word. Indeed, if the church had rightly done its teaching job images would not be needed one bit, averred Calvin.[80] And whereas images come entangled with the temptation toward idolatry, God's word rightly understood does not. Rather than make use of carved, painted, or graven images, Calvin believed we should look for the image of God in our neighbor or even in creation, images that because they are made

---

78. Ibid., 64.

79. Dyrness, *Reformed Theology*, 73, quoting Calvin, "Argument," in *Commentaries on the First Book of Moses Called Genesis*, 62.

80. Ibid., 80, quoting Calvin, *Institutes*, I, ch. 11, paragraphs 12–14, pp. 112–15.

by God can be enjoyed. Nevertheless, we must remember that creation itself cannot contain God.[81]

Despite his rather negative attitude toward Christian artwork and images, Calvin did not overtly encourage iconoclasm. In fact, at one point he even condemned those who destroyed images in Lyons.[82] He knew that art could indeed benefit the young and illiterate, but believed that God's Spirit had surpassed images by giving special revelation, the Scriptures.[83] And, if Calvin's attitude toward Christian and churchly artwork seems dour we do well to remember the chaotic and tumultuous context of his own day.

ULRICH ZWINGLI (1484–1531)

During thirteen days of 1524 a committee of citizens, led by Zwingli, went through every church in Zurich and stripped them of their artwork. Paintings were burned along with woodworkings. Statues were shattered. Crucifixes were dislodged. (Because they were not used for prayer or contemplation, and so were not locations for idolatry, Zwingli maintained and protected stained glass.) Wooden choir stalls, intricately carved, were pried out and burned. Seventeen distinct altarpieces were destroyed. Colorful frescoed walls were whitewashed. Soon after, a traveler returning home to Zurich cried out, "there was nothing at all inside, it was hideous." Contrastingly Zwingli himself wrote, "In Zurich we have churches which are positively luminous; the walls are beautifully white." Later in 1525 Zurich abolished observance of the mass. We can note that whereas Zurich was only some 500 miles from Rome, ideologically it might as well have been on the other side of the universe.[84]

Ordained a Catholic priest in 1506, Zwingli was promoted to Zurich's Grossmünster cathedral church in 1519. It was not until after an entire year of Zwingli's Bible preaching that in 1522 the Reformation began in Zurich, initiated when his Reform-minded group ate sausage during Lent. In January 1523 Zwingli published his *67 Conclusions*; like Luther's own *95 Theses*, these were intended to stir discussion. Zwingli is known for having led the Radical Reformation although he would not always agree with how far others took his ideas. Having espoused a memorialist position on the Lord's

---

81. Ibid., 75–76. Coulton, *The Fate of Medieval Art*, 438.
82. Coulton, *The Fate of Medieval Art*, 411.
83. Ibid., referencing Calvin's *Institutes*, I, xi, 5.
84. Miles, *Image as Insight*, 102–3.

The Reformation

Supper, Zwingli is the true father figure for low-church Protestants. Almost 500 years later he remains influential, including his minimalist aesthetic perspective.

Zwingli, negatively motivated, was disgusted by many Roman Catholic practices, not least of which concerned images; hereon he was following a pattern of critique established by Erasmus and other humanist scholars.[85] There were many humanists teaching in Northern Italian universities, none more influential than Erasmus. A man of far reaching vision, Erasmus wanted a *Christianismus renascens*: to revive the entirety of Christianity. However, because he was not himself a member of the Catholic curia, was not a power broker within the Catholic Church's institutional system, Erasmus had broader ideological aims as against immediately ecclesiastical aims; he was less concerned with modifying the particulars than he was with overhauling the whole. This overhaul would occur when the people, especially middle-class literates, read the New Testament and the church fathers and consequently perceived and lived life in more pristine ways. Erasmus, like many revivalistic church leaders even today, believed that "the pure philosophy of Christ" was that which existed before Gregory the Great's era. All that had occurred since Gregory's time was degenerate. It is no surprise then that, as Garside wrote, "the humanists' desire for a *Christianismus renascens* ultimately meant nothing less than an attempt to get out of the whole ecclesiastical environment created by medieval Christianity and to return to the religio-cultural environment of the early church and antiquity *as they conceived it*."[86] It was this attitudinal perspective that Zwingli embraced while attending the various schools and universities of his education. At Basel, Bern, and Vienna, Zwingli studied with men who were noted humanist scholars. During his ten years at Glarus he constantly corresponded with humanists. At Einsiedeln he was "to all intents and purposes a thoroughgoing disciple of Erasmus," where he did two years of "virtually complete immersion in Erasmian thought."[87]

Thus, again for our aesthetic purposes, while it is clear that Zwingli affirmed an Evangelical—Bible-emphasizing, Christ-as-unique-savior, New Testament-as-new-law—vantage point, he did so "from the humanist philosophy of Christ."[88] Like Erasmus, Zwingli was psychologically and

---

85. Garside Jr., *Zwingli and the Arts*, 34.
86. Ibid., 35. My italics.
87. Ibid., 33.
88. Ibid., 35.

intellectually removed from the ecclesiastical environment. Subsequently it was "virtually impossible for him to disengage questions of substance from those of form." Hence, the reform for Zwingli must not only be spiritual, as it had been primarily for Luther, but institutional and liturgical.[89] So for instance, whereas Luther was content to have images torn out of people's hearts, Zwingli wanted them altogether torn out of churches. (Like Calvin, he was fine with artwork and images outside church walls.) He once wrote of images,

> Men kneel, bow, and remove their hats before them; candles and incense are burned before them; men name them after the saints whom they represent; men kiss them; men adorn them with gold and jewels; men designate them with the appellation merciful or gracious; men seek consolation merely from touching them, or even hope to acquire remission of sins thereby.[90]

Also of significance, and this was his positive motivation, Zwingli was ardently committed to follow the Bible and no other source. If the Bible did not teach something, neither should the church. If the Bible did not commend something, neither should the church. And since, in Zwingli's interpretation, the Bible did not commend the use of art (nor even music, as shown further below), neither should the church. Jesus never commanded that ceremony or physical setting be central to Christian worship. What the Bible did teach, and what Jesus himself taught, was that worship ought be done "in spirit and truth" (John 4:24). For Zwingli, walking in philosophical terrain plowed by humanism, "in spirit" meant nonmaterial.[91] Again, Zwingli primarily learned to interpret Jesus hereon through humanist, particularly Erasmian, lenses. Erasmus's beliefs inculcated a radical distinction between flesh and spirit. Garside explains, "Outward observance in worship was without value, because it was corporeal; true Christian discipleship meant the spiritual life, an almost exclusive inner experience, whose external expression in public worship was in itself relatively insignificant."[92]

In establishing some foundations for understanding today's Evangelical environment we must be measured. In our historical investigation

---

89. Ibid., 36.

90. Christensen, *Art and the Reformation in Germany*, 22.

91. Begbie, *Resounding Truth*, 116. We can now see why he interpreted the Lord's supper as a memorial, one not making Christ present but only a sign that commemorates and points to Christ.

92. Garside Jr., *Zwingli and the Arts*, 36.

The Reformation

we cannot bear false witness. The vacuous nature of much of low-church aesthetics owes to many causes and features that follow Zwingli and the sixteenth century, as our later chapters will establish. Those caveats notwithstanding, the subjectivizing tendencies of contemporary Evangelicalism have important roots in Zwingli's reforming moves. For instance, that worship in spirit in truth is to be a non-corporeal practice, an internal, spirit, heart, and mind dynamic, yet neither a bodily nor aesthetic dynamic, comes directly from Zwingli and those like him. Zwingli illustrated this attitude thusly:

> No prayer is more pleasing to God than that which recognizes Him truly and calls on God truly with heart free from doubt, not with hypocrisy, but with right, true acknowledgment and recognition. Thus [Exod 14:15] Moses calls earnestly on God within his heart and does not move his lips. So also Hannah did not cry aloud [1 Sam. 1:13]. So, too, Christ [Matt. 6:7] prohibited much babbling and has taught that we should pray in spirit and truth [John 4:24] where He frees us also from particular localities; that not in one locality better than another may God be well and correctly called upon, but in all localities where God is called upon in spirit and truth, there does He say: Here am I.[93]

That the Scriptures broadly, or Jesus particularly, thereby meant that we cease to be embodied beings who live in space and time strains credulity. Yes, the central matter, as it always was for Jesus, is the state of the heart. No, our hearts are never eviscerated from our bodies, just as our bodies are never taken out of space and time. Zwingli pressed too hard, even while we can appreciate the gist of his teaching: God wants our hearts, not just our words or actions. Yet, God also wants our words and actions. Zwingli's yearning to root his practice in biblical categories is exemplary. That he stringently limited our possibilities for following Christ to spiritual and internal dimensions works against the both Bible's witness and human nature.

Certainly, we must recall Zwingli's historical context: grotesque spiritual abuses, mindless repetition, rote observance lacking true volition, and works-righteousness beliefs that permeated Christian worship; these were all at issue in the critiques of the humanists, Zwingli, and other Radical Reformers. Still further, the polemic of it all cannot be ignored. When men of purported Christian character and status call each other all manner of rude

---

93. Ibid., 40, translating and quoting Zwingli's *Samtliche Werke*, vol. 2, 348, lines 5–16.

and corrosive names, when they put into print emotional outbursts that ought be reserved for one's own private remonstrations at best, we are not surprised that the arguments take on a force that is greater than their surface logic or persuasion. Again, the Reformation's polemical temperature was white-hot. It is no surprise then, based on Zwingli's teachings about true spirituality, teachings arguing that Christian religion is less about the body than the spirit, that the church organ in Grossmünster was dismantled and destroyed. On Zwingli's command, even *a cappella* congregational singing in Zurich ceased until the end of the sixteenth century. Zwingli interpreted Paul in Colossians 3:16, "teaching and admonishing one another in psalms and hymns and spiritual songs, singing with grace in your hearts to the Lord," to mean that we should not sing vocally, but *only in our hearts*.[94] Hyper-spiritualized and hyper-subjectivized, instead of taking more measured steps Zwingli made a clean sweep of Zurich: churches were entirely sanitized of any significant aesthetic. Whitewashed walls lacking musical echoes, these pleased Zwingli's eyes and ears. That was, after all, his biblical model.

When squared up with an oak bat, a ninety-five–mile-an-hour fastball travels further than one traveling eighty miles per hour. The same energy is taken and directed in another direction, but it continues at a higher rate of speed. The issue of Zwingli and music is particularly fascinating. Luther loved and commended music, both inside and outside the church, as a gift from God. Calvin, knowing that music stirred the people's hearts and emotions toward God, encouraged congregational singing of the Psalms.[95] Zwingli altogether prohibited music. Music allowed people to be seen and heard in their worship, and that enabled hypocrisy and public displays of piety, things Jesus forbade. People were singing things they did not even understand. With ostentatious display, thought Zwingli, professional choirs tainted the heartfelt quality of the worship. Garside believes that this has greatly to do with Zwingli himself having been a proficient musician. At every school whereat he attended or taught Zwingli was lauded as an amazingly talented singer and musician. He played multiple instruments. His voice was so lovely a Dominican monastery in Bern invited him to join their ranks.[96]

---

94. Ibid., 45.
95. Begbie, *Resounding Truth*, 107–8.
96. Garside Jr., *Zwingli and the Arts*, 41–47, and especially 73–75.

The Reformation

WRAP-UP: IMPLICATIONS FOR SUBSEQUENT PROTESTANT AESTHETICS

Our study being primarily historical and not constructive, we nevertheless do well to briefly observe some important abiding dynamics at work in sixteenth-century Protestant theo-aesthetic views. First, it is obvious but still worthwhile to note that the less caustic the Protestant leader's critique of Rome was the less he was likely to want to jettison the use of all images or a defined churchly aesthetic.[97] Present even today is the low-church attitude, "if the Catholics do it that way, we won't," regardless of the wisdom of the practice at issue. Many forget, the Reformation is over. Agreed, as Calvin put it, "the church is reformed and ever reforming"; this side of eternity as Christ's body we are never all that we are called to be. Yet, the geographical and linguistic separation, the personal and political power struggles, the work of ecclesial realignment, the tasks of spiritual and theological restructuring, those are all dynamics that were completed a long time ago. It is simply no longer a viable reason that aesthetics be disregarded because "we don't want to be Catholic." There may be other well-grounded arguments for aesthetic minimalism, but that ought not be one.

The aesthetic secular-sacred dualism instilled by Calvin and Zwingli is simply no longer viable. In their varied ways, both men were comfortable with the use of art and images outside the church, but not inside. This is not only a little ironic, given that a significant Reformation impulse was to convert the secular-mundane spaces and places of life into arenas for God's glory. It seems that art, images, architecture, and music were the exceptions to the Protestant sacralizing impulse. For Zwingli, music was acceptable outside the church building, but not inside it. Calvin only allowed specified and limited forms of music within church walls. Though I am one willing to make all manner of diverse arguments about the structure and use of sacred space, the Reformation's secular-sacred aesthetic dualism has caused both enormous damage to the way millions of believers have lived, and today live, their lives, and to the church's witness to the world. Because, again, we no longer live inside the torrid polemic that characterized the Reformers' era, we need to be more holistic, more savvy about our intentional shaping of liturgical space. We wound our mission and witness when we work a

---

97. This with the caveat that while all structure and space has its aesthetic quality, aesthetic design itself implies intent. Today, frequently design is of little import compared to utility for many Protestant churches.

secular-sacred split. We are called to bring all things under submission to Christ, to use all things to his glory, whether inside the church or not.

The general Reformation Protestant preference for word over image, preaching over liturgics was appropriate for its day; we've repeatedly referenced the prevalent abuses. However, it is too easy to neglect the fact that *words are symbols*, too. They are symbols on paper and they symbolize meaning inside our minds. I believe words are consistently more precise than images. Thank you, Lord, for your Word and your words! Nevertheless, words do not always pristinely convey meaning. Words require their linguistic and literary and historic contexts. Spoken words involve the interpretation of body language. Words themselves are limited. Words profoundly help us touch upon reality, but we need no longer believe that words are the only way to communicate, glorify God, or facilitate our worship.

Finally, we briefly note that undoubtedly owing to their respective historic contingencies Zwingli and Calvin both struggled to consider that physicality is good because created by God. Undoubtedly, both men appreciated creation's beauty. That, however, is different from understanding and inculcating a more careful and biblically grounded creation theology into the worship setting. Spiritual worship (John 4:24) never meant that we should cut ourselves off from our communal surroundings, abandon the role and place of our bodies, or turn so ardently inward that our worship experience becomes a private one. Is it possible that the practice of so many Evangelical churches today—to turn the lights down low and turn the worship band's volume up so high so that we can neither see nor hear anyone around us—is a faint continuation of the ardent inward turn of the Reformation?[98] We need to think more carefully on these matters.

WHAT THE REFORMATION TEACHES US TO SEE:

- beauty can be turned idolatrous and dangerous
- beauty can be abused

---

98. Thiessen, ed., *Theological Aesthetics*, 155, believes that the impact of both the Reformation and the Counter-Reformation "influenced the beginnings of the Enlightenment, i.e., the turn to the human subject from a formerly theocentric world-view, the radical stress on rationalism, and the critique of religion."

The Reformation

WHAT LUTHER TEACHES US TO SEE:

- anything can become dangerous, but that does not make all things evil
- images are a matter of conscience
- biblical scenes should be used to edify the church
- physical creation is good
- empty ritual is destructive
- music can edify the church

WHAT CALVIN TEACHES US TO SEE:

- words are more important than images
- creation is a theater for God's glory
- secular, not religious, images are acceptable
- the Bible teaches us to see creation's beauty as God's glory

WHAT ZWINGLI TEACHES US TO SEE:

- the church should have no images
- spiritual, not ritualistic, worship is what is important
- singing should be in our hearts, not with our voices

8

Jonathan Edwards (1703–1758)
The Wonder of God's Beautifying Beauty: The Holy Spirit

SHOULD CHRISTIAN REFLECTION ON beauty be solely rooted in the Bible? Or, can Christians use philosophical categories to process and frame beauty? Put differently, are there any guidelines for both defining and/or expanding our theo-aesthetic musings? We ask such questions here to reiterate that interpretation is critical in and for life. We have to learn to see beauty. *Beauty requires lenses*. We do not perceive or see beauty from nowhere. None of us are neutral. We see from a particular vantage point and we look through already-cut lenses. And honestly, some of those lenses more readily help us than others. To make my point, let me suggest an analogy.

My father-in-law, Dennis McNutt, told the story of his time as a young missionary kid in West Africa in the 1940s. When his parents showed a picture of people to indigenous West Africans they could not see the faces in the photo; they had never seen a picture and did not know how to look at it. They had to be taught that those were human faces in the photograph before they would believe it. Their interpretive lenses had to be educated. O'Donohue clarifies, "The quality of our outlook determines what we come to see." And, if we don't know how to perceive beauty we may look right through a gorgeous subject as if it didn't even exist. "The imagination," O'Donohue avers, "is like a lantern." "When our eyes are graced with wonder," he continued, "the world reveals its wonders to us."[1] Frequently, beauty surrounds us, but if our imagination is listless, we may overlook a delicate wonder shining right in front of us.

The Reformation—for all its appropriate criticism, for all its necessary correction, and for the genius of its biblical redirect—dulled people's aesthetic imaginations. The seventeenth- and eighteenth-century Protestants, having taken their epistemological cues from Reformation leaders, tended to filter truth and reality through biblical lenses. Once justification by faith was implanted within the Protestant world view other pressing questions arose, like "what is the assurance of salvation?" and "what is the difference between salvation and sanctification?" Protestant theological energy was spent cleaning up the lingering foment of Protestant versus Catholic, and Protestant versus sibling Protestant, controversies. Over the next two centuries Protestants were industriously codifying their beliefs and plowing those into their own established traditions. Theological reflection on beauty, creation, and human creativity was mostly shelved. That background makes Jonathan Edwards's theo-aesthetic flourish even more astounding.

Born into the Puritan heritage in the new colonies, Edwards was for over two decades an influential pastor in Massachusetts. Living in the heyday of the Enlightenment, Edwards both studied and was fascinated by the then-recent intellectual developments. Yet, unlike many of his contemporaries who abandoned a biblical orthodoxy and fell into the embrace of Deism, Edwards critically incorporated new developments into his own world view. While Edwards's Reformed tradition was fertile ground for his own theological development he also took Enlightenment insights and used them for, rather than against, a biblically informed perspective on life. Willing to learn and open to listen, Edwards awakened both his mind to perceive and his eyes to see.

Today Edwards is renowned both for his role in the first Great Awakening—it began in his own Northampton church in 1734—and for his famous sermon, "Sinners in the Hands of an Angry God" (1741), a sermon that was idiosyncratic with his preaching style. In the annals of theology, Edwards is frequently called the most famous American theologian ever. We will survey his vantage points on God's beauty, the Holy Spirit, and Christian affections. Truly, Edwards was a man whose eyes were graced with wonder.

1. O'Donohue, *Beauty*, 145.

For Him Who Has Eyes to See
GOD AS BEAUTY

Even before Edwards was born, Puritan spirituality and lifestyle took as its central concerns ethics and behavior. Edwards, for as Reformed as he truly was, made a distinctive shift within his own immediate Christian tradition: God was beautiful. Or more narrowly constructed, the first of God's perfections was beauty. Again, to note how innovative this foundational move was let us recall that Puritans emphasized God's holiness. In Edwards's day Puritans believed holiness should manifest not in quietude but in work and action that itself was morally holy. Concurrently, Puritans sought to redeem the time God gave them so they stressed "maximum effectiveness" through living godly disciplined lives.[2] Yes, like a good Puritan divine, Edwards was disciplined and fastidious, even in his youth.[3] And yet his own fixation on practical holy living makes it even more remarkable that Edwards made beauty central to his own theological framework. Beholding and appreciating beauty is a quieter, not an activist, discipline. "His stress on the primacy of the aesthetic over the moral and legal in our experience of God," clarified Douglas Elwood, "places the old Calvinism on a very different footing."[4]

Even into the twenty-first century which Protestant denomination argues that beauty is central to following Christ? What Evangelical theologian argues that God's beauty is the primary way to frame reality and Christian living? We are 2,000 years into Christian history and beauty still barely registers on the Christian imagination. Edwards's commitment to God's being primarily beautiful, again, is novel for a low-church Protestant. Kin Yip Louie said, "Puritan New England is not known for its cultivation of fine arts."[5] Withal, Gerald McDermott holds that Edwards "related God to beauty more than anyone else in the history of Christian thought."[6]

---

2. Ryken, "The Original Puritan Work Ethic," 89.

3. Marsden, *Jonathan Edwards*, 53. As a young man this pronounced religious drive saw Edwards fluctuate emotionally. For instance at nineteen years of age Edwards wrote "that this being so exceedingly careful, and so particularly anxious, to force myself to think of religion, at all leisure moments, has exceedingly distracted my mind, and made me altogether unfit for that, and everything else." Ibid.

4. Elwood, *Jonathan Edwards*, 3. Louie nevertheless cogently argues that Edwards remained solidly theologically Reformed. Edwards was not so much introducing a new vantage point for Enlightenment philosophy as he was developing further nuance within Reformed theology. Louie, *Jonathan Edwards*, 15, 64–93.

5. Louie, *Jonathan Edwards*, 18. See also 3–14.

6. McDermott, *The Great Theologians*, 115.

Jonathan Edwards (1703–1758)

For Edwards the beauty of God was not merely a focal point for piety and devotion, nor was God's beauty just a theological rubric by which life's beauty could be interpreted, true though those were. Beauty went deeper than that for Edwards. God's beauty was "fundamental to his understanding of God, as the first of God's perfections, as key to the doctrine of the Trinity, as a defining aspect of the natural world, as basic to the phenomenon of conversion, as visible in the lives of the saints, and as marking the difference between the regenerate and the unregenerate mind."[7] Beauty moved in and from God and then out into creation itself. Beauty was indeed central to Edwards's theological framework.

God is beautiful. What did that assertion express for Edwards? It meant primarily excellence and holiness, terms synonymous in Edwardsian theology.[8] Excellence did not mean simply worthiness, near-perfection, or the aesthetically sublime. Using philosophical categories, Edwards held that excellence involves being, a philosophical term. Let's see how this stacked up for Edwards.

Being is clearly greater than nonbeing; it is better to exist than not. But to be *a* being incorporates volition: willing. Volition in turn enables choice and love; if one could not choose one could not sincerely love. God himself is a being who exists, chooses, and loves. What God is in himself he wants for creation. Thus, Edwards held that true beauty, deepest beauty, manifests in agreement, consent, and love; terms all incorporating mutuality and resulting in *primary beauty*, as Edwards called it. We see primary beauty in that God chooses to love us. Furthermore, primary beauty manifests itself in that God chose to invite us into an uncoerced relationship of love with both him and one another. Primary beauty is communal; it incorporates beings who choose to mutually serve and love one another.

By way of contrast, *secondary beauty* involves beauty in the material world.[9] Creation, the physical realm, manifests myriad instances of proportion, symmetry, harmony, relations, and equality—aesthetic categories as old as antiquity. However creation cannot express primary beauty because nature—itself a thing, not a being—is not capable of agreement, consent or love; material things lack mind and volition. This dualistic, primary and

---

7. McClymond and McDermott, *The Theology of Johnathan Edwards*, 93.

8. Mitchell, *On the Experience of Beauty*, 1–2.

9. Secondary beauty, Edwards maintained, could also appear in society through the categories of architecture, wisdom, structure, and organization. Cf. Sammon, *The God Who Is Beauty*, 4–5. Here lingers the older Calvinist scheme whereby human-made beauty is relegated to a subordinate status to natural beauty.

secondary, schema did not cause Edwards to disdain physical beauties (he believed secondary beauty can lead us to primary beauty), but he did understand them to be less than spiritual beauties. "The world is the language; spiritual beauty is the meaning," encapsulated Louie.[10]

God shines through secondary beauty, Edwards averred. He once remarked, "The beauty of the world is a communication of God's beauty."[11] Edwards's penetrating theological reflections on God's beauty and the beauty of nature led McClymond and McDermott to assert that in his theology Edwards was espousing his own version of *analogia entis*: analogy of being.[12] Thus, for Edwards there is a correspondence between God and his creation, it is "*a cosmos in which God and creatures are both alike and unlike in important ways.*"[13] Edwards believed all created things testify to the existence of God; hereon he is echoing the intellectual constructions of antiquity. Both Pseudo-Dionysius and Augustine believed that the very existence of a thing, the fact of its being, is testimony to the existence of a greater cause: God. On this hierarchy Edwards developed his own typology. Here are samples:

> Every last part of the creation is emblematic of the divine, an effulgent crystal with supernatural meaning: even the tiniest leaf in a flower is a word from God, the sun shows forth God's glory, the clouds and mountains bespeak God's majesty, and the green fields and pleasant flowers testify to "his grace and mercy."[14]

Elsewhere he wrote,

> The great markers of the days and seasons burst with meaning. The sun, for example, which makes plants flourish when it shines after rain, is a type of the Sun of Righteousness who heals the soul's afflictions; the stars are types of the saints in glory, and the moon is an image of earthly glory and all the good of earthly life, which like the moon ever changes, rising and falling, waxing and waning.

---

10. Louie, *Jonathan Edwards*, 80. This schema in mind, Edwards held that human persons are greater than angels because we can love God with our affections whereas angels only can by nature. Cf. ibid., 151.

11. Edwards, "1722, The Miscellanies," 384, in *Works of Jonathan Edwards* (hereafter *WJE*) online.

12. We will address *analogia entis* more carefully in our chapter on Balthasar, who makes that theological frame central to his theology of beauty.

13. McClymond and McDermott, *The Theology of Johnathan Edwards*, 105. My italics.

14. Ibid., 127.

Jonathan Edwards (1703-1758)

Birds flying in the sky are also types of the saints in heaven, but "to a fairer degree" than the stars.[15]

Edwards did not systematically develop his reflections on how everything somehow pointed to God, but so thoroughgoing was his typological thinking that Edwards believed even false religions typified something true about God because God had implanted truth about himself therein. For example, human sacrifice pointed ultimately toward Christ's ultimate sacrifice.[16]

Again we point out that Edwards broke with the larger sweep of Reformed and Puritan theology to think so dynamically, so philosophically, and to see the world around him as *wondrously radiating the presence of God*, as being imbued with something of God's own self, God's Spirit. On the one hand Edwards went against the then-budding position of Deism which depersonalized God and squeezed the mystery out of life.[17] On the other hand Edwards would not breach biblical orthodoxy and move into pantheism, as happens with some theologians today. He was too committed both to his own Reformed tradition and to a biblical world view to blur the boundaries between God and creation. God was present in and through creation, but God was not creation. Edwards knew that creation does not exist of its own accord. "The universe," he believe, "is created *out of nothing every moment* and if it were not for our imaginations, which hinder us, we might see that wonderful work performed continually."[18] His heightened sense of God's presence thus evident, he still exercised restraint. "Edwards never compromised his assertion of the radical transcendence of God." McClymond and McDermott continued, "Paradoxically, [Edwards maintained that] God was immanent by virtue of his transcendence, and transcendent by virtue of his immanence."[19] Edwards's experience of nature's vibrant beauty coupled with his commitment to God's transcendence represents a presence-and-absence tension that is unique even among Protestants today.[20]

---

15. Ibid., 127-28.
16. Ibid., 129.
17. Marsden, *Jonathan Edwards*, 77.
18. Ibid., 74, 109. My italics.
19. McClymond and McDermott, *The Theology of Johnathan Edwards*, 105.
20. That Edwards did so, and that he employed an implicit *analogia entis* view of reality, prefigured the later monumental work of the Jesuit Hans Urs von Balthasar. Cf. ibid., 105.

For Him Who Has Eyes to See

As Edwards's aforenoted relational configurations on primary beauty implied, God's triune nature also figured into his aesthetic formulation. God, the Trinity, is primary beauty's archetype and wellspring because God is not only one. Edwards reasoned that one "alone cannot be excellent, inasmuch as, in such case, there can be no consent. Therefore, if God is excellent, there must be a plurality in God; otherwise there can be no consent in him."[21] Because the intelligent and volitional "other" in God is capable of agreeing, consenting to, and loving the "still other" in God—the Son to the Father, the Spirit to the Son, and so on—God is *not only love itself*, as commonly understood (1 John 4:8, 16), but *beauty itself*. The archetype of community, God is thus both the "foundation and fountain of all beauty."[22] Hence, by the Spirit, the Son consents to and loves the Father, and the Father reciprocates. Mitchell aptly summarized Edwards, "The Trinity is an infinite society of being infinitely consenting to being."[23] The beauty of being, primary beauty, is found in agreeing to and making oneself vulnerable to the other. Believers, in order to become disciples and flourish, must consent to and defer to both God and one another. It is beautiful to be in consensual relationship.[24] Believers thus participate in God's beauty when they willingly prefer and serve one another; in this way *God's beauty is a beautifying beauty*. What God does for God as God—love and serve the other in God—is given to created beings who can reciprocate that service and mutuality to and for one another. God's beauty then involves harmony, proximity, proportionality, and relationship—categories that are extended out into creation and humanity. But God's beauty is also virtuous and holy; it involves love, care for the other, righteousness, integrity, charity, and reciprocity.

That God is beautiful was not merely theoretical for Edwards. He experienced this beauty, this divine light, both inside church services and outside in nature. Within Edwards's Northampton church in October 1740 George Whitefield preached a sermon and noted that "Mr. Edwards wept during the whole time of the exercise."[25] Edwards loved church revival. He loved the transformation that God could work in a believer's heart within

---

21. Edwards, "Scientific and Philosophical Writings," 84, *WJE*.
22. Mitchell, *On the Experience of Beauty*, 105.
23. Ibid., 13.
24. Marsden, *Jonathan Edwards*, 3, avers that Edwards nevertheless maintained a traditional aristocratic, hierarchical, perspective on society.
25. Gaustad, quoting "Whitefield's Journal" in *Religion in America*, 196.

Jonathan Edwards (1703–1758)

a church service. But Edwards loved too the beauty out in creation. A teenager, he was already aware of God's presence shining through nature's beauty. He would walk in the fields contemplating God's sweetness, majesty, and grace.[26] Again, however, nature's beauties are always viewed as less than God's higher and truer beauties. For instance,

> The beauty of trees, plants, and flowers with which God has bespangled the face of the earth, is delightful; the beautiful frame of the body of man, especially in its perfection, is astonishing; the beauty of the moon and stars is wonderful; the beauty of [the] highest heavens is transcendent; the excellency of angels and the saints in light is very glorious: but it is all deformity and darkness in comparison of the brighter glories and beauties of the creator of all, for "behold even to the moon, and it shineth not" (Job 25:5); that is, think of the excellency of God and the moon will not seem to shine to you, God's excellency so much outshines [it].[27]

Edwards delighted in nature's beauty, but always as a projection of a truer reality in another realm, emanating from a still more real beauty: God.[28] Key for Edwards on God's beauty is that he believed it was something that one could experience; it was not an abstraction for mere speculation. Harkening to the philosophic constructions of antiquity, Edwards believed God's beauty objectively exists; beauty is no mere subjective interpretation. Rather, as an extension of God's saving goodness, beauty can be apprehended. Edwards once clearly delineated his sensibilities about God's divine light. It was a spiritual light that consists in

> a real sense and apprehension of the divine excellency of things revealed in the word of God. A spiritual and saving conviction of the truth and reality of these things, arises from such a sight of their divine excellency and glory; so that this conviction of their truth is an effect and natural consequence of this sight of their divine glory. There is therefore in this spiritual light . . . a real sense of the excellency of God and Jesus Christ, and of the work of redemption, and the ways and works of God revealed in the gospel. . . . He that is spiritually enlightened truly apprehends and sees it, or has a

---

26. Edwards, "Typological Writings," 58, *WJE*. See also "Sermons and Discourses: 1723–1729," 476, *WJE*.

27. Ibid., 421.

28. Louie, *Jonathan Edwards*, 216, summarizes Edwards and locates him historically: "Edwards's aesthetics is an idealistic interpretation of Calvin's dogma of the world as theatre of God's glory."

sense of it. He does not merely rationally believe that God is glorious, but he has a sense of the gloriousness of God in his heart.[29]

Reason is indeed important, Edwards argued in the same text. It is reasonable to suppose that a God who exists would want to communicate himself to his creation through grace, knowledge, and wisdom.[30] However, sensory perception and participatory perception trump reason when it comes to the knowledge of beauty. We should see how novel, how innovative, this makes Edwards. The Reformed tradition emphasizes the mind and the beauty of our God-given intellect. Edwards loved the mind but said there was something greater: sensory perception. It is the latter that enables us to know beauty.

True to his Puritan moorings, Edwards brought around full circle his reflections on God's beauty and light to a holy life lived for God,

> This light, and this only, has its fruit in a universal holiness of life. No merely notional or speculative understanding of the doctrines of religion will ever bring to this. But this light, as it reaches the bottom of the heart, and changes the nature, so it will effectually dispose to a universal obedience.[31]

God's beautiful light is variously experienced in the word of God, in one's heart, and in one's reason. By God-given reason and particularly via the Bible[32] people can know something about God's existence and can understand (Christian) matters of religion.[33] But there is a deeper knowledge, a vivified knowledge—one we today might describe as existential—available concerning God. It is a knowledge pertaining to the senses; and so Edwards called it a sensible knowledge. It is a transforming knowledge. I think it fair to summarize Edwards hereon and call it an experiential and visceral kind of knowledge. It is a living knowledge precisely because it is vivified in

---

29. Edwards, "Sermon and Discourses 1730–1733," 413, *WJE*.

30. Edwards was confident that human minds can understand God's creation. Cf. Louie, *Jonathan Edwards*, 73–74, 105.

31. Edwards, "Sermons, Series II, 1733," 295, *WJE*.

32. McDermott notes that while Edwards repeatedly professed allegiance to *sola Scriptura* he nevertheless operated with a tacit recognition "that the Bible can be read only through and with tradition." Church tradition was more significant than Edwards usually admitted. McDermott, "The Emerging Divide in Evangelical Theology," 376.

33. Edwards often used the word *religion*. Unlike contemporary Evangelicals he did not juxtapose religion against relationship. Rather, religion involves the true practice and lifestyle of faith in Christ.

relationship with God. Truly, both Edwards's perceptions of, and reflections on, God are themselves beautiful.

In all of this formulation Edwards was being quite philosophical, though clearly in ways that did not violate accepted Reformed tradition or Scripture. McClymond and McDermott note Edwards's philosophic-Platonic indebtedness hereon: the spiritual alone is capable of primary beauty; secondary beauty "mirrors and shadows the beauty of primary beauty"; beings with mind and volition are superior to non-sentient creation. Edwards was unique for maintaining a rather patristic view of reality and beauty in a post-Reformation era.[34]

THE HOLY SPIRIT AND BEAUTY

Harkening to his Reformed tradition, Edwards believed that the Spirit was the bond of love between the Father and the Son.[35] By extension of that bonding action, the Spirit is also he who unites believers to God. Edwards was emphatic that God is a communicating being. Prefiguring future Pentecostal and Charismatic spiritual and theological constructions, Edwards made the then-remarkable step of arguing that God's communication is not merely about information, but of himself. When God shares his Spirit with us he is sharing himself with us. This communication is one of consent: the Spirit is the consent between the Father and the Son.[36] "The Holy Spirit is the act of God between the Father and the Son infinitely loving and delighting in each other. Sure I am, that if the Father and the Son do infinitely delight in each other, there must be an infinitely pure and perfect act between them, an infinitely sweet energy which we call delight."[37] Thus, those in Christ experience God himself, the Holy Spirit. God does not merely infuse us with grace. God pours his Spirit into believers:

---

34. McClymond and McDermott, *The Theology of Johnathan Edwards*, 94.

35. That compared to a more resolutely communal model whereby the Spirit is himself his unique self, and not merely a bonding (whether personal or somewhat impersonal) agent between Father and Son. The technicalities hereon are so complex that they cannot be visited here.

36. McClymond and McDermott, *The Theology of Johnathan Edwards*, 198, argue that Edwards did not narrowly ground his Trinitarian doctrine in the divine essence, following the older pattern of Augustine. Rather, Edwards affirmed a more social model of plurality. The Spirit was the bonding agent in that more social model.

37. Edwards, "1722, The Miscellanies," 260, *WJE*.

> The Spirit of God is given to the true saints to dwell in them, as his lasting abode; and to influence their hearts, as a principle of new nature, or as a divine supernatural spring of life and action. The Scriptures represent the Holy Spirit, not only as moving, and occasionally influencing the saints, but as dwelling in them.... he becomes there a principle or spring of new nature and life.[38]

Mitchell interprets Edwards such that "union with Christ admits one into the very society of the Trinity."[39] Again, this is a real and authentic experience of God, and not merely a legal appropriation of Christ's saving work. Working within his Reformed tradition, Edwards's development here is fascinating and highly personalized: the believer experiences *God himself*, via the presence of the Holy Spirit.

Edwards does not argue that believers experience God's essence; Edwards avoids confusing the creator with the creator, even if he does not clarify the boundaries or mechanisms for this intimate indwelling (i.e., if we are experiencing God himself are we not experiencing God's essence?). And still, believers receive God himself, the Holy Spirit, as a gift given through Christ's person and work. Saints experience "excellency and joy by a kind of participation of God." And, "God puts his own beauty, i.e., his beautiful likeness upon their souls.... The saints are beautiful and blessed by a communication of God's holiness and joy ... by the gift of the Holy Ghost, and his dwelling in them."[40] Christians' hearts and souls experience the indwelling of the beautiful one, God's Holy Spirit.

Edwards's theology on the vivifying effects of God's Spirit is beautiful. Christ didn't only atone for our sins, achieve forgiveness for us, or secure our eternal life, truly glorious as are those all. There is more. Astoundingly, we are given the gift of God's Spirit. Indeed, Edwards averred that saving grace "is no other than the Spirit of God itself dwelling and acting in the heart of a saint."[41] Steven Studebaker notes that for Edwards "the gift of salvation (the Spirit) is equal to the value of its cost (the suffering of Christ). In both circumstances a divine person is the currency of redemption."[42] God's gracious act of salvation is beautiful and his giving of his beautiful Spirit to

---

38. Edwards, "Religious Affections," 200, *WJE*.

39. Mitchell, *On the Experience of Beauty*, 40. Eastern Orthodox theologians argue the same.

40. Ibid., 28, quoting Edwards in "God Glorified," *WJE*, 5.

41. Edwards, "Writings on the Trinity, Grace, and Faith," 46, *WJE*.

42. Studebaker, *A Pentecostal Trinitarian Theology*, 159.

indwell the believer is beautiful further still. The Apostle John commented on the "grace upon grace" (John 1:16) that extends from Christ Jesus, but Edwards has a model wherein there is *beauty upon beauty that extends from God's Holy Spirit.*

The Holy Spirit's presence as gift opens believers up to a fuller, richer, more intuitively enhanced way of being Christian. When God's Spirit takes up his abode in a person that person's heart is ignited. "The sense of the heart," as Edwards so commonly put it, results from God's indwelling Spirit. This is not the actualization of some latent human attribute or quality, as pop psychologists might espouse it today, it is a brand new disposition appearing within the self. The unregenerate do not enjoy this sensibility. Rather, there is a new aesthetic and spiritual sensibility, a new way for the mind to perceive reality. This sensibility is "an active tendency of the entire self that determines the direction of all the functions of the human self," said Sang Lee.[43] Whether or not twenty-first-century contemporaries would agree with Edwards on these fruits and manifestations of the indwelling Spirit as being so certain (or narrow), Edwards was resolute on the facticity of this theological framing. We see him processing that reality when he quoted Job 38:7, "the morning stars sang together, and all the sons of God shouted for joy," and when observing creation's beauty he journaled, "it was always my manner, at such times, to sing forth my contemplations."[44] Edwards knew resolutely that God both lived in his heart and changed his experience of life. Life in Christ is not only intellectually meaningful, it is experientially beautiful.

Further remarkable, Edwards held that *the Holy Spirit is very the beauty of God*.[45] For some this may seem outlandish, but we recall Edwards's definition of beauty as that which involves consent. Beauty is less an abstraction than it is persons in consensual relationship. The Trinity is a society of being in relation to being. Through loving acts God subsequently extends that relationship to creation and especially to the saints through the Holy Spirit. Developing this Edwards wrote,

> It was more especially the Holy Spirit's work to bring the world to its beauty and perfection out of the chaos, for the beauty of the

---

43. Lee, *The Philosophical Theology*, 150.

44. Marsden, *Jonathan Edwards*, 78.

45. Again, this is historically novel. Aquinas, who developed "the most sophisticated philosophical aesthetics in the West until the rise of modern aesthetics," posited that the Son is the archetype of beauty. Louie, *Jonathan Edwards*, 26.

world is a communication of God's beauty. The Holy Spirit is the harmony and excellency and beauty of the Deity; therefore, 'twas his work to communicate beauty and harmony to the world, and so we read that it was he that moved upon the face of the waters.[46]

Edwards believed that this beautiful indwelling elicited within believers a new awareness of God's beauty, Christ's beauty, the beauty of divine things, and the beauty present in nature. In short, the Spirit of God produces *a new and heightened aesthetic sensibility.* This sensory work, to Edwards's understanding, was not a by-product of new life in Christ, it was the first effect in regeneration. This sensory work causes believers' hearts to "have a relish of the loveliness and sweetness of the supreme excellency of the Divine nature."[47] In all of this we see that in Edwards's theology *God's beauty beautifies.* Or still more precisely, God's Spirit beautifies because he is the beauty of the Godhead. Patrick Sherry summed up Edwards thus, "Edwards derives the Holy Spirit's mission as beautifier from his role within the Trinity . . . being the harmony and beauty of the Godhead, [the Spirit] has the particular function of communicating beauty and harmony in the world."[48] Edwards is so novel here, on the Spirit as the beautifier, that neither twenty-first–century Pentecostals nor Charismatics have developed the implications for their own pneumatological constructions. Edwards was a man far ahead of his times!

God, the beautiful being who freely shares being, pours his Spirit into the saints who are then both beautified and more attuned to the beautiful. Saints, with their hearts tuned by God's Spirit, are capable both of perceiving more creational beauty and more of God's beauty at work in life than can the unregenerate. And, those beauties, as they appear in nature, are emanations of God's own glory and beauty.[49]

Another way to see the verve of God's Spirit within Edwards's theological framing concerned imagination. It takes some imagination—imagination filtered by a heart lit afire by God's Spirit—to see God within and

---

46. Edwards, "1722, The Miscellanies," 384, *WJE*.

47. Edwards, "1743, Documents on the Trinity, Grace, and Faith," 20, *WJE*.

48. Sherry, *Spirit and Beauty*, 93.

49. "The word 'emanations' . . . clearly means 'communications.'" Edwards, "Ethical Writings," 96, *WJE*. In his body of writings Edwards used emanation(s) 102 times; yet, it is not entirely clear whether Edwards was using that in an established Neoplatonist sense, or whether that term is a kind of holdover category that, by the eighteenth century, permeated theological discourse. The parallels with and echoes of Pseudo-Dionysius are nevertheless astounding.

behind the beauty of creation. Things are not always as they initially seem. An imagination inflamed by God's Spirit pauses to look for more, to see how and whether God's grace might be present.[50] Frequently, art students aver, when we know something about the artist herself the art itself has a more abiding meaning. Edwards was aware of that same dynamic, if he didn't put it in exact words, when he said that

> the source of prejudices was that people get so used to perceiving things in common ways that they "make what they can actually perceive by their senses, or by immediate and outside reflection into their own souls, the standard of possibility or impossibility; so that there must be no body, forsooth, bigger than they can conceive of, or less than they can see with their eyes; nor motion either much swifter or slower than they can imagine."[51]

This willingness to consider that there is possibly is more at play than surface level made Edwards committed to a life of honest learning. He knew that age can petrify a person's vantage point. A constant of human nature is that we become committed to our way of being and tenaciously cling to that, something characterized as "the curse of knowledge." Contrastingly, Edwards, his imagination made vivid, said, "Resolved, if ever I live to years, that I will be impartial to hear the reasons of all pretended discoveries, and receive them if rational, how long so ever I have been used to another way of thinking."[52] In all of this we can see that there can be epistemological ramifications for new life in the Spirit. God's Spirit not only opens us to beauty's existence in ways we never experienced before, it produces internal sensibilities that can make us open to learning across our lives' duration. Edwards had still more to say on the effects of God's Spirit living inside our hearts.

50. Edwards's own imagination having been lit by God's Spirit is particularly intriguing given that he, a man of his own era, believed that human imagination consistently moved to the vain and fallen; Puritans did not appreciate novelty or experimentation. To cite an earlier quotation, "The universe is created out of nothing every moment and if it were not for our imaginations, which hinder us, we might see that wonderful work performed continually." Marsden, *Jonathan Edwards*, 74. Christians of his day had not yet begun to explore how our imaginations mirror God's own.

51. Edwards, "Of the Prejudices of Imagination," 196–97, quoted in Marsden, *Jonathan Edwards*, 80. This also evinces Edwards's Enlightenment commitments to learning truth, in whatever form.

52. Edwards, "Letters and Personal Writings," September 23, 1716, 781, *WJE*. On a similar line, Meister Eckhart believed that whereas time makes us old, eternity keeps us young. O'Donohue, *Beauty*, 20.

For Him Who Has Eyes to See
HOLY SPIRIT-UAL AFFECTIONS

Living in the twenty-first century we are bombarded with competing truth claims about human nature and reality. For instance, some say we are essentially one with the universe and we only need to realize that to find bliss. Others claim the goal of life is to become self-actualized, whatever that means. Sociocultural studies show that Christians are as affected by their surroundings as other groupings. Therapeutic, self-help, find-your-happy-place configurations sometimes preempt gospel presentations in all manner of Christian churches. However we think about Edwards's theological formulations on God's Holy Spirit, we err to imagine he was espousing unique versions of pantheism or mysticism. The man was a Puritan. True, he was establishing ways of appreciating, celebrating, and processing beauty, but he was not thereby abandoning his Reformed tradition to become an eighteenth-century Romantic.[53] Put differently, while Edwards was quite comfortable thinking through and writing in philosophical terminology, he did so in ways that maintained biblical categories. He knew that all things must be tested with Scripture. He was a pastor who constantly fed his church with biblical teaching.

Before we survey him on beautiful affections, it is also worth noting Edwards in light of past formulations. Greek Stoics, classical Neoplatonists, Jewish and then Christian Neoplatonists, Christian desert monastics, and Eastern Orthodox mystics all believed that we need to tame our passions in order to experience true virtue, peace, and wholeness (however understood). Hence, there is a long line of philosophers and Christians who argued that the chief problem confronting humanity is that we are beset by passions: the wounds to and in our souls. Each of those groups proposed, in varied manner, ascetic prescriptions to tame and/or root out the passions. Even the abiding classical philosophical belief that reason ought to trump emotion is itself part of this approach to human nature. Edwards thus stands in a long line of philosophers and theologians who seek some seminal transformation of the human self, yet Edwards did so in ways that were again quite innovative.

Ringing true to his Reformed moorings, Edwards believed that true beauty is rooted in the holy God alone. There was no notion of self-help therapy with our influential Puritan theologian. Jesus Christ is God's only Son and Savior; he alone brings forgiveness, justification, restored

---

53. Davidson, "Narcission."

relationship with God, new life, the Holy Spirit, and hope. That may all be fairly obvious, but we do well to be careful. More, Edwards did not stop with a forensic—having to do with the divine courtroom—understanding of salvation. God forgives, but he also wants to transform our hearts. This affective (pertaining to our emotions, feelings, choosing and willing) orientation finds unique expression in Edwards. All people have dispositions, precritical attitudes that shape our decision-making. Aristotle famously argued that we are chiefly what we love. And we love even before we think. Truly, our loving trumps and guides our thinking. (When Jesus said "where your treasure is, there your heart will be also" [Matt 6:21], was he echoing Aristotle?) Having received and accepted Aristotle through Augustine's formulations, Edwards believed *not that people have dispositions so much as dispositions have people*. These dispositions, these affections, or still better the bent of our heart, reveal who we really are. Summarizing Edwards hereon McClymond and McDermott wrote, "It is disposition that renders a person either pleasing or displeasing to God. God chiefly looks not to outward actions but to inward dispositions."[54]

More particularly, Edwards believed that our affections could genuinely experience beauty. Touched by God's Spirit, touched therefore by God's beauty, believers can experience the *suavitas*—smoothness, affability, pleasantness—of God. Aware of Enlightenment philosophers' writings on human knowledge, Edwards knew that we do not only know things by reason, we also know things by signs. Signs are pictures of ideas in the mind. We also, however, know things by apprehension of our senses, or what Edwards called sensible knowledge. Also called *heart knowledge*, sensible knowledge included "all agreeableness and disagreeableness, all beauty and deforming, all pleasure and pain, and all those sensations, exercises, and passions of the mind that arise from either of those [various dualisms]."[55] (Edwards did *not* posit head versus heart in his schema; they were just different ways the one self knows.) This experiential knowledge was especially important for Edwards as he assessed genuine from false religious experience. Edwards used an analogy about honey to make his point. Someone can learn that honey is sweet by reading about it in a book or hearing so from someone. It is another kind of knowledge to sample honey's sweetness

---

54. McClymond and McDermott, *The Theology of Jonathan Edwards*, 5.
55. Edwards, *Miscellany* #782, in Mitchell, *On the Experience of Beauty*, 22.

on one's tongue. The latter is experiential knowledge. Tasting actually imparts the sweetness to the knower.[56]

Just as there is sensible knowledge of natural things (i.e., honey's flavor) so there is sensible knowledge of supernatural things. Using grace, the Holy Spirit awakens unbelieving people to the reality of religious matters. At first an unbeliever only experiences conviction of sin or the reality of God's existence upon hearing God's word preached. After salvation, however, into Christian believers, those whom Edwards regularly called saints, God's Spirit infuses a deeper spiritual work, one that results in the believer experiencing God's *suavitas*. The saints have "a sense of the divine spiritual excellency of the things of religion."[57] The saints can sense God's beauty in creation, in other saints, and in the words and work of God. In this there is an interplay between natural sensible knowledge and supernatural (a.k.a. spiritual) knowledge; God's Spirit infuses grace and touches the Christian with the result that a sensible, experiential consequence follows. These experiences, Edwards taught, could be intense and "complexly beautiful."[58] Further still, these experiences can shape and transform the saints's own affections. Touched by the beauty of God, our hearts can be increasingly transformed and made beautiful.

Edwards preached and wrote about the profound nature of such affective experiences. He believed said experiences involve the whole person with the result that the person is transformed. True religion, something Edwards earnestly wanted his parishioners to experience and embrace, changes a person's affections. People can attest to feeling God's grace and Spirit, but if their lives are not moving toward holiness, toward excellency of heart, then it is likely their experience is not authentic. Putting his theologizing into practice, Edwards went on to develop twelve negative and twelve positive signs for discerning religious experience. By these we can see, again, that Edwards did not believe beauty was only "out there" in nature, but also an attribute within the Christian believer. We will summarize these to denote the attention to detail that Edwards gave this matter.

Negative (Ambiguous) Signs That Do Not Guarantee Authenticity

1) Intensity of religious experience, including extraordinary events

2) Bodily effects

---

56. Edwards, "Divine and Supernatural Light," 14, *WJE*, in ibid., 22–23.
57. Edwards, *Miscellany* #782, in ibid., 26.
58. Ibid.

Jonathan Edwards (1703–1758)

3) Talking about one's experience

4) People exciting themselves (i.e., "enthusiasm")

5) The ability to quote Scripture (the devil can do that)

6) An appearance of love

7) Having only one religious affection (versus several together)

8) The resulting comfort and joy (a.k.a. a precise pattern of emotional responses)

9) Spending inordinate time in religious matters and worship

10) Being predisposed to praise and glorify God

11) Exceeding assurance about one's experience

12) Supposed spiritual discernment of other people

Positive Signs of Affections Touched by Grace

1) The work is supernatural, not natural; i.e., there is a new internal dynamic, a new spiritual perception, a new disposition wrought by the Holy Spirit

2) A love of God for God and not for benefit of the human person

3) A love of morality and its own sweetness, beauty, and holiness

4) Spiritual knowledge: the mind understands spiritual things and recognizes God's beauty in life

5) Conviction and assurance of the reality of divine things

6) Evangelical humiliation regarding sin

7) Transformation of the soul

8) Mirroring the spirit and temperament of Jesus Christ (a.k.a. the fruit of the Spirit)

9) Tenderness of heart and spirit (a.k.a. not violent, combative, or critical)

10) Symmetry and proportion of Christian affections and characteristics

11) Increased intensity for Christian affections and character

12) Christian practice (a.k.a. faith produces work)[59]

---

59. Following Mitchell's overview, ibid., 59–74.

His above positive signs, rooted in and driven by the Holy Spirit (#1), all have beauty in their midst. Especially given that there is a new means of perception (#1), and given that the Spirit is himself God's beauty, we can see that Edwards's discerning sieve was itself permeated by the category of beauty. At the expense of being redundant, that he framed the Christian life around beauty, and understood the Christian life to be the means of beautiful life was radical for his day. Indeed, it presents a challenge for us today. The sources of Edwards's theo-aesthetic formulations are unclear.[60] He wrote in ways that resounded with older medieval and patristic models, themselves having sprung from philosophic sources of antiquity. And yet, we see at work in Edwards's articulations concerning beauty newer, more psychological and relational veins. For example, with him hierarchies still exist but they are less about spirit and matter, invisible and visible, and more about the relational and ethical realms in life. Dyrness summed Edwards's theology thusly:

> Perhaps Edwards's most important contribution to theology was the replacement of a traditional substance metaphysics with a more relational and dynamic conception of reality. This enabled Edwards to portray the Puritan understanding of typology in a radically new way. Reality for Edwards is a network of dispositional powers, or as Edwards like to say, "habits." He defined habits as patterns according to which existences are caused by God.[61]

---

60. *Why* he emphasized beauty is less clear. Kristeller reveals that initial taxonomies about the fine arts began in France in earnest in the mid-eighteenth century. So perhaps Edwards was aware of those developments. Kristeller, "The Modern System of the Arts," 96. Dyrness believes that Edwards was working from his Reformed tradition: "his views contain a highly original formulation that carries forward the best insights of Calvin and the tradition he represents." Dyrness, *Reformed Theology*, 284. Louie, *Jonathan Edwards*, 17–18, 47–62, clarifies that recent scholars have argued, pro and con, about the influence on Edwards of Francis Hutcheson (1694–1746), a Scottish-Irish Presbyterian who wrote about beauty and aesthetics. Although Edwards was aware of recent published innovations on aesthetics he was writing about aesthetics before he read others; he was also being novel more than he was relying on other writers. Edwards wanted to relate religious affections to beauty, and visa versa, more than develop a precise aesthetic philosophy. Louie, *Jonathan Edwards*, 31, 187.

61. Dyrness, *Reformed Theology*, 276.

Jonathan Edwards (1703–1758)

WRAP-UP

To conclude this chapter, we note that Edwards's theo-aesthetic reflections had no effect upon Puritan architecture, liturgical aesthetics, or craftsmanship. The Puritans continued to have very plain churches with plain worship services focusing on preaching the Bible. There was, on Edwards's theo-aesthetic lead, no great shift in how Puritans shaped culture for their day and age.[62] In history, Edwards's theology was only rediscovered, led by Perry Miller, in the twentieth century. Nevertheless, Edwards represents how one can be faithful to ancient biblical constructs in ways that are culturally relevant, sensitive to the particulars of beauty's varied appearance, and appreciative of God's presence in and through his creation.

WHAT EDWARDS TEACHES US TO SEE:

- Protestants can learn from philosophy
- God is both beautiful and beauty itself
- creation, though less so than spiritual realities, is beautiful
- creation shines with God's beauty
- in every moment God sustains creation
- beauty involves freedom
- God's beauty beautifies
- beauty can truly be experienced with our heart and senses
- believers experience God's Spirit
- God's Spirit is the very beauty of God
- God's Spirit heightens the believer's aesthetic sensibilities
- God's Spirit enflames our imaginations
- our dispositions reveal our true identity
- beauty is a fruit of the Spirit

---

62. Dyrness, *Reformed Theology*, 58–59.

9

Immanuel Kant (1724–1804)
The Beauty of the Human Person's Ability to Perceive Beauty

"Whatever floats your boat." "One man's trash is another man's treasure." "To each his own." "Whatever's right is right." "There's no accounting for taste." "Beauty is in the eye of the beholder." Whoopie Goldberg pushed even further: "Art *and* life are subjective. Not everybody's gonna dig what I dig, but I reserve the right to dig it."[1] Regarding popular attitudes about art and aesthetics such sayings are now commonplace. Previously we've noted this dynamic, but it bears repeating: in substantial ways we are the products of the past. Over centuries we learned to believe that taste is relevant to the subject, the viewer. Honestly, the belief that aesthetic taste is merely subjective is so steeped in the Western psyche that my college students are surprised to learn it was not always that way. Specifically, in both antiquity and the medieval era philosophers and theologians believed that beauty was objective and universal. For most today such a position would seem bizarre. So, what brought about this seismic shift? Among other causes, the philosophy of Immanuel Kant.

We ought be judicious. As we will see, Kant himself did not believe that beauty is merely subjective. And there were other philosophers writing during the Enlightenment who pushed the "taste is a matter of private opinion" position harder. But Kant is significant hereon because he

---

1. "Quotes about taste." My italics.

Immanuel Kant (1724–1804)

was writing only decades after aesthetic study had been promoted in the university setting by Alexander Gottlieb Baumgarten (1714–1762).[2] In response Kant asked and answered questions in order to drive aesthetics into newer and more sophisticated territory. Baumgarten took the classical definition, "beauty is that which, when seen, gives pleasure," and instilled it with a narrower meaning: beauty is that which, when experienced *by the senses*, gives pleasure. Disagreeing, Kant wrote to correct Baumgarten and suggest a more sure and dynamic foundation for aesthetic appreciation.

Kant was ambivalent about artwork. He loved poetry but did not think painting or music were very interesting. When once he heard inmates in a nearby prison singing hymns he wrote the police chief a complaint letter. Other than a portrait of Rousseau given to him by a friend, he owned no artwork.[3] Knowing that about him, it is peculiar that Kant took up the category of aesthetics. More motivated by a commitment to logic and duty than inspired by the emotional effects of beauty, Kant nevertheless helped to turn aesthetics in new directions by *thinking about thinking about* the aesthetic experience. Alternately put, rather than ask "what is beauty?" as had been the preoccupation of antiquity and the medieval era, Kant asked both "precisely how do we perceive beauty?" and "what transpires in the human mind when beauty is perceived?" He was interested in how and on what basis human beings made judgments across life's differing vistas: goodness, agreeableness, and aesthetics. Kant's concern was not how beauty was "out there," but how beauty is processed "in here" by the human person. Kant thus addressed and resolved (so he believed) philosophical rather than theological questions. He did not rhapsodize on how beauty participates in or shines forth God; indeed, even though he had been raised by German Pietists (Christianity was the arena *within* which, if not the world view *against* which, Western philosophers have worked for two millennia) Kant was discreet if not agnostic concerning God's existence.[4] Why

---

2. Baumgarten, who invented the term *aesthetics*, was motivated to develop his aesthetic theories by the burgeoning of art across Europe. Amid a rising tide of artistic flourishing, he asked and tried to answer the questions, "really, what is beautiful?" And, "just what constituted excellent art?" Cf. "18th Century German Aesthetics." Kant had thoroughly read Baumgarten's writings.

3. Scruton, *Kant*, 5.

4. Exhibiting a rather paradoxical tension, Kant believed God existed but that we cannot know anything about him. There is no special revelation from God to humanity, there is no absolute proof or evidence left behind by God, and there are no arguments that unassailably demonstrate God's existence. And yet, Kant knew he could not ground his arguments in mere opinion, naked reason, or experience. Therefore, he espoused

then is a philosopher being surveyed in a study on theological aesthetics? Because the way hundreds of millions of Christians perceive beauty today was profoundly shaped both by Kant and those who for two centuries now have unpacked Kant's implications. Even today Kant is known as the one of the, if not *the*, greatest Enlightenment philosophers.

The fourth of nine children, Immanuel Kant was born into German-speaking Königsberg (today's Kaliningrad, western Russia), a Baltic seaport city of some 50,000 people in the then-Prussian Empire. Under the reign of Prince Frederick the Great, Königsberg began to embrace the high culture of Europe, and so the university became a hub of philosophical study. Educated first as a young boy at a Pietist school, at age twenty-two Kant graduated from the university after six years of study. Because he was unable to secure a teaching position at the university he spent the next twenty-five years tutoring private students, writing, and publishing his own minor works on mathematics, physics, and metaphysics. Finally, in 1770 he was given a professor's chair of metaphysics and logic at Königsberg.

Regarding aesthetic judgments, the two pre-existing substantial schools of thought Kant sought to correct and even reconcile were empiricism and rationalism.[5] Exemplified by Baumgarten in Germany and David Hume (1711–1776) in Scotland, empiricism maintained that human beings are what we are owing to our experience of reality. Our senses perceive evidence in the world around us and that sensory information is the grounding point,[6] the processing basis, for how we construct our reality. Again, for the empiricists beauty is perceived and processed primarily by the five senses, not cognition, though cognition is involved. On the other hand,

---

arguments (e.g. God is the basis for morality, the soul is immortal) for the transcendent that gave his philosophical perspective a surer and more abiding footing. *He believed in God because he concluded by reason that he must.* God alone guarantees the upright bases of our moral configurations; God alone unswervingly exists as the *telos*, the destiny, for human community. A merely finite foundation would snap under the pressure of the demands of reason; only the eternal and transcendent can undergird the human need. Older academic tradition portrayed Kant as a "metaphysical destroyer": there is nothing real beyond the bounds of reason. More recent studies assert that Kant was trying to protect religion from unduly sophisticated and skeptical philosophers. See Palmquist, "Kant's Religious Argument."

5. We will not and cannot exhaustively portray these schools or Kant's interaction with them, or even Kant's own broader sophisticated philosophical perspectives. Our focus will remain upon aesthetics.

6. Traditionally, philosophers want either to understand what the grounds—bases, beliefs, foundations, provable assertions, reason, imagination, emotions, narratives, chance, God—are for our processing reality and/or to suggest what those are.

rationalism, exemplified for Kant by the Germans Gottfried Wilhelm Liebnitz (1646–1716) and his student Christian Wolf (1679–1754), maintained that human understanding exists prior, *a priori*[7] in technical philosophy, to sensory experience. The human mind has innate principles, categories, concepts, and constructs that exist, that are in operation, even before the person begins to sensorially process reality. Put differently, there is an "I" that both exists and can reason even before sensory experience becomes operant. (Even today these two schools of thought are studied and debated for their merits and pitfalls.) Again, Kant believed both of those schools were erroneous. He took what he believed to be true from each school, modified some of their tenets, and synthesized them.[8]

KANT'S AESTHETIC

As Kant put it there are four aspects of the aesthetic experience: disinterestedness, universality, purposiveness, and necessity. We will survey each not only to understand how Kant construed and understood the aesthetic experience (an exercise of its own worth), but also to glimpse the possibilities of explaining the human experience of beauty. To clarify, we are not considering Kant in order to present his understanding as normative but to see how profound, how intertwined, and how multifaceted the experience of beauty truly is. Kant was right at least on this much: beauty is a mysterious dynamic, and if we are to make intellectual sense of it, if we are to ask ourselves what occurs in the perceptual moment of beauty, much careful unpacking is required. Whereas the classical position, again, was, "beauty is that which, when seen, gives pleasure," Kant believed beauty is "in here," in

---

7. *A priori*: a principle or knowledge that is self-evident prior to experience or observation.

8. Forgive my seeming paternalistic, but Kant was *not* merely taking the best of each position and combining them. So many Millennials, those born since 1980, postmodernists or PoMos as I denote them, motivated by fairness, think it good practice to combine the better halves of positions or beliefs; and they will do so even if those halves are mutually contradictory. Instead, Kant reflected philosophically as an employed professor for eleven years before he began to write his philosophical triumverate: *Critique of Pure Reason* (1781, 1787), *Critique of Practical Reason* (1788), and *Critique of Judgment* (1790). With extreme precision (though many argue thereabout; Kant is often obscure and scholars debate whether that is because he was just clumsily obscure or because he was attempting to express incredibly complex and integrated ideas) he was delineating the process of perception as it applied to aesthetic experience. His method was no mere glomming together of competing philosophical perspectives.

the human person, and something we experience. Hence, we might expect that Kant was espousing mere subjectivity: taste is entirely personal and relevant to each one's likes and dislikes. However, he did not state such a baldly relativist position.

For Kant beauty was *not* something rooted in the object. Beauty did not adhere within the thing being viewed, heard, or sensed.[9] Instead, beauty was, for Kant, the feeling that we feel when we view an object. Thus, we connect our feelings of pleasure or delight to our perception of said object. We enjoy feeling our pleasurable feelings. We particularly enjoy sensory-feeling when we believe we are experiencing beauty. We are only this far in and we can already see that Kant upped the ante when it comes to the classical definition of beauty: his emphasis is not just on our experience but on our feeling the experience. For Kant this feeling is a sensory one.

Kant also believed that aesthetic judgments must be entirely devoid of conceptual formation. He called this state of mind, or state of being, *disinterestedness*. It is easy to see the term *disinterestedness* and think Kant meant indifference or ambivalence, but he did not imply that (frankly, how could we make a determination if we did not care to do so?). Before Kant's time the classical philosophical-theological tradition taught the need for *apatheia*: calming one's emotions or being devoid of passion altogether in order to make wiser judgments, or being untouched by desires and movements of the soul that bring affliction (e.g., covetousness, greed, lust, jealousy, anger). But again, Kant was not processing thus. To put it in more contemporary terms, Kant was being far more cognitive than soulish or existential. By disinterestedness Kant meant devoid of concepts. Disinterest in German (*uninteressiertheit*) meant without "any kind of desire, aim, or purpose, or any social, moral, or intellectual considerations."[10] Judgment of beauty is aesthetic (sensory), not cognitive and not immediately logical.

Kant wanted us to have disinterestedness so that our aesthetic perception and judging can be pure. In making aesthetic judgment, that is when determining whether something is beautiful or not, we may not approach the object with prior conceptual commitments filtering our assessment. So, for instance, if we were observing a horse, to use an example Kant did, we could not truly say we perceived beauty if we viewed the horse while being

---

9. Throughout this chapter I will use the dynamic of vision to describe the aesthetic process. To include the other senses would make for consistently clunky and convoluted grammar so I will stick with vision.

10. Wenzel, *Kant's Aesthetics*, 19.

Immanuel Kant (1724–1804)

already committed to the concepts/categories that a horse is only beautiful if its hair is auburn, or if it has a long flowing mane, or if it has lustrous eyes. If we did employ concepts and categories in that way we would be making judgments of agreeableness, not beauty; we might *like* the categories of auburn, flowing manes, or lustrous eyes, but those in themselves do not necessitate beauty. Agreeableness, a quality or attribute that we enjoy or like, does not necessitate beauty. Again, aesthetic judgment must be a-conceptual in Kantian philosophy. And it was not even that, by insisting that we excise or empty our conceptual framework, Kant wanted us to have a full-throttled "a ha!" emotional-sensory moment when we perceive the beautiful; art aficionados, perhaps unwittingly borrowing from Kant's thoughts hereon, today enjoy being surprised by beauty and so seek to be neutral as they move toward a piece of art or a vista in nature. No, Kant simply believed that to employ concepts, categories, and pre-existing definitions was to *de facto* rule out the possibility of making a judgment about beauty.

Also concerning disinterestedness, Kant argued that *beauty cannot be defined*. Each instance of beauty is unique, Kant believed. If we were to say that all steepled churches were beautiful we would be basing our aesthetic judgment on previously existing concepts of steeples and churches, and their mutual relations, not on our disinterested perception. We could however appropriately say, "*this* steepled church is beautiful." Judging a specific church (or rose, or guitar, etc.) for beauty is possible because it does not involve our need for previously existing concepts. And, Kant reasoned, it is just not true that all described and defined anythings were always beautiful simply because they had previously established qualities.[11] Again for example, it is just not true that all red apples are beautiful, even if they are of our favorite variety, Red Delicious. Aesthetic judgment, Kant insisted, must be disinterested and therefore particular. Disinterestedness is also valuable because it makes possible a true judgment of beauty. For instance, Kant did not believe the conclusion that "painting is beautiful" could be accurate if the painting gave one pleasure; pleasure would be the operant category in lieu of a perception of beauty. Rather, one could with warrant say, "that

---

11. It makes sense that Kant believed it is easier for us to be disinterested with things in nature than man-made things. With the things of nature we do not usually "consider their functions or purposes. We do not construct and make flowers. What looks like a purpose or function in nature may just be a coincidence." By way of contrast, with the products of human craftsmanship, "we set the functions before we built the objects." Ibid., 70.

painting is pleasurable because I find it beautiful." To argue that a painting is beautiful because it gives us pleasure would be a judgment of agreeableness, not aesthetics.

Thus far, in establishing, or more precisely requiring, disinterestedness, Kant believed he was distancing himself from the empiricists. Empiricists like Baumgarten had argued that when an object has prescribed beautiful qualities the subject (viewer, perceiver) would sensorially experience that object as beautiful. For the empiricists the beautiful object would touch, or would be touched by, a person's senses such that one would conclude the object is indeed beautiful. Empiricists embraced the existence and accuracy of pre-existing categories that define, or contribute toward, beauty. Earlier in our study we saw that classical philosophy and theology, as those sought to define beauty, embraced believed-to-be-objective categories like radiance, clarity, proportion, integrity, and perfection.[12] Empiricists like Baumgarten believed that aesthetic judgment involved the interaction of those categories with the human senses such that beauty was deduced; moreover, Baumgarten had argued earlier that there are rules in place for determining beauty, rules so fixed and understood that aesthetics were a kind of science.[13] By insisting that each instance of beauty is particular and unique, and by insisting that there are no objective, true-for-everyone-everywhere categories for beauty, Kant was thus distancing himself from the empiricists. He even believed that judgments of taste cannot be proven by argument, which again would use previously existing mental concepts upon which or about which to argue.[14] Disinterestedness was the first aspect of Kant's aesthetic. Universality was his second.

Perhaps like me you have been involved in an argument about something's beauty. Los Angeles's Getty Museum houses Pierre-Auguste Renoir's *La Promenade*. Painted in 1870, *La Promenade* portrays a scruffy man escorting an elegant woman through foliage, perhaps a garden. Even though I initially did not appreciate impressionistic paintings, the first time I saw

---

12. Wenzel clarified, "According to Kant, beauty can never be reduced to the concept of perfection." Kant is hereby distancing himself from Baumgarten, Liebnitz, and Wolff, those who thought beauty was perfection, or that perfection was a possible ground for beauty. Perfection would necessitate rules for deducing and assessing perfection; but *there are no rules with beauty*; it is a subjective matter. Ibid., 65.

13. Ibid., 5.

14. Studies on Kant's aesthetics are numerous. Thus far these sources informed my own delineation: Wenzel, *Kant's Aesthetics*, 19–26; Kemal, *Kant's Aesthetic Theory*, 24–40; Grant, "Aesthetics and the Philosophy of Art"; and, Burnham, *Kant: Aesthetics*.

Immanuel Kant (1724–1804)

this Renoir piece I was enchanted by the beauty of the demure woman's blistering white dress as its light shot out at my eyes. The space surrounding her looks electric, it shimmers with movement perhaps due to a breeze blowing through the glade or perhaps Renoir was ingeniously portraying the movement of light across the surface of leaves and clothing. The motion of the painting's light (and just how can a static painting make light seem like it is moving?! What magic!) reminds me of what summer heat looks like as it radiates up and off asphalt. Over the years I have taken twelve classes of students to the Getty with me and I have had students look at that painting, pause, and then shrug, "meh." What was decidedly obvious to me, the painting's beauty, was not at all apparent to others. I have tried to convince students to see what I see, to look longer, to peer with a sense of wonder, and still they disagree and move on to view other paintings. Sometimes my students do not, but I always do, experience the clear sense of beauty when I view *La Promenade*. It is my expectation that everyone who ever has the privilege to see that painting will conclude similarly, "wow, what a marvel of beauty!" That totalizing perspective, Kant maintained, is called universality.

Concerning aesthetics, Kant believed everyone who ever makes an aesthetic judgment will conclude that the object is beautiful for everyone; it is a universal claim. Believing that the object is beautiful, we also believe that everyone ought to believe the same. Because we are disinterested in our judgment—again, Kant's four aesthetic aspects occur simultaneously, even though we have to carefully explain each one sequentially at the discursive level—there is no prior concept or category that is unique to our judgment. We are judging subjectively objectively. Devoid of conceptual bias, lacking prior formal framework, the person—the subject—is viewing the object objectively: we believe our perspective is true for everyone. Such judgments are by definition universal in their sweep. Judging without bias, judging in a state of disinterestedness, we believe we share the same perspective as everyone else, all of whom are similarly judging disinterestedly and universally. In short, we have asserted, Kant said, "a universal rule that one cannot produce."[15] Since nothing is the source of your judgment and nothing is the source of everyone else's judgment, we'll all arrive at the same disinterested and universal judgment: that the thing is truly beautiful.

---

15. Kant, *Critique of Pure Reason*, Section 18, 237, quoted in Wenzel, *Kant's Aesthetics*, 79.

Still, with that rather oxymoronic perspective established, we need be fair to Kant. He did not remotely believe that everyone will view every object equally, or that everyone would always agree that given objects were beautiful. He knew we are different persons with differing interpretations. And yet he was adamant that each person's aesthetic judgment *must be made with universality*. For example, if our mother said that a black BMW was beautiful she could not mean that it was only beautiful *to her*. She would either be lying to herself or to us, or she would be entirely misunderstanding what it meant to say a BMW, or an anything, was beautiful. If she said that that black BMW was beautiful *only to her* she would be making a judgment about agreeableness, not beauty. Beauty is something that holds for everyone, at least the way Kant believed he was framing it. Burnham summarized Kant hereon, "Although we may say '*beauty is in the eye of the beholder*,' that is not how we act. Instead, we debate and argue about our aesthetic judgments—and especially about works of art—and we tend to believe that such debates and arguments can actually achieve something."[16]

What occurs inside the person, what transpires at the subjective level, such that he or she could conclude that something is universally beautiful? Or, what is the internal mechanism for such a determination? Is it, like Nietzsche and Freud later espoused, an act of arbitrary will? Is the mechanism as simple as one person choosing? Indeed, Kant had thought that through, too. We do not all judge similarly about the beauty of a given object, but we all arrive at our conclusion by similar means. (Still again, we see that Kant is trying to chart a course between bald subjectivity and fixed objectivity. And again, he was not doing so to be "fair" to both sides but because he believed he was legitimately describing the process.) The human person has unique capacities. Concerning aesthetics, we are able to make judgments that involve our capacities to both reason and to exercise imagination. Beauty is not, as we have repeatedly seen, arrived at by force of reason; concepts and predetermined categories are eliminated or corralled. And yet, beauty is not gauged by random sensation; a museum curator does not (should not) call a statue beautiful simply because it strikes her sensations as pleasurable. Kant believed judgments of taste involve a harmonious exchange of both our understanding and our imagination.

Oxford philosopher James Grant says that understanding Kant hereon becomes arduous because Kant does not provide examples of what he meant. Scholars of Kant, however, believe that what Kant meant was that

---

16. Burnham, *Kant: Aesthetics*.

Immanuel Kant (1724–1804)

beauty is sensed "when your own pleasure comes from the harmonious free-play of your imagination and reason." Free play is where your intuitions are allowed to work within the bounds of reason.[17] Our minds are always working with understanding and sensation, cognition and feeling. These dualities mix, interact, overlap, and penetrate one another so that new combinations arise. All people have these dualities, but they do not all operate the same within every person. We all know people who live on one side of that duality more than the other; to wit, we tend to think of engineers as living in their cognition and actors as living in their imagination.

When we think critically we use our reason, our cognitive faculties, to take things apart to understand them. Consider a golf ball, for example. We know that its diameter is 1.68 inches and that its weight cannot exceed 1.62 ounces, as established by the rules of the United States Golf Association. If it is larger, smaller, lighter, or heavier than that it might be a facsimile of a golf ball, but no knowing golfer would ever call it a true golf ball. That is, there are established rules—concepts, categories—in place for determining what is and what is not a golf ball. The golf ball cannot be either everything or nothing, and it cannot even be only a round object. Imagination may have brought a golf ball into existence, but now there are fixed categories that determine a golf ball. (As we will see, Kant does not only think free play is at work in evaluating objects for beauty but also in the production of beautiful objects.)

Beauty, however, is neither established nor perceived by fixed rules. For Kant, still again, we approach aesthetic encounter with disinterestedness. That quality at hand, we are then free to encounter an object without bias. When I look at a rose with disinterestedness, Wenzel wrote, "in pure contemplation I am free from" prior considerations so that I am liberated from "such worries or pressures. I just enjoy looking at the rose and find it beautiful. I do not need to possess, understand, or bring into existence the object of my contemplation." He continued, "What matters is what I make of this representation in myself, not how I depend on the existence of the object."[18] It is a precognitive practice of forgetting oneself in order to freely contemplate the object. Kant did *not* mean practicing a kind of zen-like losing of the self. Rather, again, he meant that we leave behind conceptual

---

17. Grant, "Kant's Critique of Judgment, Lecture 2," referencing Guyer, *Kant*, [no page] on free-play.
18. Wenzel, *Kant's Aesthetics*, 19.

commitments so that our imagination freely encounters the given object. Let me try to exemplify what scholars think Kant was after.

In a class I teach entitled "Beauty and the Christian Life," I give my students two different exercises. Each exercise, one somewhere outside in nature and one someplace inside a church service, aims for the student to sit and "soak" in the experience. I ask them to not sit and make critical judgments about nature or the churchly surroundings—"the ocean is too placid," or, "there's an utter lack of artwork"—but to sit still and existentially soak in the surrounding environment, whatever that environment may be. Among other things I want,[19] now employing Kantian terms, them to experience the free play of their imaginations and their reasoning. In a written paper after they complete the exercise I ask them to evaluate, "What did it feel like? What sensations did it evoke inside you? What did it mean for you to just relax and enjoy the moment? Did being still make you more open to experiencing beauty?" Of course they do employ their reason, but I want them to do so with space for their imagination to roam. Their imaginations can be turned on, but not in ways so fantastical or ridiculous that they lose contact with reality.

On the one hand, our culture does not encourage us to be reflective and reasoned enough. Some folks often go through our daily lives, or even our churchly and devotional experiences, unaware of what is actually occurring to us and in us. On the other hand, especially for certain hyper-cognitive types, some people rarely turn off their critical brains and just enjoy the moment; they can be in a constant race to the next event such that they race through the present moment of grace. Pausing for the free play of understanding and imagination to occur is not an easy thing to do. Aware of this conundrum, Wenzel clarified, "Sometimes, in particular cases, it is difficult to draw the line between a free, pure, and disinterested satisfaction on the one hand, and a satisfaction into which some interest is mixed, on the other." Are you sure that liking a man or woman "does not depend upon imagining what you would gain from being at the side of this person?" The line can be difficult to draw.[20]

The harmonious and free play of our intuitions/imagination and reason/understanding results in judgments that are universal in scope. Indeed,

---

19. For example, pausing to observe and listen to their surroundings, pausing to allow God's Spirit to speak to them, stopping simply to rest, practicing the discipline of pausing, and finding beauty in the very act of not doing something.

20. Wenzel, *Kant's Aesthetics*, 20.

we are often not aware that we are even in a state of free play, we are often unaware that we are synthesizing varied intuitions, but this is something all people practice, believed Kant. "That *everyone* can do this follows from the criterion being an objectively necessary one," Wenzel clarified Kant's position, "that everyone can only apply it to *himself* follows from the subjective nature of our feelings." Once again we see the subjective-objective tension, this human-amid-established-reality dynamic, that Kant attempted to maintain in his theory of aesthetics; indeed he did this across the sweep of his philosophy. Let us move to the third aspect.

With keen insight Kant believed that beauty *appears* to us to have purpose but in truth lacks definite purpose; this is known as Kant's problem of purposiveness without purpose. Contrastingly, there would be true purpose in an instantiation of beauty if the beautiful thing were a matter of craftsmanship. Both the ancient Hebrews and ancient Greeks held understandings whereby the beautiful object could have utility and not just be something to behold. A ceramic carafe could be beautiful not only because of its wonderful symmetry and its coloration, tactile qualities pertaining to form and appearance, but also via the grace by which it poured liquids; in each of those ways the carafe could exhibit and express beauty. Kant, by distinction, believed beauty must appear to have purpose, but in fact be purposeless. Stated differently, Kant believed that the goal or *telos* (ultimate end) of beauty is pointless.

Let's try an analogy. In the cool early morning you may look at a hydrangea plant and be delighted by its beauty: the broad, velvety and soft-but-lush petals send out vibrations of light blue and violet, the petals are arranged in grapefruit-sized, snow cone-shaped clusters, and the morning dew rests gently atop thousands of the petals in order to magnify and bend the light as it moves across the plant's surface. You may look at that hydrangea and think, "what a visual feast! This hydrangea exists to make me, and all other onlookers, happy." (More in keeping with this book, a theist may look at the hydrangea and think, "God's creativity is boundless and his playfulness sweeps my imagination up toward his glory! What can be behind the universe but a genius designer?!" Such musing redounds with gratitude.) But in so doing you have, Kant believed, only projected your longing for purpose together with you aspirations and beliefs on to the hydrangea. In Kantian truth, the hydrangea's beauty has no purpose. It looks to be purposeful, but in truth is not. It may appear to have purpose, but that it so appears may just be a coincidence. It is also possible that we are erroneous in discerning a purpose.[21] The hydrangea petals' coloration even may attract certain insects for the sake of pollination, but neither the leaves nor the insects perceive the presence of beauty. Burnham put it carefully,

> A "definite purpose" would be either the set of external purposes (what the thing was meant to do or accomplish), or the internal purpose (what the thing was simply meant to be like). In the former case, the success of the process of making is judged according to utility; in the latter, according to perfection. Kant argues that beauty is equivalent neither to utility nor perfection, but is still purposive. Beauty in nature, then, will appear as purposive with respect to our faculty of judgment, but its beauty will have no ascertainable purpose—that is, it is not purposive with respect to determinate cognition. Indeed, this is why beauty is pleasurable since, Kant argues, pleasure is defined as a feeling that arises on the achievement of a purpose, or at least the recognition of a purposiveness.[22]

Beauty is therefore purposive with purpose. Beauty looks like it should have a reason, a cause, a goal, but in fact in the thing itself, in the reality of the thing as it exists, there is no purpose for its being beautiful. The transcendence of beauty that you perceive is due to your field of perception, the disinterested free play of your understanding and imagination processing the hydrangea's appearance, not the plant itself. Were the hydrangea plant's beauty to exist but not be perceived by a sensing-knowing being, there would be no beauty. Our self, our perceiving, our imaginatively processing the thing's there-ed-ness, and its form are all combined in the existence of beauty. This is complex. But that complexity makes the apprehension of beauty more, not less, beautiful!

Hence, Kant described his philosophy as *transcendental idealism*: there are qualities in the human self that exist *a priori* to our relations in and to life; these qualities allows us to go beyond ourselves and out into reality in order that we may perceive and understand reality. *We are not* transcendent (above, outside or beyond reality), but we are transcendental: we *are* capable of going beyond ourselves in a perception and knowledge of life that makes possible beauty.[23] Kant is far more renowned for extending this

21. Wenzel, *Kant's Aesthetics*, 70.

22. Burnham, *Kant: Aesthetics*, "The Third Moment," working from Kant's *Critique of Judgment*, "Introduction," section VI.

23. "Transcendental idealism: a term applied to the epistemology of the 18th-century German philosopher Immanuel Kant, who held that the human self, or transcendental

same line of argumentation and reasoning with regard to our moral framework. Nothing else in nature manifests a moral compass. Lacking entirely in regret and with zero resulting guilt a red-tailed hawk plunges her talons into the heart and spine of a western gray squirrel and then eats it, bits of entrails by bits of entrails. We human beings are not wired like that hawk, and that we sense morality attests to our having *a priori* qualities, qualities that transcend all others we find in nature. Kant thus believed morality and beauty both pointed to something profound present in the universe.

When it comes to human art the matter becomes understandably more complex for Kant. He would agree with us that some purpose had to exist prior to the painting of the picture. The artist must have wanted to paint a specific mountain and not all mountains at once, or that the artist wanted to convey a mood of peacefulness and not anxiety. Does not the existence of those prior ideas, motivations, and reasons connote the existence of purpose? Kant qualified, no—just because an artist has the idea of a serene mountain vista in her mind does not necessitate the existence or appearance of beauty. The artist could have had any number of purposes for painting and yet beauty could still be absent. Purpose does not equate to or necessitate beauty.

And still Kant knew there is a difference between beauty as it appears in nature and the beauty that is produced by people. He called these kinds of beauties "free" and "dependent." Free beauty occurs in nature and is wholly lacking in prior conceptualization; the hydrangea does not think in order to grow and sprout flowers. However, with dependent beauty we

---

ego, constructs knowledge out of sense impressions and from universal concepts called categories that it imposes upon them. Kant's transcendentalism is set in contrast to those of two of his predecessors—the problematic idealism of René Descartes, who claimed that the existence of matter can be doubted, and the dogmatic idealism of George Berkeley, who flatly denied the existence of matter. Kant believed that ideas, the raw matter of knowledge, must somehow be due to realities existing independently of human minds; but he held that such things-in-themselves must remain forever unknown. Human knowledge cannot reach to them because knowledge can only arise in the course of synthesizing the ideas of sense. Transcendental idealism has remained a significant strand in later philosophy, being perpetuated in various forms of Kantian and Neo-Kantian movements of thought." "Transcendental Idealism" in *Encyclopedia Britannica*. Scruton, in *Kant*, 23, also helps hereon: Transcendental idealism presupposes "a very special kind of harmony between the capacities of the knower and the nature of the known. It is possible because of this harmony that a priori knowledge is possible. It follows from this theory that the 'forms of thought' which govern the understanding, and the a priori nature of reality, are in exact correspondence. The world is as we think it, and we think it as it is." Oh, the philosophical debates that ricochet around this position!

already know for example that paintings are painted for some purpose following some kinds of rules and resulting from some kind of thought; in this way we view a painting differently than we view a hydrangea. Believing that, Kant esteemed the free beauty of nature over human artwork. Free beauty is more pure than dependent beauty. Scruton encapsulated Kant hereon, only by contemplating free beauty "are our faculties able to relax entirely from the burdens of common scientific and practical thought, and enter into free play which is the ground of aesthetic pleasure."[24] Students of Kant note that the issue of purposiveness without purpose, especially as it concerns human artwork, raises serious problems.[25]

Kant's fourth aspect in the judgment of beauty is necessity. In Kant's aesthetic formulation we have seen rather subjective elements or aspects simultaneously at work: disinterestedness, universality, and purposiveness without purpose. As we have noted, those three are interrelated. For Kant their ground is the *a priori* element at work in aesthetic experience: *sensus communis*, common sense. This deserves clarification. Common sense was first proposed in history by Aristotle for whom it was "a central cognitive faculty that combines our five senses." Word definitions change over time and today we English speakers use common sense primarily to convey a kind of intelligence concerning everyday matters. When we say "it is common sense to buckle one's seat belt while riding in an automobile," we are referring to shared understanding of what is unilaterally wise. Another, more precise, definition of common sense is "a healthy understanding that is opposed to skepticism or nonsense." Not surprisingly, Kant held a more technical definition than we regularly employ. For him common sense was more like Aristotle had used it. That is, the *sensus communis*—something inherent and internal within all individuals—is the "effect of the free play," and "a sense by which we feel our own state of mind." Hence, it is common

---

24. Scruton, *Kant*, 87.

25. Wenzel, for example, notes that Kant's theory would make children more capable of aesthetic judgment than adults, precisely because the cognitive formation of children, that is the concepts and categories they bring to judgment, is less congealed, less mature. Wenzel counters that it is necessary to have some kind of criteria at work in judging both artwork and music. "After all, do we not need an understanding of musical composition, variation, counterpoint and the like, to appreciate the music of Bach? Do we not need to be educated and experienced in such matters to be able to appreciate this kind of music appropriately? That is, can we always, as Kant demands, abstract from concepts and still be left with the possibility of appreciating the object properly?" *Kant's Aesthetics*, 70. There is a fine line between free and dependent beauty. Wenzel, 72, adds, "Fluctuation is easily possible."

because we all use it. It is common, and even universal, in that when we exercise it we believe it applicable to everyone. That we all use it and that it is common within everyone makes it a necessity: there is no escaping it (not that Kant would want to!). Again, common sense is a dynamic that exists *a priori* in every human mind. Indeed, for Kant the other three moments/aspects of aesthetic judgment occur via the operation of common sense.[26] Common sense is our *a priori* ability to be disinterested, to postulate universal aesthetic judgments, and to see purposiveness without purpose in beautiful things.

Earlier we noted that Kant's perspective on human knowing is called transcendental idealism. He supposed a clear correspondence between human cognition and reality. For example, Kant believed that when we listen to music we *hear* the unity among its parts. The notes themselves do not know or experience a unity. The unity we hear is one we hear as the notes are played. We hear it only because our imagination, in process of free play, brings our perception of the notes "under the indeterminate idea of unity." Scruton recounted Kant hereon:

> Only beings with imagination (a faculty of reason) can hear musical unity, since only they can carry out this indeterminate synthesis. So the unity is the perception of mine. But this perception is not arbitrary, since it is compelled by my rational nature. I perceive the organization in my experience as objective. The experience of unity brings pleasure, and this too belongs to the exercise of reason. I suppose the pleasure, like the melody, to be the property of all who are constituted like me. So I represent my pleasure in the music as due to the workings of a "common sense," which is to say, a disposition that is at once based in experience, and common to all rational beings.[27]

So, there is a necessary something to our experience of beauty: that we have an *a priori* dynamic, one that operates in the same way among us all to process beauty (indeed to make any judgments at all). Again, the objective ground is that we all have a subjective, though existing prior to experience, ability to make aesthetic judgments. Still, more than one philosopher has found this confusing if not circular. Indeed, Kant's philosophy of mind is

---

26. Wenzel, *Kant's Aesthetics*, 80–85; quotations from page 84. Cf. Burnham, *Kant: Aesthetics*.

27. Scruton, *Kant*, 85–86, following Kant's *Critique of Aesthetic Judgment*, section 153.

often overlooked among contemporary philosophers.[28] Nevertheless, at this chapter's later conclusion, several appreciative but critical interactions with Kant's philosophy of aesthetics will be noted.

With painstaking detail Kant himself plumbs the depths of each of our above noted four aspects—disinterestedness, universality, purposiveness without purpose, and necessity. His desire to explain these aspects, or moments, at the epistemological and philosophical levels is variously excruciating, obtuse, and sophisticated. At bare minimum, he has shown us that in the process of perceiving beauty there is much transpiring between the subject, the subject's knowing and experiencing, and the thing considered. We will consider him on one more matter that abides in aesthetic circles today, the sublime.

THE SUBLIME

In popular parlance, the word *sublime* indicates the overwhelmingly beautiful, a superior quality inherent within a person or object, something elevated or impressive, or even the dreamy, as in, "his sparkling blue eyes are just sublime!" For Kant, however, the sublime is a category that expresses other specific qualities. The contingencies of human nature and existence being what they are, we have a tendency to flatten words and ideas to their lowest common denominator; unfortunately, this also tends to flatten our experience and understanding of not only beauty, but life itself. Elsewhere I wrote, "If 'the devil is in the details,' so also are the beauty, truth, and meaning of an idea or position."[29] We do well to furnish our vocabulary with terms that help us touch more carefully upon the mystery of beauty. Kant can help us.

The sublime, in Kant's repertoire, conveys the mighty, large, and overwhelming. Sublime artwork or natural forces, Wenzel clarified, "are almost frightening, and they make us aware of our physical limitations in comparison with them."[30] Gesa Elsbeth Thiessen abridged Kant and described the sublime thus: "the sublime connotes what is awe-inspiring, overwhelming, threatening and mysterious. It is achieved by including into a work of art elements of the fantastic, of melancholy, and sometimes of transience and

---

28. Wenzel, *Kant's Aesthetics*, 85.
29. Rybarczyk, *The Spirit Unfettered*, ix.
30. Wenzel, *Kant's Aesthetics*, 106–7.

morbidity."³¹ Kant provided several examples of the sublime: the dome of St. Peter's basilica in Rome, the Egyptian pyramids, ominous and towering mountains, crashing thunder and flashing lightning, lofty waterfalls, rushing mighty rivers, erupting volcanoes, devastating hurricanes, overhanging cliffs, and the vast and starry heavens above.³² With the exception of St. Peter's and the pyramids (might he have described certain roller coasters or rocket ship rides as touching upon the sublime?), each of Kant's examples are from nature. This makes sense since the sublime is expressed through size and power. More acutely, and in keeping with Kant's aesthetic sensibilities as noted earlier, the sublime forces us to consider our own physical limitations.

But it's not because that it is powerful or overwhelming that we call it sublime. There is more. With the sublime Kant argued that we enjoy knowing we can see it without being harmed. We are able to witness the awesome, dreadful, and brutalizing power of nature from a safe distance, we can see its ability to devastate all the while we ourselves are beyond its reach. We enjoy being able to touch upon the magnificent without getting crushed, we delight in putting our fingers close to the fire without getting burned. Hence, with the sublime there is both a negative and a positive quality: danger and safety, violence and peace, the unpleasant and the pleasant. And unless we suppose that Kant is willing for himself, or for us, to become enrapt in the thing-as-such, say in the surging force of nature, we must see that for our Prussian philosopher the event had everything to do with our dynamic *a priori* ability to perceive. Again, he's turning the tables on the older classical-patristic-medieval formulations that emphasized beauty's objectivity.

We are what is important, for Kant, even to the extent that our presence and perception transcends the thing we are witnessing. For Kant, Burnham argues that when we witness the sublime the thing-as-such is not the real object, "at all." Burnham continues.

> Instead, what is properly sublime are ideas of reason: namely, the ideas of absolute totality or absolute freedom. However huge the building, we know it is puny compared to absolute totality; however powerful the storm, it is nothing compared to absolute freedom. The sublime feeling is therefore a kind of "rapid alternation" between the fear of the overwhelming and the peculiar pleasure

---

31. Thiessen, ed., *Theological Aesthetics*, 158.
32. Kant, *Critique of the Power of Judgment*, sections, 245, 252, 256, 269, 270.

of seeing that overwhelming overwhelmed. Thus, it turns out that the sublime experience is purposive after all—that we can, in some way, "get our head around it."[33]

What we experience with the sublime is our perception of the sublime. Yes, we get to witness the something that is larger than ourselves, but all the while we know that there are things larger than that awe-inspiring thing confronting us! We know, for instance, that while a hurricane is devastating it cannot compare to the energy inside the sun or inside the totality of the universe. And, as Burnham pointed out, the cumulative power of the universe itself falls short before both the existence of reason and our feeling of absolute freedom. (I think that is an amazing realization!) In part then, the sublime involves our feeling of superiority over nature, even though we realize our own limitations. Kant wrote, "thus in our mind we find a superiority to nature even in its immensity." He continued, "Thus humanity in our own person remains unhumiliated, though as mortal creatures we have to submit to the dominion of nature."[34]

Describing the sublime, Kant listed multiple categories and concepts that inhere the human mind: a voice of reason that moves us to consider the totality of the issue, the ability to think in totalizing (all-encompassing, wondrous) ways, a sense of the transcendent, the ability to sense and imagine that there is more than what appears on the surface, and the awareness that we are independent of nature.[35] Clarifying just that little portion of Kant's philosophy we can see why he was a father of Enlightenment philosophy: in significant ways he made the individual human person the final measure, indicator, or arbiter of reality.

WRAP-UP: KANT'S AESTHETIC PHILOSOPHY— IMPLICATIONS AND BRIEF INTERACTIONS

Kant's aesthetic philosophy, because it is intertwined with his sweeping transcendental idealism, deserves extensive and sophisticated interpretation. By suggesting resultant implications and by making cursory interactions thereon, we open ourselves to profound critique. Nevertheless, not

---

33. Burnham, *Aesthetics*, "The Sublime."

34. Kant, *Critique of Judgment*, *The Dynamical Sublime*, sections 261 and 262 in Beck, ed., *Kant: Selections*, 379.

35. My summary of Wenzel's own overview, *Kant's Aesthetics*, 107, where he follows Kant's *Critique of the Power of Judgment*, sections 254, 255, 257, 261, and 262.

Immanuel Kant (1724–1804)

only out of homage to Kant, but to better if only briefly understand ourselves, we must make a few remarks.

Subjectivity. Kant did not think so, with his insistence on the *a priori* dimensions of human nature, but his philosophical musings on the aesthetic experience helped to turn a societal understanding of aesthetics *from* the definitions of beauty *to* the perceiver's experience, alone. After Kant it will be excruciatingly difficult to argue cogently that beauty is "out there" in discernible and universally understood categories. He correctly asserted that in important ways we are experiencing *our experiencing* of the beautiful, but he erred to believe that each and every person uses their perceiving common sense in personally unique ways. It is erroneous, despite popular culture's now many clichéd mantras—"like a snowflake, you are unique," "no one walks in your shoes," adages all so glib and so vapid because they are consistently severed from transcendent moorings—to believe that each person either creates or interprets his or her own reality. For all of the problems of postmodernism,[36] it is correct when it asserts that human beings "do"—perceive, interpret, narrate, construe, navigate—reality in groups: families, clans, friendship circles, linguistic clusters, religious affiliations, and other varied subcultures. Those groupings, indeed, view beauty and practice aesthetics in their varied and respective ways, but individual persons do not solely by themselves practice aesthetics. Individual persons who "do" reality, or even aesthetics, on their own consistently get moved out, whether by intentional social ostracization or by unintentional forces of social marginalization, and become rendered irrelevant. A man might vary from some specifics of his group's norms but he will not differ entirely, else he would no longer associate, or be allowed to associate, with his group. For instance, if her musical band likes a certain genre of music a woman drummer may like other noted bands or artists or instruments within that

---

36. Postmodernism generally asserts that "all truth is local." In other words groups—not individuals, as Kant surmised—create and establish their own boundaries for processing reality. Conceived differently, to a committed postmodernist philosopher, there is no truth that is true for everyone everywhere. Postmodernists believe that there are only local constructions and interpretations of truth, but that each of those are finally illusory. Of course, a committed postmodernist would *rarely* accept that postmodernism is also just one more locally constructed narrative. In my classes I teach that postmodernism is helpful as a descriptive tool but is prescriptively disastrous. In other words, postmodernism helps us understand that we do reality together as people groups, but it has no solutions for what besets us. Its remedies (e.g., each group should do what it believes or feels is best for itself—a solution that only buttresses the ability of the powerful to finally devour the weak) are medicines more destructive than the original disease.

genre. But if she altogether rejected her band's genre she would not likely be an accepted member of her own band for long.

Specifically as it concerns aesthetics, scholars are increasingly showing that differing people groupings do in fact perceive form in similar ways. All cultures value symmetry, harmonies of color and sound, excellence, and elegance, even if they seek out and portray symmetry, harmony, excellence, and elegance in different ways. Again, with the benefit of 200 years, we see that Kant overstated things to emphasize individual perception as he did.

Furthermore on subjectivity, that Kant sought to root our shared experience of aesthetic judgment in some *a priori* inherent category of common sense is not enough. The precise how and what of that common sense needs a firmer ground than Kant established. He wanted to suggest there is something transcendental about us, something derived, if uncomfortably so for Kant, from a god behind or beneath human nature. We will briefly note that whereas his transcendental "ground" is better than other and later postulations[37] Kant didn't go deep enough. We would want to ask him other foundational questions: "Which god? Why? For how long? To what end?"

*Disinterestedness. Kant insisted that perception of beauty is done, and should be done, with disinterestedness.[38] One wonders, is that even possible? Is it feasible to turn off one's past experiences, one's accumulation of prior knowledge, or one's acculturated way of processing life? Kant did not know this in his day, but we now know today that our very physio-neural network becomes trained. Especially while we are infants and then through our years as children, our nervous systems, through repeated firings and processings, get trained or "hard wired" to process information in preestablished and routinized manners. For instance, it becomes increasingly easier to communicate in one specific language because our brains repeat that information processing until our language engine gets built, shaped, and strengthened. By repeated use and exercise, brain tissue actually becomes strengthened in some areas and weakened in other areas. Hence, when we go to learn another language, we find it very difficult; this is because we

---

37. Our real ground is our *will*, as variously expressed by many post-Enlightenment philosophers. Again, such a postulation often ironically produces a "go card" for the strong to eat the weak. That "all groups may do and believe want they want" is fine until one group wants to annihilate an adjacent group; then what arbitrates? World views that locate the ground of our being in human nature, however understood, finally result in nihilism.

38. Burnham notes that disinterestedness is the part most attacked by other scholars. *Aesthetics*, "The Judgment of the Beautiful."

have built neural "highways" for doing language that makes it arduous for another language to travel across. So, there is a physiological challenge to Kant's valuing of disinterestedness.

Then there is the philosophical challenge: is it helpful to be disinterested? Does one truly appreciate a painting more when one is, amid disinterestedness, utterly surprised by it? Or, is it not the case that as one learns to look at distinct genres one more deeply enjoys a painting's particularities? When one understands how the genre portrays reality, when one realizes how that genre is intentionally recasting our perception of reality, are there not more rather than less delicacies to appreciate? We saw earlier that Thomas Aquinas believed we perceive beauty more readily when our perspective is educated and trained. William James (1842–1910) once wrote "Men have no eyes but for those aspects of things which they have already been taught to discern ... in poetry and the arts someone has to come and tell us what aspects we may single out ... and what effects we may admire, *before* our aesthetic nature can 'dilate' to its full extent."[39]

Universality. Kant argued that when one makes a judgment about beauty we presume one's judgment thereon is true for everyone everywhere. Kant was astutely thereby touching on the very nature of human existence and knowledge. We cannot honestly talk about truth claims and simultaneously be committed pluralists. A PoMo, or a pluralist, who believes truth is whatever one wants it to be is either disingenuous or deceived. Missiologist Lesslie Newbigin once poignantly said, "The relativism which is not willing to speak about truth but only about 'what is true for me' is an evasion of the serious business of living. It is the mark of a tragic loss of nerve in our contemporary culture. It is a preliminary symptom of death."[40] Our perception of the truth might vary, but truth itself does not. I teach that *perceiving versus being* dynamic is called catholicity: in our varied groupings we see and assent to the truth but we express that truth with our own cultural-linguistic categories. For instance, gravity exists whether we know to call it that or not. But the truth of gravity remains. Genius that he was, Kant knew that our perceptions of beauty and morality functioned similarly: they were universal, true, and abiding for everyone everywhere. Only when Western society learned, over the course of generations, to divorce aesthetics from the rest of reality did we learn to imprison morality within a box of relativity.

39. James, *Principles of Psychology*, vol. 1, 443. My italics.
40. Newbigin, *The Gospel in a Pluralist Society*, 22.

Hence, one obvious implication of Kant's philosophy is not only that beauty requires interpretation, but so does truth. This is because, as Kant so astutely understood it, human cognition is equally elusive, equally difficult to describe and understand. That we can sense and perceive but only sufficiently describe those with enormous difficulty goes toward the transcendental nature of reality itself. As Christians we would, for starters, suggest that reality is characterized by the transcendental since it participates in something, or someone, who himself far transcends the categories of this existence.

Purposiveness without purpose. Kant's evaluation on this theme is brilliant. Indeed, there is something present in beauty that requires paradoxical language. We realize—or are taught to realize—that more is shimmering inside beauty's presence than any one single category. Classical philosophy and theology knew to express this "more" with the word *excessus*. For my part, I am quite reticent to finally define beauty, but if I had to use one word it would be *excessus*. There *is* something there but it defies neat categorization; it comes in many packages, shines in diverse ways, and is not content to sit still. Kant was spot-on, there are no rules for beauty. That beauty "seems to have a purpose but finally does not" trends in the same direction as *excessus*: we see something (don't we see it?) that we cannot finally nail down. In our scientific era—or maybe our era is becoming post-scientific (since Western people are not as adamant as in generations past to explain everything with scientific, cause-and-effect concepts)—we love function and purpose. We want to know the direction, sweep, aim, end, goal, and conclusion of something. And yet, *beauty defies purpose*. It should have a purpose, but in and of itself it does not. As Evangelicals, we know that at the very least beauty's purpose is to produce gratitude. Still, our heartfelt thanks for beauty's presence in no way gives beauty the laud, the acclaim, the stillness, and the wonder it deserves. Our gratitude is not response enough for beauty. Beauty points us to something that we discern the presence of but that we cannot see. Kant's purposiveness without purpose moves us toward expressions of the ineffable. Truly, we need adept, more encompassing, more transcendent terms than Kant gives us to express what we are experiencing when we experience beauty.[41]

---

41. Once I set out to establish these kinds of categories as they pertain to *glossolalia*. Rybarczyk, "Reframing Tongues."

Immanuel Kant (1724–1804)

WHAT KANT TEACHES US TO SEE:

- thinking about the aesthetic experience is a worthy endeavor
- beauty is inseparable from the subjective experience of it
- our judgment of beauty must be disinterested
- there are no objective categories or rules for beauty
- if it is beautiful it must be universally so for everyone
- perceiving beauty involves both understanding and imagination
- beauty *appears* to us to have purpose but in truth lacks definite purpose
- human beings have innate capacities to experience beauty
- the aesthetically sublime overwhelms us
- the sublime allows us to touch danger without being harmed
- the subjective experience is more important, but not removed from, the objective reality (which cannot be fully known)

10

Paul Evdokimov (1901–1970)
Beauty through Iconic Lenses

IN MY UNIVERSITY CLASSES I frequently invite foreign students to share aloud both their perspectives about life in Southern California and their experience of Christianity here. I am intrigued to hear what they see about us. For everyone everywhere, there are elements to our lifestyle and our world view about which we are not always cognizant. Coming from different cultures, my foreign students are able to single out American values and practices, elements that are not always obvious to us.[1] Mostly, by inviting foreign perspectives, I am fascinated to learn about varied cultural vistas, but I have also realized that being an aesthete requires a willingness to stop, listen, observe, and learn. Beauty is not merely viewed by individuals. We all see and appreciate beauty within a perceptual and en-valued framework that is shared by so many around us. Others can help us see things that we overlook.

Pertinent for this chapter, Western Christians are almost entirely ignorant of Eastern Christianity. Most Westerners would be shocked to know that Eastern Europe received the gospel over 1,000 years ago—Armenia was the first nation to convert en masse to Christ Jesus—and that most people today in Eastern European countries consider themselves Christian. In the first century when the house churches in Rome were growing,

---

1. Commonly, foreign students remark about the trendy ways students dress. Regarding our faith, they regularly note how individualized is the way we Americans do Christianity.

Paul Evdokimov (1901–1970)

Eastern churches also were spreading across what are today the lands of Israel, Jordan, Syria, Turkey, Iraq, Iran, and Egypt, varied regions that over time would become the domain of the Byzantine Christian Empire. The spread of Islam in the sixth and seventh centuries and then particularly the hegemony of the Ottoman Empire (fourteenth to twentieth centuries) meant that Eastern Christians were repeatedly the targets of genocide; under that constant pressure, by the fourteenth century Russia became the *de facto* center of the Eastern church such that Russian Orthodox denizens referred to Moscow as the "third Rome."[2] This chapter will consider the theoasthetic insights of an Orthodox theologian, Paul (Pavel) Evdokimov, not only because he wrote an entire volume on beauty, something that made his theological work unique, especially for his era, but also because he was well aware of the aesthetic-philosophic developments occurring around him. A professor in Paris, a city that then dominated the artistic scene, Evdokimov was keenly attuned to the quickly changing artistic milieu.[3] Thus, we will see what he thought about beauty and aesthetics, uniquely positioned as he was: an Eastern Christian inside a Western context. As we will see, Evdokimov kept his ardent commitment to Orthodoxy, but he nevertheless studied Western philosophy and understood the swirling cultural contexts of the mid-twentieth century. He lived and taught in the very throes of the "anxiety and rage of the modern challenge to God."[4]

Born in St. Petersburg, Evdokimov was Russian Orthodox. When Paul was four years old, his father, an officer in the tsar's army, was assassinated by one of his own soldiers. Young Paul, educated as a boy in a Russian military school, began his theological studies at Kiev. However, a few years after the 1917 Bolshevik Revolution, with his remaining family Evdokimov emigrated through Constantinople into Paris where he earned his bachelor's degree in philosophy at the Sorbonne. Afterward he studied with the famed Russian émigré theologians Sergius Bulgakov and Nikolai Berdyaev, at St. Sergius (of Radonezh) Theological Institute, a Russian Orthodox school in Paris. Eventually, he earned his doctorate in philosophy at the university of Aix-en-Provence. During World War II he both helped the French Resistance by hiding people whom the Nazis sought to arrest

---

2. Byzantium was the second Rome under Emperor Constantine. The "third Rome" appellation carried with it notions of divine providence, blessing, and chosenness. See Meyendorff, *Rome, Constantinople, Moscow*.

3. See his comments in *The Art of the Icon*, chapter 7: "Modern Art in the Light of the Icon," 73–95.

4. Plekon, "A Theologian of God's Beauty."

and served in a Protestant relief hostel as an administrator and counselor, concerning which Michael Plekon notes that "It was as natural for him to mediate disputes, listen long into the night to stories of tragedy, [and] to lead evening prayers for a very mixed, ecumenical community."[5] A lay theologian,[6] he began his teaching career in the mid-1950s first at St. Sergius Theological Institute. Later he taught at the Ecumenical Institute in Bossey, Switzerland, and then at the Higher Institute of Ecumenical Studies in Catholic Theology in Paris. Having established fraternal relationship with Roman Catholics, Evdokimov was invited to be an official observer at Vatican II (1962–1965).

It helps to set the stage to know that Evdokimov's entire theology is aptly summarized as iconographic. He himself once framed his perspective as iconosophy: iconic wisdom, or the wisdom of viewing reality through an iconic lens.[7] Broadly put, Evdokimov's entire theological outlook was aesthetic: he believed everything has the potential to be, and could be understood as, an icon—an image, a mirror, a touchpoint, a doorway—for the eternal and the spiritual, in short an aesthetic avenue for God's presence. Evdokimov's was a position that is dramatically opposed to the subjectivizing perspective of Kant, even though Evdokimov is clear that the subject is involved in perceiving beauty.

Christ, in Orthodox theology, clearly came to forgive us our sin but that was done with an eye toward our final culmination: that we become like Christ, human while fully permeated by the divine. Jesus' *theandric* (man-God) nature is *the* foundation for most Orthodox theologians. Athanasius of Alexandria (296–373) once famously wrote, "God became man that man might become god." This doctrine is known as *theosis*: the complete suffusion of our being with the grace of the Holy Spirit such that we become all that God has for us to be: like him.[8] By the plan of the Father and the agency of the Holy Spirit, the second person of the Trinity,

---

5. Plekon, "A Theologian of God's Beauty." This together with Plekon and Vinogradov, eds., *A Paul Evdokimov Reader*, 2–4, and remarks in Plekon's website is the basis for this biographical information.

6. Across Orthodox history most theologians are ascetics, monks, priests or bishops.

7. Evdokimov, *The Art of the Icon*, 95, following Berdyaev.

8. Sometimes the word for *theosis* in English is "deification" or "divinization." This cannot be misconstrued. The Orthodox know that only God is God. We, however, can become "like" God. They teach that whereas Christ *is* God by nature, we become *like* God by grace.

the Word, became flesh; hence, the incarnation—the divine in and through the human—is the archetypal foundation for Orthodox understandings of beauty and aesthetics. We little-Christs, Christians, are called to be like Christ not only as moral beings, but across our entire existence, including our bodies. Jesus Christ is the perfect icon of the Father (Col 1:15) and we are called to be icons of Christ. Clearly, *theosis* can only be accomplished by the grace of the Holy Spirit, and yet we are necessarily involved. With their *theosis* doctrine the Orthodox thus emphasize human freedom more so than does the post-Augustinian West: by God's free and loving design, we are free to choose, free to say yes or no to the ongoing operations of God.[9] This dynamic of divine-human synergy[10] will be made apparent further below.

Lastly by way of introduction, the Orthodox celebrate the mystery of reality. While in an earlier chapter we saw that the Areopagite was ultimately committed to apophatic formulation—that the "no" we can say about God always surpasses the "yes" we can say about God, that what we *do* know about God is always surpassed by that which we do *not* know about God —in Evdokimov we see echoed the argument that mystery is less a problem than it is part of the solution.

ICONS

Western Christianity did battle with, conversed with, and finally found harmony with elements of various successive philosophies: Renaissance humanism, rationalism, empiricism, romanticism, existentialism, and postmodernism. In each varied case the overarching concern of Western philosophies has been human nature and the self. Contrastingly, Eastern Christianity has never much processed the West's philosophical

---

9. A famous Orthodox hymn exemplifies this position: "Do not say that it is impossible to receive the Spirit of God, Do not say that it is possible to be made whole without Him, Do not say that one can possess Him without knowing it, Do not say that God does not manifest Himself to man, Do not say that men cannot perceive the divine light, or that it is impossible in this age! Never is it found to be impossible, my friends. On the contrary, it is entirely possible when one desires it." Symeon the New Theologian (949–1022), Hymn 27, 125–32, quoted in Krivocheine, *St Symeon the New Theologian*, Foreword.

10. Synergy: co-working, mutual effort; God's energy working with our energy. The Orthodox are clear, God is always first mover; there is nothing we can do to save ourselves.

developments, developments largely understood by the Orthodox as devolutions, plagues on the history of Western thought. Instead, the Orthodox inherited a distinctly Platonic world view where questions pertained less immediately to the human self and more broadly to a matter-spirit dualism. In our earlier chapters we saw Gregory of Nyssa, Augustine, the Pseudo-Areopagite, and even Thomas Aquinas each working within this Platonized framework. They all struggled with how beauty can reside within and shine through everyday stuff; after all, physical matter breaks down, changes, and becomes overrun by disease, mildew, and rot. Worse, matter is the locus for darkness, evil, and sin. With that matter-spirit dualism in mind we can better understand why icons—the spiritual shining through the material—carry the spiritual-theological[11] weight that they do for the Orthodox. Evdokimov, like all Orthodox theologians, sees the problematic nature of matter and physicality overcome by God's Son. Similarly, in an icon God's beauty can shine through painted matter.

The Apostle Paul repeatedly exclaimed this iconic dynamic: "But we all, with unveiled face beholding as *in a mirror* the glory of the Lord, are being transformed into the same image [icon] from glory to glory, just as from the Lord, the Spirit" (2 Cor 3:18). "For God, who said, 'Light shall shine out of darkness,' is the One who has *shone* in our hearts to give the light of knowledge of the glory of God in the face of Christ" (2 Cor 4:6).[12] The word *icon* and its dynamic of shining through also appears in, "For whom He foreknew, He also predestined to become *conformed to the image* [icon] of His Son, that He might be the first-born among many brethren," (Rom 8:29). And yet again, "And He is the *image* [icon] of the *invisible* God, the first-born of all creation. For by him all things were created, both *visible and invisible*, whether thrones or dominions or rulers or authorities—all things have been created by Him and for Him; the mystery which has been hidden from the past ages and generations . . . which is *Christ in you*, the

---

11. For the Orthodox spirituality and theology are two sides of the same coin. Their spirituality puts their theology into worship and practice, and their theology gives definition to their spirituality. Theology for the Orthodox is not a set of ideas that are somehow distinctly bracketed from daily or ecclesial life or "real" life as some might think of it in the West. Theology for them also is not a fence of ideas to keep out error. Theology is a life source, a fountain of truth to enrich the lives of the Orthodox faithful. A problem, when I travel to Eastern Europe and as I read studies of life there, is that the Orthodox priests too easily get stuck in the rituals of Orthodoxy. They do not draw enough from the wells of their own theology and intentionally teach that to the faithful.

12. Evdokimov, *The Art of the Icon*, 222. My italics in this verse and the subsequent ones.

hope of glory," (Col 1:15–16, 26a, 27b). Those Pauline passages all attest to how physicality—human beings or Christ Jesus—can mirror or shine forth something else—God's glory, God's divinity, and God the Father. Scripture verses are important to Evdokimov's theology of aesthetics, but his theological perspective is much broader, much more encompassing.

The West, again in contrast, sees the incarnation as necessary for the atonement; God became one of us in order to save us. Evdokimov, exemplifying Orthodox theology, views the incarnation as an act of solidarity and ontological healing for a creation created for fellowship with God. Something—sin and evil—had invaded God's good creation. The result was that a fracture, a gaping abyss, was introduced into the very being of human nature: we alienate ourselves from God, from one another and from ourselves, and then fittingly we die. Christ Jesus came not only to forgive our sin and evil, he came to heal that fracture, to fill that abyss. In his ontology Christ heals us: he was both human and divine; the two natures are consubstantial.[13] Evdokimov put it thus, "the Incarnation is God's response to his already established presence in humanity, to his image in humankind. So atonement is a matter not so much of human nature *making amends* as of its *being mended*." In the East atonement is "usually discussed in physical and ontological rather than ethical and juridical terms; and the end is not 'redemption', or even 'salvation' (in the 'salvationist' or individual sense), but *apocatastasis*, universal restoration and healing." "To this divine end humankind is in its essence cast in the divine likeness."[14]

---

13. Evdokimov, *Orthodoxy*, 85, 144–48, 251–52; *The Art of the Icon*, 208.

14. Evdokimov, *Orthodoxy*, 95–96. Original italics. He clarifies in note 18, page 96, that he is following the patristic fathers on this. In *The Art of the Icon* (5, 134, 136) and in *Orthodoxy* (48, 214–17, 337–38) Evdokimov discusses hell, the freedom of people to reject God unto the end, and those who may be lost for eternity. The reader errs to think that the Orthodox view salvation in the kinds of deterministic predestinarian theologies of Augustine, Luther, Calvin, and the like. The Orthodox are far too emphatic on both God's own humility, especially as made evident in Christ's own emptying of himself (Phil 2:5–11) such that God in his own humble nature will never force salvation or relationship, and human freedom as a God-given gift, to frame salvation in deterministic or universalizing categories. *Apocatastasis* will happen, Evdokimov believes, but it may not include everyone or everything: "the final *apocatastasis*, the summing up of heaven and earth. This is the divine plan, the undoubted purpose of the Incarnation, excluding no one in its scope. Nevertheless, the end remains hidden and unpredictable; at the most we can be receptive and hopeful." *Orthodoxy*, 71. He also carefully qualifies the doctrine of predestination in *In the World, of the Church*, 15–18. "According to the Fathers' saying, 'God is not able to force anyone to love him.'" Ibid., 16.

Evdokimov reads the Bible *in light of* his grand theological commitment—the incarnation—more than he reads the Bible *to infer* his theological commitments.[15] Hence, everything in the economy of salvation (this life, the universe, humankind and our redemption) stems from and orbits the incarnation. For instance, Jesus was not born in the image of Adam. Rather, human beings were created in the image of the incarnate one. "God sculpted the human person while looking at his Wisdom, the celestial humanity of Christ."[16] God's perfect man, even from before creation, was Jesus, the Word made flesh; we were all created in the image of *the* image: the Son who shows the Father. God made us for himself, so he could take up his abode in us, make us to be his living temples, and all of that after the image of his own Son having been made flesh, himself the perfect embodiment of heaven on earth.[17] Or, to illustrate it alternately, Evdokimov believed Jesus' kingdom of God stories were told with this divinity-shining-through-matter dynamic in mind: "The *material* images of the Gospel parables and the *cosmic matter* of the sacraments are not accidental. The simplest things conform to a very precise destiny. Everything is an *image*, a likeness, a *participation* in the economy of salvation; everything is a *hymn*, a doxology."[18]

With an icon the transcendent becomes immanent, the eternal enters time. That this can happen is not only by virtue of God's sovereign and loving power, but because God had originally created reality and human beings so that those may share relationship with God. By the Holy Spirit a painted icon mirrors the mysterious matter-spirit dynamic of time and eternity's preeminent icon: Jesus Christ. The same Holy Spirit who overshadowed Mary and brought the Word into her womb, the same Spirit who empowered Jesus' ministry and raised him from the dead, that same Spirit who gives gifts to the church and makes all things new can make an icon become the locus of a mysterious presence.

---

15. To be fair, all Christian traditions, even those believing they are ardently committed to a Bible-only foundation, work their theology thus. It is not possible to read the Bible without prior commitments, even if those commitments are inherent within and inferred from the Bible. Scholars refer to this dynamic as the hermeneutical circle: the process that constantly interprets and reinterprets both the Bible and life with ever-increasing (hopefully) nuance and insight.

16. Evdokimov, *The Art of the Icon*, 47, where he follows Gregory Palamas and Clement of Alexandria.

17. Ibid.

18. Ibid., 59. My italics.

Paul Evdokimov (1901–1970)

The Council of Chalcedon (451), representing both the Eastern and Western halves of the church, averred that the two natures of Christ exist together variously without confusion, separation, division, or change. John of Damascus (d. 749) reasoned that the "energies of the two natures, the created and the uncreated, penetrate each other," in a *perichoresis*, an exchange of idioms.[19] Indeed, for Evdokimov, Christ's humanity "is the image of his divinity. Jesus did not say, "He who has seen me has seen God," but rather, "He who has seen me has seen the Father."[20] This is because the Son is the image of the Father. Evdokimov, following his mentor Bulgakov, said that Chalcedon affirmed Eastern Orthodoxy's central truth: Jesus' theandric nature.[21] The eternal, invisible, all-powerful God became visible and voluntarily limited in Jesus of Nazareth, the Word become flesh. The Word who was "in the beginning, with God," and who indeed "was God," "became flesh, and dwelt among us" (John 1:1, 14). The average Western Evangelical would read John's gospel thereon and think, "God became flesh in order to teach me how to live, pay for my sins, die for me, and give me access to eternal life." Such a reading would harmonize with the Evangelical believer's broader philosophical individualizing milieu, even if she or he was neither aware of nor understood that milieu. The average Orthodox believer would read John's prologue and think, "God entered creation! Material has been sanctified by his enfleshment. My very body's resurrection is assured because Christ Jesus' body was raised up." Without realizing his or her own philosophic matrix, it would just make sense for the Orthodox believer to focus on how in the incarnation God resolved and healed the matter-spirit conundrum.

Truly then, with Evdokimov it seems like we've left the lake of beauty for the ocean of theology! Frankly, Evdokimov said that the aim of the patristic fathers, his own theological guides and mentors, was *epignosis*: the "awareness of God." Developed as a theological category, *epignosis* meant the translation of everything in and for the presence and glory of God. Not only do icons serve a theological or worshipful purpose, so does everything in life.[22] More on that will be developed later in this chapter. Yet if we fail to

---

19. The whole small 'o' orthodox church (Catholic, Orthodox, Protestant) embraces a trinitarian doctrine of *perichoresis*. The three in the Godhead enjoy mutuality, mutual penetration, communion, and union without any of the three losing their own unique identity.

20. Evdokimov, *The Art of the Icon*, 208–9.

21. Evdokimov, *Orthodoxy*, 45.

22. Ibid., 24.

understand Orthodoxy's christological foundation for iconography we will miss the theo-asethetic weight that they believe icons carry. *Icons are more than religious art, they are theological statements.* For the Orthodox icons are theology in paint rather than ink.[23]

That foundational theological mining done, there are practical aspects to iconography. Very stylized, icons typically portray their subjects with large eyes; the focus of most icons is the main subject's eyes. The viewer makes contact with the hypostasis, the mysterious self, and the energies of the subject portrayed especially through the eyes. Hands and feet are small, but bodies are lithe and elongated, they appear very light; this helps to convey the sense of eternity and transcendence of their life in Christ. Bodies are draped in gowns and garments in order to preserve the subject's modesty. Evdokimov described this elegance:

> The bodies drawn to underline their svelteness seem to float in the air or melt into the ethereal gold of the divine light; they lose all carnal character. The icon represents a world apart, renewed, in which persons with eternity written on their faces live freely together with the divine energies. These saints are energized by *epectasis*, the stretching out of a universe that dilates without limits in the heavenly spaces of the Kingdom.[24]

Is the subject (e.g., Christ, apostle, prophet, Mary, saint) actually present through the Icon? By grace of the Holy Spirit, as many Orthodox theologians put it, or by the energies of God, as Evdokimov more commonly puts it, the Orthodox believe yes. The Christian East holds a world view that is very *porous*, just as we saw in earlier chapters on Gregory of Nyssa and the Pseudo-Areopagite. Divinity can shine through physicality, eternity can soak through the temporal. The transcendent can shimmer in and through the immanent. Invisible things permeate visible things again both because God delights in making himself known and because he created reality such that it is capable of receiving his presence and sharing that. Everything, then, can be iconic. True enough, in an icon—or anything else—we cannot experience God's full glory because of our finitude and weakness. And yet, when we do, or when the Orthodox do, experience God's energies the

---

23. Another Orthodox noted, "'Theology in imagery,' the icon expresses through colors what the Gospel proclaims in words." Quenot, *The Icon*, 12.

24. Evdokimov, *The Art of the Icon*, 221. The reader is reminded that *epectasis* was a doctrine espoused by Gregory of Nyssa.

experience is inexpressible.[25] Especially when there is faith operative in the believer's heart, something of the eternal realm is intuited with and in the icon, "known through nonknowing," felt to be present in ways that cannot be articulated. Jesus himself pointed to perceptive knowing, "Those who have ears to hear, let them hear." Thereon Evdokimov clarified, "This saying most certainly assumes another saying: 'Those who have eyes to see, let them see.' The proof is the blinding light that comes from him who is present, and that proof is the icon."[26] Per Evdokimov and the Orthodox, for those with faith, for those open to receive, there is something more going on with an icon than mere line, color, or form. There is presence. And it follows the proper response is worship of the Triune God, best expressed in silence.[27]

Icons are not painted so much as written (*graphos*). Again, the iconographer's vocation is to faithfully convey—to write not just illustrate—the mysterious truth of the subject shown. Evdokimov put it thus: "St. Gregory of Nyssa said that 'silent art knows how to speak.'"[28] To preserve icons' theological purpose and to try to prevent error, Nicea (325) established rules for icons. One, icons can only be about something from history. So, for instance, they cannot be imaginary, say about purple dinosaurs, Jesus in Eden's garden standing beside unicorns, or fictional events construed by the painter's creativity. Understandably then, prominent iconographic themes come from the Bible: prophets, apostles, angels, scenes from Jesus' life (e.g., his baptism in Jordan, healing the sick, crucifixion, resurrection), or scenes from the apostles's lives (e.g., Pentecost). However, post-biblical subjects can be written: saints, patriarchs, priests, ascetics and monks; though usually these are portrayed as subjects looking directly at the viewer and not so commonly put into a scene.

Another rule is that the artist is not allowed to sign his or her work. Icons are understood to be a gift from, to, and for the church, not an opportunity for individual creativity to be displayed. However, within the established rules, the artist-iconographer is free to bring in perspective and feel

---

25. Evdokimov, *The Art of the Icon*, 231–38. No one can see, apprehend, or understand God's essence, not even the angels in his presence. Out of his fullness, however, God nevertheless shares himself with his creation and does so by virtue of his energies. This philosophic doctrine traces its roots most famously to Gregory of Palamas (1296–1359). For more on God's essence see *The Art of the Icon*, 36.

26. Ibid., 238.

27. Ibid., 236–37; Evdokimov, *Orthodoxy*, 318.

28. Evdokimov, *The Art of the Icon*, 150.

and nuance that can give the icon its own personal quality. St. Seraphim of Serov is known to have intentionally made "an error or two" when he painted an icon, just so it better expressed a more natural demeanor.[29] Normally iconographic education is an embodied process involving teacher and student. However, there are instruction manuals that guide artists in their holy work.[30] Each iconographic school is free, within the rules, to "carry their own identifiable characteristics."[31] On the process of painting, Evdokimov said something that rings fairly constant in the art world: artists seek to "rise above and go beyond empirical things to their intelligible structure," grasping their unity. In doing the craft the artist looks for "something more." However, what Evdokimov meant by that had a distinctly Orthodox ring to it. Iconographers, Evdokimov's ideal artists, seek to *symbolize* reality, not deflate or destroy reality. He noted that the Greek stem *-bolos* means "throwing." The devil, *diabolos*, "throws apart" and wreaks chaos. A symbol, in contrast, "throws together" and is "a bridge that links the two shores: the invisible and the visible, the earthly and the heavenly, the empiric and the ideal."[32] Stop signs and algebraic signs are symbols, but they are arbitrary; those signs have meaning because we have all agreed that they do. Icons, in contrast, participate in the reality of their subject. An icon "performs the function of revealing the 'meaning' and at the same time it is the expressive receptacle of the 'presence.'"[33]

Symbols, again, gather and present the subject portrayed. Abstract art throws apart the subject, the person, rather than bringing it together. Indeed, Evdokimov was a harsh critic of abstract art. He argued that abstract art is doomed from the start because it tries to depict the real without using the forms or bodies of the real: "As a result, we have nothing but a false magic of the moment. Ghosts can still offer us a certain aesthetic pleasure. They haunt the leftover crumbs of the fragmented world but are of very little interest." Viewers are not welcome in the world of abstract art because

---

29. Ibid., 210.

30. These manuals, mostly from the sixteenth to eighteenth centuries, are often illustrated. They variously show traditional compositions for the iconographer to follow, features of certain apostles and saints to be replicated, how to prepare materials, the use of binding agents, and how to prepare and use different sealants and varnishes. Evdokimov, *The Art of the Icon*, 215–16.

31. Ibid.

32. Ibid., 86.

33. Phan, *The Iconographical Vision of Evdokimov*, 276.

such art is depersonalized.[34] So committed to the personalism of the symbol, the Council of Trullo (692) even "prohibited the use of 'the figures and shadows,' of the Old Testament, that is, the lamb, fish, etc., as symbols of Christ. The prefigurations must be replaced by the human face of Christ."[35]

Further regarding the rules of icon painting, an artist must display a certain level of excellence since "this basic talent is the vehicle which carries everything else."[36] A bad icon, Evdokimov asserted, "is an offense to God."[37] And yet more important than technical ability is the iconographer's spiritual sense, a quality of holiness. To enhance that quality in centuries gone by iconographers were required to be part of monastic communities. She or he variously had to be sensitive to the things of God, characterized by a life in the Holy Spirit, shaped by prayer, manifesting a capacity for contemplation, living in faith, and holding the ability to see inside the subject/person.[38]

Western Christians, unwittingly influenced by the *Libri Carolini*,[39] may well ask, "didn't the Old Testament prohibit making images?" The Orthodox would respond, "the Old Testament prohibited both worshipping images and making images of the invisible God. However, since God himself entered space and time and became flesh we are now free to portray him using matter. Moreover, we do not worship images. To do so would be idolatrous." The object, because it reflects someone holy, may be venerated, but true worship (*latreia*) is "reserved for God alone."[40] An ancient

---

34. Evdokimov, *The Art of the Icon*, 86–88.

35. Ibid., 213. Orthodox Christians frequently do wear crosses around their necks.

36. Ibid., 213.

37. Ibid., 188.

38. Evdokimov, *The Art of the Icon*, 213, 222, 226–29, 234, 236. I have a friend who paints icons. With quite vivid terms she talks about how the Holy Spirit will speak to her about the specifics of the particular piece she is working on.

39. As we saw in our chapter on the Reformation, the *Libri Carolini* were documents that favored words over images and that took a position against the Second Nicene Council (787) and its promulgation of images. Evdokimov argued that the *Libri Carolini* "were based on a most unfortunate and inexact Latin translation of the Greek texts of" Nicea. The *Libri Carolini* accused the Ecumenical Council at Nicea of legitimizing the worship of images, something Nicea did not do. Western Catholic Councils (Frankfurt 794 and Paris 824) disparaged Nicea and said "Christ did not save us by paintings." To which Evdokimov says, neither did Christ save us "by a book, we might add." *The Art of the Icon*, 167.

40. Meyendorff, *Eastern Christian Thought*, 183. Neither Mary nor the saints may be worshipped. Evdokimov makes clear that icons may not be worshipped. *The Art of the*

icon defender, Leontius of Neapolis, made the defense against idolatry even stronger: "We do not make obeisance to the nature of wood, but we revere and do obeisance to Him who was crucified on the Cross.... When the two beams of the Cross are joined together I adore the figure because of Christ who on the Cross was crucified, but if the beams are separated, I throw them away and burn them."[41] Evdokimov put it even more philosophically, the icon does not contain the prototype's *hypostatic* or *personal* presence. The hypostasis is neither imprisoned in the icon nor is it incarnated in the icon. Yet the divine energies radiate out, "Being a material point in this world, the icon opens a breach through which the Transcendent shines, and the successive waves of this presence transcend all limits and fill the whole universe."[42]

Icons are apostolic, so asserts Evdokimov. The church's first iconographer, Orthodox tradition avers, was St. Luke.[43] He painted three different icons of Mary and her son Jesus, an icon that is known as the *theotokos* icon. *Theotokos: theos*—God; *tokos*—bringing forth. Mary is thus revered as the mother of God. Icons of the *theotokos* have the young Jesus, sometimes a babe and sometimes a young boy, on his mother's lap, or sometimes positioned adjacent her womb. *Theotokos* icons are some of the most prominent icons in Orthodox churches because they symbolize the incarnation. God became flesh in and through Mary's womb.[44]

HUMAN NATURE AND THE REALM OF CREATION

The Christian East, far more so than the West, holds a theo-anthropological position that is decidedly aesthetic. In God's creation human beings are unique. Whereas animals are fleshly and angels are spiritual, people alone are both flesh and spirit. It was with humankind in mind that God created the earth. True, angels enjoy God's holy presence, but the Scriptures nowhere teach that they can be filled with God's Spirit or are temples of the

---

Icon, 201.

41. Ware, *The Orthodox Church*, 40, quoting Leontius in *PG*, XCIV, 1384D.

42. Evdokimov, *The Art of the Icon*, 196.

43. Ibid., 177.

44. This doctrine was affirmed at the ecumenical (West and East) Council of Ephesus in 431. By mother of God the Orthodox mean that in space and time God came through Mary. They could not and do not mean that Mary preexisted either God or Jesus Christ.

Paul Evdokimov (1901–1970)

living God. Only on the sixth day, the culmination of his creative process, did God finally create his masterpieces, man and woman. The union of flesh and spirit (we again see Platonic thought lurking beneath and behind), human beings were, and are, thus microcosms of the universe, intersections of materiality and divinity. Created good, physicality was originally meant to be a location for spirit, animal nature to be a residence for godly nature. Then God gave them, the apex of his creation, dominion over creation. He wanted them to be like him: an artist who shapes and designs and colors, a writer who names and guides and reveals.[45]

Harmonious with their own mystical perspective, the Orthodox believe that before the fall Adam and Eve enjoyed a kind of visceral, intuitive, transcending relationship with God. The whole of their physical senses were designed, even hardwired and lit, for penetrating knowledge of and sharing with God.[46] This kind of sharing and knowledge the Orthodox call *theoria*: an open and unmitigated experiential knowledge involving communion and deep mystical union. Even today, our knowledge of God is not first rational, but intuitive and mystical. There is awareness, Evdokimov argued, even if it cannot be articulated.[47] We saw this earlier, but the Orthodox believe God created human beings with a *perichoretic* (mutual penetrating) capacity for relationship with himself and one another.

That God gave them dominion, made them to be artists, and that he instilled within them an inherent capacity for awareness, knowledge, and capacity for relationship with himself all goes to the Orthodox doctrine of *imago dei*: humans being are uniquely made in God's image. We were created in his image, but we were given a task: to grow into the likeness of God. St. Basil (330–379) once wrote, "Man has received the order to become god by grace."[48] In Genesis 1:26–27 we see the Hebrew tandem, *selem* and *demut*, image and likeness, used to refer to our created nature. Originally that tandem, that duality, was used to emphasize how we were both distinct from and superior to animals; that was perhaps especially for an ancient Egyptian context wherein animals were accorded divine status.[49]

---

45. Evdokimov, *The Art of the Icon*, 47–51. A succinct presentation of an iconographic theo-anthropology is available in Ware, "The Human Person as an Icon of the Trinity."

46. Evdokimov, *The Art of the Icon*, 184.

47. See for instance Lossky, *The Vision of God*, 59. Evdokimov, *Orthodoxy*, 25.

48. Evdokimov, *The Art of the Icon*, 185, quoting Gregory of Nazianzus in *Laudem Basilii Magni, PG* 36, 560 A.

49. Lossky, *Image and Likeness of God*, 123.

The Orthodox, embracing christological, pneumatological, anthropological, and iconographical perspectives, turn image and likeness into an entire undergirding theological framework and believe that our God-given task is to become like God. God gave us the capacity, in his image, but we are called to become ever more like him. "The blessedness of [Edenic] Paradise was only the germ whose end is the deified state."[50] We have a capacity that is called, and enabled by Christ and his Holy Spirit, to go further. We are all called to be *Christophers*—those becoming the form of Christ.[51] As we saw earlier with the Nyssan, this process of becoming like God will stretch out into eternity such that after the resurrection our entire being will become ever more beautiful, both like Christ and the triune God.

Capacity to become implies the existence of freedom. If we were fated for salvation no need for freedom would exist. True salvation is perichoresis: sharing, communion, and love, not coercion or force. Thus, when he created God took a risk in giving us free will, but he knew that there is no love without freedom.[52] God yearns that we use our freedom toward him rather than toward sin, death, and selfishness. "As the modern person in his or her nakedness confronts death, the divine choice offered is starker than ever: 'I have set before you life and death, blessings and curses. Choose life so that you and your descendants may live' (Deut 30:19)." This choosing is perpetual in Orthodox theology: "It is in freedom that the person is realized, being freely opened to the grace that presses on every soul in secret, without ever constraining it. 'The Spirit begets no will that resists him. He transforms by divinization only the one who desires it.'" Freedom is difficult and dangerous, hence there is the necessity of discipline, even ascetic discipline, that is normative and expected.[53] Freedom is foundational in Evdokimov's anthropology.

Then we sinned. Sin introduced within us a fracture, injected us with a disease—mortality. Our physical, sensory, and sensual nature, in short our animal nature, was disordered and debased.[54] The fall wounded, bent, and perverted the *imago dei* that we are, but it did not destroy it. If many

---

50. Evdokimov, *Orthodoxy*, 95.

51. Evdokimov, *The Art of the Icon*, 191.

52. Ware so avers in *The Orthodox Way*, 58–59, and in *The Orthodox Church*, 231, "the idea of personal and organic union between God and humans is a constant theme" in John's gospel, Paul's Epistles, and 2 Peter 1:4.

53. Quotes from Evdokimov, *Orthodoxy*, 51 and 80. For more on freedom see also *Orthodoxy*: 48–51, 68–71, 79–84, 274–78, 315–19.

54. Evdokimov, *Orthodoxy*, 98.

Paul Evdokimov (1901–1970)

in the West, post-Augustinian Catholics or Protestants, view human nature as totally depraved, the Orthodox do not. Not only does Scripture attest to the ongoing presence of God's image in sinners,[55] the Orthodox are too aware of the beauty that even non-believers make and do, too aware that non-Christians perceive and sample truth, to finally give up on our original created nature. The Orthodox *never* assert that we can save ourselves. We are sinners. The fall was "a cosmic catastrophe." Our sin introduced darkness into the universe. Victimized by our sin, nature is now resistant, and we corrupt and befoul the very matter we were to nourish, care for, and bring back to God.[56] At funerals the Orthodox pray, "*I bear the marks of my sins* but I am in the image of your unspeakable glory."[57] More, the Jesus Prayer, perhaps the most prayed prayer in Orthodox spirituality, is adamant, "Lord, Jesus Christ, Son of God, have mercy on me a sinner." The effects of the fall are real.

This is all very ontological-metaphysical and less legally courtroomish. And yet God created us to be his vessels, his mirrors, his images. Not only has God clearly not given up on that commitment, it is not possible for us to lose that inherent capacity. Human persons may wrench, pervert, mangle, and corrode the *imago dei*, who we are as created by God, but we cannot stop being what he made us to be. "No evil will ever be able to efface the original mystery of humankind," Evdokimov commented, "for there exists nothing that can annihilate in it the indelible stamp of God." We can even become demonic caricatures of our God-given selves, but this does not finally efface the image.[58] Summarized Evdokimov, "Nothing in nature is impure in itself."[59] Whether or not Evangelicals agree, the christological-incarnational element cannot be missed if we are to understand Evdokimov's aesthetic. We also cannot miss this: the universe is en-graced with capacity for God. Evdokimov wrote, "In Orthodoxy theology *grace is involved in nature from the very beginning*, in the act of creation itself." And more, "Nature is truly 'supernature,' deiform and god-bearing *in its very origins*. In his essence humankind is struck in God's image, and that ontological deiformity explains how grace is 'co-natural' with nature, just as nature is conformed to grace. They are complementary and penetrate

---

55. Gen 9:6; Acts 17:28; 1 Cor 11:7; 2 Cor 3:15–18; Col 3:10; Jas 3:9.
56. Evdokimov, *The Art of the Icon*, 99–103, the latter from whence the quotation.
57. Plekon and Vinogradov, eds., *A Paul Evdokimov Reader*, 199. My emphasis.
58. Evdokimov, *Orthodoxy*, 99.
59. Evdokimov, *The Art of the Icon*, 111.

each other, thus sharing their very existence."[60] Creation broadly and humankind particularly shares in a certain God-given "resemblance" to God's self.[61] It is no surprise then that spirituality pervades every human being. Christians, monotheists, polytheists, pantheists, and atheists all make sense of reality with some appeal to, or denial of, a transcendent presence.

Our Western world view, here in the twenty-first century's advent, makes people, whether theistic or not, live a life characterized by a secular-sacred split. For example, while studying our galaxy is understood to be a matter for secular scientists, prayer is widely understood to be something inherently sacred. Or, more decidedly, there is now the secular world as it is after the fall—merely natural and finite—as contrasted to the world as it was before the fall—God's garden walk, perfect and pristine. By way of enormous contrast, in the theological East "Grace is co-natural, supernaturally natural to nature. Nature possesses an innate need for grace, a gift that spiritualizes it from the start." Evdokimov followed the Roman Catholic patristic scholar Henri de Lubac (1896–1991), "In the West, human nature is taken to comprise intellectual and animal life, spiritual (supernatural) life being added to and even superimposed on the purely human economy." "Grace was understood in the West as extrinsic to the creature; if the supernatural order had to be superimposed, then nature must be essentially foreign to it." Again, in contrast, in the East, "the image of God was there to begin with, and it is the 'natural' humanity that was added."[62] Evdokimov continued, "Grace is co-natural, supernaturally natural to nature. Nature possesses an innate need for grace, a gift that spiritualized from the start." Stated simply, human nature was and is charged with grace.[63]

This engraced dynamic is not flat or uniform throughout nature. There are different degrees within nature and life. Christ, the supreme human-divine person, is the archetype of deity in the flesh. Human beings, again,

---

60. Evdokimov, *Orthodoxy*, 95. My italics.

61. Plekon and Vinogradov, eds., *A Paul Evdokimov Reader*, 196.

62. Such a perspective, again, tends to see matter as problematic. Some patristic theologians echoed the Platonic world and held that woman is inferior to man. The first man, they argued, was androgynous and became male in order to propagate the species because of (or anticipating) the mortality introduced by the fall. Odd and not biblical, this all reflects the larger Platonic, Greek philosophic milieu that struggled to make sense of materiality, change, and even the inherent problems of intercourse and childbearing.

63. Evdokimov, *Orthodoxy*, 96–97. He follows de Lubac's *Surnaturel*, in my second quotation. On page 97, note 21, Evdokimov quotes the Roman Catholic patristic scholar, Daniélou, *Platonisme*, 63.

in their ability for the divine to shine through their material selves are above and beyond the angels.[64] In this regard, different people are drawn to God by different gifts and virtues. Some may hunger for the vision of God while others yearn for his goodness. Some may long for God's justification whereas others ache for his pure love. There is room for each to be and become Christlike. Hence there is room for diversity, "'Where your treasure is, there will your heart be also,' says the Gospel. But what attracts the heart is by no means the same from person to person."[65]

In all of this, the Orthodox tend to emphasize who we are *in creation* more so than who we are because of *the fall*. Again, this is a matter of first commitments, milieu, and method. Eastern Christians are not Western Christians, disconcerting though that may be to some. But what this means for Evdokimov and the Orthodox East is that beauty is a shining of God's grace in a universe created by God. Beauty is not an accident that happens in a fallen, darkened, totally depraved world. Beauty is the ongoing melody of God through creation and creation's continually echoed harmony to God. To reiterate an earlier point, "everything is a *hymn*, a doxology."[66] Evdokimov put it even more poetically, "The psalms describe a sort of sacred dance in which the mountains jump around like rams and the hills like lambs, (Ps 114:4). This is not a simple allegory but the secret aspiration of every living thing, [a] hymn of glory to the Creator." The biblical view of creation is dynamic, energized, living, vivified, vigorous, perpetually created.[67] Maybe we have, but God hasn't stopped caring for his creation. God is too abundant, too exuberant, too self-giving, too much love to ever abandon his creation. Every subtle sunrise is God saying, "I'm still here. I love you. I only have good for you." Every poignant crescent moon is the divine artist whispering, "only love, I only have love for this life." Fittingly, "According to St. Nicholas Cabasilas, God has a 'crazy love' (*manikon eros*) for man."[68] In, through, and still with, creation, Evdokimov believed God not only said, "Let there be light," but "Let there be beauty."[69]

64. Evdokimov, *The Art of the Icon*, 110–11.

65. Evdokimov, *Orthodoxy*, 17.

66. Evdokimov, *The Art of the Icon*, 59. My italics.

67. Ibid., 107. Along more philosophical lines he added that with Greek philosophy and contemporary philosophic materialism, "every static conception of being is its profanation, a regression back toward the state of inanimate dust, toward the brink of nothingness." Ibid.

68. Ibid., 49.

69. Ibid., 8. He is insistent, 108, that God did/does not do these things out of necessity,

An important caveat is due. Creation is a cosmic liturgy, a grand worship service wherein each glorifies God according to its own capacity and shares in God's presence according to its own God designed qualities. However, this is not pantheism. Neither is it a novel version of process theology whereby God is the material or energy or soul of the world. But his beauty is communicated through the world's forms. This is a mystery. "It is," Evdokimov noted, "a sort of theo-materialism whose beauty is manifested through the forms of this world."[70]

Constituted as people are by God for God, our nature itself being engraced and capable of mirroring God's identity, we can see why Evdokimov had a world view that makes room for and celebrates the work, endeavors, goodness, and truth of non-believers. This question can be very difficult for Evangelicals: how do we make sense of the existence of goodness, beauty, and truthfulness we can see evident in non-Christians? As my college students regularly ask me, how come so many non-believers lead lives that are better, more generous, more compassionate, or full of more beauty than the lives of self-professing Christians? Reformed Protestants answer this with common grace; God's grace is present in and through creation, such that goodness, truth, and beauty nevertheless abide in a fallen world. How common grace is present is a more arduous question. Some answer "by God's power"; others aver "by God's mysterious providence"—God guides history such that "He causes His sun to rise on the evil and the good, and sends rain on the righteous and the unrighteous" (Matt 5:45). So then, is God causing unbelievers to live more moral lives, to make more beautiful artwork, than Christian believers or not? Obviously, no theological system is foolproof. For their part, the Orthodox also believe God is sovereign over history, but they place far more weight on human freedom than do the Reformed. All people are made in the image of God. It follows that people make, do, and occasionally are themselves truth, goodness, and beauty. Those qualities do not save non-believers. Only Jesus Christ saves. Or in a more Orthodox category, Jesus Christ alone is resurrection life. But that non-believers are not believers does not denigrate the reality of the goodness, truth, and beauty that they appropriate or celebrate.

We've seen repeatedly that the aforenoted spirit-matter duality is deeply ensconced in Orthodox theology. Where Evdokimov took some personal risk was to extend the notion of porosity, of the iconosophic

---

but only out of freedom.

70. Ibid., 29.

nature of reality, into more abstract categories. Evdokimov argued that God's presence shines through culture. When God told Adam and Eve to "fill the earth and subdue it" (Gen 1:28) he wanted them to "turn it into God's Temple." That cultural mandate noted, all of life is thus meant to be an icon for God's glory. "For God so loved the world that he sent his only begotten Son" (John 3:16) shows that God's redemptive aim was not just the church.[71] For centuries Eastern Orthodox theologians have reasoned that the Orthodox church service, the liturgy, is an icon of God's presence. Evdokimov ratified and celebrated that belief, too.[72] Moreover, Orthodox theologians have practiced *epignosis*, bringing all things in and through the knowledge of God, concerning *symphonia*: the working together of church and state. During the Byzantine era the accepted Orthodox belief was that the emperor and the patriarch are both to serve the glory of God. In their respective realms, the emperor and patriarch, like different pieces of an orchestra, were to play a symphony together. That might work if and when both patriarch and emperor acclaim Christ as Lord. Himself, Evdokimov knew he lived in an increasingly post-Christian world. He lived when Statists—Nazis in western Europe and Communists in eastern Europe—wrought genocide and sought to rule Europe. He was well aware of how the artistic world perverted form and line in the *avant-garde* city of Paris.[73] And yet he still believed possible for the world outside the church to be an icon, for the goodness and beauty of God to shine forth in the world. There was thus, with Evdokimov, the possibility of synergy between culture creation and holiness.[74]

71. Ibid., 53–54.

72. For example, *Orthodoxy*, 8–12, 19–27, 114–16, 214–31, 245–77.

73. His critique hereon was harsh. The modern mentality presented "false transcendencies" that were "metaphysical miscarriages." "Every artist has the terrible liberty of representing the world in the image of his own devastated soul, and this tendency by no means excludes even the vision of a gigantic latrine in which dismembered monsters squirm around." Poetry and music, both, also collapse in this mess. "In the past things questioned the artist." "The modern artist, however, questions his own soul, then looks at the world and applies his disintegrating vision to things. He thus becomes an accomplice to the ancient rebellion which tries to get free from every meaning, from every preexisting and normative principle." It is a return to the original chaos. It is all very nihilistic, and rooted in a nihilistic world view. "It is like Francisco Goya's painting of Saturn devouring man's substance." "The way is dark, suffocating, and its outcome is very uncertain." "It is probably from this occult point of view that demons must see the world, a point of view emptied of the inaccessible image of God." *The Art of the Icon*, 78–79.

74. My own students find it difficult time to see or accept that non-believers, when they serve or heal or deliver from evil, can do the work of the kingdom. None of that

For instance, it is not hard to recognize such a synergy when cultural and governmental leaders openly and transparently do things for the sake of righteousness. "In the past," Evdokimov clarified, "holy princes were canonized not for their personal holiness but for their faithfulness to the charisms of royal power exercised in the service of Christian people." But it is harder to discern this synergy when it is not immediately Christian or churchly, or when action and enterprise are performed in the non-Christian public square. Nevertheless, he said that the world has its "own charisms." The world has gifts, endeavorings, and workmanship that also glorify God and serve as touch points for the kingdom of God. Evdokimov cast it thus,

> The scientist, the thinker, the artist, the social reformer etc. can find the charisms of the Royal Priesthood, and each one in his own area can become a "priest," can make his research a priestly work, a sacrament transforming every form of culture into a theophanic meeting place. This work thus becomes a way to sing God's name through science, thought, social action (the sacrament of the brother) and art. In its own way, culture joins the liturgy; it becomes a doxology, and we hear the "cosmic liturgy."[75]

Not every good deed is doxological. It is not the case that every piece of art brings praise to God. Many states and politicians fail to change anything, much less culture or the world.[76] But the church has the possibility of helping enflame culture toward theophanic (God-manifesting, God-presenting) ends. Evdokimov did not offer evaluative criteria for assessing said cultural work, but he did believe it possible for the world to be a venue for God's shining. He wrote,

> The paradox of the Christian faith is that it stimulates creativity in the world but, at its final stage when its eschatological dimension comes into play, the Christian faith shatters the world and makes history overflow its boundaries. At this point, it is not the way that is impossible but the impossible that is the way. . . . 'Divine power can invent . . . a way that is impossible.' That impossible way is the fiery eruption of the 'totally other' coming from the depths of the world itself. All forms of culture must stretch out toward this

---

saves their souls, but it does harmonize with what God wants for his creation. Such activities are how the *imago dei* shines forth.

75. Evdokimov, *The Art of the Icon*, 69. On "priest" and "cosmic liturgy" he quoted Gregory of Nyssa, *PG* 44, 128 B.

76. Evdokimov, *The Art of the Icon*, 68–69.

> limit which is at the border between two ages.... The world in the Church is the 'burning bush' in the very heart of existence.[77]

The church should celebrate when the world works toward godly ends. True, the church cannot lose its saltiness, it cannot adapt to the world's mentality. The church must remember that its calling is not to become like the world.[78] Nevertheless, Evdokimov opens up possibilities for thinking theologically both about how the world is and does beautiful things, even when not motivated by Christian doctrine or commitments. The eschatological vision of the Revelation sees all the nations walking into the new Jerusalem carrying their respective glory, honor, and genius as gifts to God. Musicians, artists, scientists, scholars, and indeed all people have their cultural gifts to contribute to God's praise. "If every person is created in the image of God and is a living icon, *earthly culture is the icon of the Kingdom of Heaven.*"[79] Evdokimov's position thus creates tensions that are not easily navigated. For some that kind of vision made him controversial, for others his vision—one rooted in aesthetics rather than ethics[80]—opens up possibilities for further development.

WRAP-UP

Manifesting a sweeping vision, Evdokimov also believed that time and space themselves, because Christ entered the former and became the latter, even though he created them both, have iconosophic possibilities. Jesus came to redeem everything, not just people. The beauty of God shines preeminently through Jesus Christ, and those made in his image—human beings. But culture, time, and space are all receptacles for the beauty, the glory, of God.[81] Many people, when they think of beauty, understandably think of the fine

---

77. Ibid., 69. He was quoting the Nyssan from *PG* 44, 128 B.

78. Ibid., 70.

79. Ibid., 70–72. Quotation from 71. Original italics.

80. That is, he seeks to find the beauty in cultural forms rather than the goodness in cultural forms. Beauty can be present even when goodness is not. He is aware that there is a distinct difference between the "old man" and the "new man," between life in the church and life in the world, between ethics and aesthetics. Cf. Evdokimov, *The Art of the Icon*, 53, *Orthodoxy* 320. We ought not press Evdokimov too hard hereon, after all his perspective is thoroughly integrated within an entire theological tradition, but he is able to see virtue in cultures even when those cultures are not themselves entirely virtuous.

81. On time and space see *The Art of the Icon*, chapters 10 and 11, "Sacred Time" and "Sacred Space"; and, *Orthodoxy* 207–21, 309–39.

arts and/or nature. Evdokimov instructs us that other categories, too, can be the location for beauty: human nature, holiness, and culture. His is a sweeping vision that teaches us to look for beauty in places we might not otherwise consider.

WHAT EVDOKIMOV TEACHES US TO SEE:

- because it is iconographic, all of life mirrors God
- Christ Jesus is God's chief icon
- the universe was created following the pattern of the incarnation
- icons express theology
- reading icons requires faith
- Christian artists must exemplify excellence
- the incarnation frees believers to make art
- human beings were created with freedom to become beautiful like Christ Jesus
- even after sin, human beings cannot stop being the image of God
- physical nature and human nature were both created to receive grace
- creation is a cosmic liturgy
- God's glory can shine through culture
- non-believers can shine forth God's glory

11

Hans Urs von Balthasar (1905–1988)
Jesus Christ: The Supreme Source of All Beauty

JUST WHAT IS SALVATION? A divine pardon of our shameful iniquities? Is having a clean slate in the eyes of God what this is all about? Should salvation be reduced to the fact that when we die we go to heaven? Or, is it possible the Scriptures suggest that God has more in store for his creation than a culminating fiery destruction (2 Pet. 3:10)[1] before it is all taken up to God's judgment seat? Truly, we Western Christians frequently cheat ourselves when we think about, and live toward, salvation. Not only do the Scriptures themselves look for a final full-fledged flourishing of the earth, Jesus the man was resurrected—bodily—from the dead. As we theologically frame beauty it is critical to remember that God became a man, and that God raised that man up in his body; both of those shout something important to us about God's designs for his physical creation: he intends to make it new. Not brand new; not so new that it is something completely different from what it is now; yourself still will be yourself, but a self made new! That newness will, if Jesus' resurrection is any indicator, involve beauty.

Beauty is an eternally constituent attribute of God's own self. When God first spoke creation into existence he plunged beauty into its very atomic structure. Beauty permeates God's good works, including the expanse of the universe. God's plans for the eternal salvation of it all involve

---

[1]. That phrase in Peter can rightly be interpreted as cleansing and sanctifying, not destroying, fire.

beauty. Beauty is God's grace extended toward sinners like you and me. If all of that is true then beauty should permeate—not stand awkwardly at the fringes of—theological construction. It is a new day, and thank God there are theologians realizing that.[2] The great theo-aesthetic giant is Hans urs Von Balthasar. A Jesuit scholar, Balthasar was arguably the first theologian to do theology from an explicitly aesthetic angle. Rather than merely incorporating beauty along the way, Balthasar believed that beauty, and with it aesthetics, is *the* way to construe the Christian understanding of reality. Before we consider his theological framing some brief biography is important.

Born into a Swiss patrician family in Lucerne, Balthasar was as a boy brilliant and eager to learn. In a letter to a high school friend he once remarked, "At that time you were frightfully industrious, while I was spending all my time on music and Danté and standing on my bed in the dormitory at night trying to get enough light to read *Faust*." And yet, he was meek despite having a substantial intellect. Peter Henrici, Balthasar's cousin, once wrote about Hans, "For all his greatness and towering knowledge, he was able to remain 'uncomplicated,' humble, indeed childlike."[3] Standing tall in height above most his peers and students, Balthasar nevertheless did not let his stature or amazing intellect become off-putting to those in his company. Balthasar recognized he was endowed with capacities that were simply given to him and he accepted them as just that, gifts. One of his gifts was linguistic proficiency. He grew up speaking German, French, and English. He loved literature and earned a doctorate therein in 1928. His *summa cum laude* dissertation at university in Zurich was entitled "The History of the Eschatological Problem in Modern German Literature." For fun, throughout his life, he read plays. He was so touched by poetry that in his own probing theology he interpreted and analyzed great poets: Danté, Goethe, Claudel, Péguy. While a student chaplain in Basel, Balthasar edited and translated a series on European culture.

For as much as he loved language and literature he was also a gifted musician. Indeed, during his early years it was unclear whether he would choose to study music or literature, though he finally chose the latter.

---

2. This is a burgeoning field of thought. Standouts here on include: Jeremy Begbie, *Theology, Music and Time*; *Beholding the Glory: Incarnation through the Arts*; *Resounding Truth: Christian Wisdom in the World of Music*; Frank Burch Brown, *Good Taste, Bad: Aesthetics in Religious Life*; William Dyrness, *Visual Faith: Art, Theology, and Worship in Dialogue*; David Bentley Hart, *The Beauty of the Infinite: The Aesthetics of Christian Truth*; Richard Viladesau, *Theological Aesthetics: God in Imagination, Beauty, and Art*.

3. Henrici, "A Sketch of His Life." Paragraph's first quote from 9.

Hans Urs von Balthasar (1905–1988)

Proficient at piano playing, as a boy he had perfect pitch and a musical memory to go with it. He loved classical music: Mozart, Schubert, Tschaikovsky, Mahler, orchestral masses, and operas. He cherished Mozart so deeply that Balthasar memorized every musical score Mozart ever wrote. Once, later in life, Balthasar gave away his record player, remarking that he didn't need it anymore since the music played clearly in his mind.

Balthasar also was characterized by deep faith. Although three of his grandparents were Protestants, he was raised in a Roman Catholic family. As a young boy he loved attending the mass, often on his own, where he was able to soak in the quiet and revel in the "overwhelming splendor." His faith was "simple and straightforward," "childlike in the best sense." Indeed, even though there were many philosophical currents opposed to Christianity during his education, he left university with an "undoubting faith." Looking back on his matter-of-fact faith and his desire to entirely serve God we ourselves can see why it made sense that Balthasar gave his life to priestly service, but his specific calling, one that claimed him during a spiritual retreat with other students, thereon hit him "like lightning from a cloudless sky." Beneath a tree in the Black Forest outside of Basel, the voice told him, "You have nothing to chose, you have been called. You will not serve, you will be taken into service. You have no plans to make, you are just a little stone in a mosaic which has long been ready." He became a priest-novitiate in November 1929 (age 24) and was ordained to the Jesuit priesthood in 1936.[4]

Eventually, after years of mentoring students and scholarly publishing, Balthasar toured as a guest speaker on philosophy and theology, even though he himself had not earned a doctorate in those disciplines, at various universities across Europe. Later in life he was a friend to, and theological interlocutor with, the Protestant theologian Karl Barth. Even though they shared much in common by way of theology—both having developed towering Christocentric theologies—and love of Mozart, the two sharply disagreed on the doctrine of the analogy of being (*analogia entis*, mentioned later below). More influential perhaps even than Barth was Adrienne von Speyr, a medical doctor and friend of Balthasar's in Basel. Speyr was a Protestant woman who converted to Catholicism and made Balthasar her confessor; so close was their relationship that it was a cause of gossip for years. A mystic, Speyr variously prayed for many who received healings, was the locus for multiple instances of stigmatization (bleeding from

---

4. Henrici, "A Sketch," 10, 13.

the hands and feet in a mirroring of Jesus' own wounds), and had visions upon visions. It was the latter especially which had a dramatic effect upon Balthasar's own eschatology.[5] Famously, or infamously, Speyr believed that Christ's atoning work was so great and so dramatic that one day in eternity hell itself would be emptied.[6]

Because he was at work in an academic trajectory known today as the Catholic *Résourcement* movement, Balthasar remains a somewhat controversial figure. We must, therefore, see him in his context. From 1869–1870 the Catholic Church held Vatican I, an ecumenical Council that was trying to deal with the then-erupting problems of modernism (rationalism, liberalism, and the rise of the higher critical method of studying the Bible) and Europe's own shifting landscape (the separation of church and state together with the rise of democratic forms of government). In a very defensive posture to the dramatic changes underway in the nineteenth century, Vatican I saw the Catholic Church declare the doctrine of papal infallibility: the assertion that the pope cannot fail when he teaches on Christian life and faith. Vatican I made it clear that the Catholic Church felt "under siege."[7] Well into the mid-twentieth century the Catholic Church was on the defensive against contra-Christian impulses. For his part, Balthasar was avowedly and proudly Catholic. He loved the patristic fathers (e.g., Augustine and Pseudo-Dionysius) and even respected (though he found dry) the Scholastics (e.g., Thomas Aquinas), but he worked with those ancient sources in a way that built bridges to, rather than openly rejected, contemporary philosophy.[8] But for more traditional and fundamentalistically minded twentieth century Catholics—when professors, theologians,

---

5. Von Balthasar once wrote about von Speyr, "I not only made some of the most difficult decisions of my life—including leaving the Jesuit Order—following her advice, but I also strove to bring my way of looking at Christian revelation into conformity with hers." And, "On the whole I received far more from her, theologically, than she from me, though, of course, the exact proportion can never be calculated." Von Balthasar later again became a Jesuit. Quoted in Wigley, *Balthasar's Trilogy*, 21.

6. Henrici, "A Sketch," 18–19, 31–33.

7. Rausch, *Catholicism at the Dawn of the Third Millennium*, 1.

8. Theologically, von Balthasar's contemporary influences were Erich Przywara, Jean Daniélou, and Henri de Lubac. Von Balthasar's historic influences are many and include: Irenaeus, Origen, Gregory of Nyssa, Pseudo-Dionysius, Augustine, Maximus the Confessor, Bonaventure, and Danté. De Lubac summarized von Balthasar's connection to the fathers, "He was nurtured by these great men and he follows in their footsteps, without servility and without falsification, because he has fully assimilated their substance." "Witness of Christ in the Church: Hans Urs von Balthasar," in *His Life and Work*, 286.

and scholars began to seek dialogue or even harmony rather than outright battle with contemporary philosophic constructs—suspicions ran rampant. Nevertheless, Balthasar was no liberal seeking to appease or accommodate liberal commitments. Rather, he was, de Lubac wrote, "strikingly original," neither "old or modern," but perhaps best summarized as "essentially trinitarian."[9] It was only during the last two decades of his life that he was finally viewed as a Catholic intellectual hero by the Vatican. In fact, Pope John Paul II decided to make him a cardinal just two days before Balthasar unexpectedly died on June 26, 1988.

Balthasar wrote extensively for most of fifty-seven years. He is most renown for his massive trilogy comprised of *The Glory of the Lord: A Theological Aesthetics*,[10] *Theo-Drama*,[11] and *Theo-Logic*.[12] Together those three series took him almost thirty years and represent fifteen volumes, amassing some 10,000 pages. Those notwithstanding, his publishing activities also include having overseen more than forty student dissertations on his own theology, and having variously written seventy other separate books, more than 500 articles and chapters contributed to edited books, nearly 100 translations of other scholars' works, and sixty volumes of the words and works of Adrienne von Speyr.[13] Prolific is a word that could not be more fittingly used than when employed regarding Balthasar. And yet, it is not just that he wrote so voluminously as he did write so insightfully and beautifully. Louis Dupré commented on Balthasar's frequently meandering and consistently imaginative style saying he "writes with the flair of an artist, a very learned one, but an artist nevertheless. In his essays he practices what his theory preaches. They are brilliant exercises in theological aesthetics."[14] Again, if Balthasar was enormously gifted at the intellectual level, he knew equally how to state his ideas in beautiful prose, as our own survey below

---

9. Ibid., 274–75.

10. First published in German as *Herrlichkeit: Eine theologische Aesthetik* by Johannes Verlag (Einsiedeln, 1961, 1967). English publication by T & T Clark (San Francisco, 1982–1991), 2nd edition, Ignatius Press, 2009. Primarily, we will follow Balthasar's aesthetic in volume I of *The Glory of the Lord*.

11. First published in German as *Theodramatik* by Johannes Verlag (Einsiedeln, 1980). English publication translated by Graham Harrison (San Francisco: Ignatius, 1988–1998).

12. First published in German as *Theologik* by Johannes Verlag (Einsiedeln, 1985). English publication translated by Adrian J. Walker (San Francisco: Ignatius, 2000–2005).

13. Henrici, "A Sketch," 31.

14. Dupré, "Balthasar's Theological Aesthetic," 206.

will seek to make evident. A heart passionate for Christ worked in concert with the melodius intellectual gifts that God had given him. Those led Henri de Lubac to call Balthasar "the most learned man in Europe" and "the most cultivated of his time."[15]

BALTHASAR'S CHRISTOCENTRIC FILTER

Like his Protestant friend Karl Barth, Balthasar believed it right and fitting to consistently run his theology through a christological filter (though Balthasar believed he was being more inclusive of the whole sweep of salvation history than was Barth).[16] This included his reflections on beauty.[17] True, Balthasar knew there were several different kinds of beauty: that found in the natural world; sublime beauty which is "overwhelming, enrapturing, and even crushing"; the beauty of eros, passionate love; the grace and restfulness of feminine beauty; the awesome experience of mythical beauty; the human-produced beauty found in art; and even "the beauty of divine revelation," to name a few. And yet, for Balthasar, *Christ Jesus surpasses all other forms of beauty*. Indeed, Jesus of Nazareth is the epitome of beauty such that all previously existing forms of beauty, Balthasar summarized, existed in a "relative hiddenness."[18] Jesus' beauty both enables and towers above all other beauty.

---

15. De Lubac, "A Witness of Christ in the Church," 272.

16. Balthasar, *Seeing the Form*, 54. Cf. Nichols, *A Key to Balthasar*, 20, where for Balthasar Jesus is the center of revelation's structure, but not its exclusive content. Moreover, Balthasar and Barth held immense mutual respect even though their theological arguments could run deep. At one time Barth even invited Balthasar to join the faculty at Basel. Balthasar particularly admired Barth for having nuanced along more biblical-christological lines John Calvin's doctrine of election. Cf. Henrici, "A Sketch of His Life," 18.

17. Prior to Balthasar's own constructions Barth had argued that Jesus' crucifixion must be seen as a lens for understanding beauty. Dupré, "Balthasar's Theological Aesthetic," 187.

18. Balthasar's listing in *Seeing the Form*, 312–13. Last quoted phrase from 310. Balthasar's theological commitments are scattered throughout his multivolume corpus. Mostly, I will follow him herein from what is the first bookend for our study, volume 1 of *The Glory of the Lord, Seeing the Form*, because his aesthetic ideas are developed at length therein. Indeed, we can only barely scratch the surface of his immense portrayal from volume 1! Oliver Davies remarks that many of Balthasar's decisive "guideline passages" are indeed found in *Seeing the Form*. Davies, "The Theological Aesthetics," in *The Cambridge Companion to Hans Urs von Balthasar*, 131. Balthasar's *Theo-Drama: Theological Dramatic Theory*, vol. V, *The Last Act*, the other bookend, will also be noted and

Hans Urs von Balthasar (1905-1988)

Now, before we extrapolate Balthasar's christocentric theo-aesthetic, we should know that he believed he was equipped to write a theology of beauty particularly because of his Roman Catholic faith. Protestants, Balthasar believed, first had traditionally focused too much on Scripture as God's revelation; well, that is when Protestants weren't busy demythologizing the Bible.[19] A Protestant reader should not take his criticism to mean Balthasar in any way depreciated the role or authority of the Bible; indeed, he was a voracious student of the Scriptures. Rather, he believed the Bible was inspired and given by God especially *to get us to Christ Jesus*: the form of God in the flesh. And secondly, to continue Balthasar's critique of Protestant theologians on beauty, the latter too consistently bent Christianity into an inward, subjective, private, and existential dynamic. Indeed, for Balthasar, Christianity inculcates and incorporates those things but Christianity is those things because it is first an objective reality. If I may play the devil's Catholic's advocate for a moment, Balthasar would say Christianity is *not* first true because subjectively "I" can experience it. Rather, Christianity is foundationally true because Christ objectively exists, and that is the case whether I or you or anyone experience him. Emphatically, for Balthasar, Christ is the perfect form of beauty. And this form exists objectively, independently of whether anyone or anything in creation recognizes him.[20] Again, Balthasar had close family relatives who were Protestants, even

---

cited because that volume, with its explorations of Christology, Trinitarian theology, and eschatology culminate Balthasar's theology.

19. Rudolph Bultmann, who presents a "real dead-end for Protestantism" (51) was a special target of Balthasar's. Cf. *Seeing the Form*, 44, 51, 55, 306, 308, 452, 474, 519, 602, 648.

20. Though I nowhere found him extrapolating it exactly thus, in my study of Balthasar I consistently perceived refractions of the ancient sacramental maxim at work, *ex opere operato* (from the work worked). With this maxim, at the Council of Trent (1545–1563), the Roman Catholics ratified that Christ is present in the sacraments by virtue of the sovereignty of God. In Christ, God had said he would be present ("this is my flesh," "this is my blood") therefore—based on God's word and promise—he is present. Earlier Augustine, against the ancient Donatist (fourth-fifth centuries) alternate position of *ex opere operantis* (by the work of the worker), maintained that the sacrament of grace, and its efficacy toward the recipients, was not dependent upon either the purity of the server or receiver, or the disposition of faith of the recipient, though the latter is today deemed beneficial lest the host be received with ignorance and/or ingratitude so that one thereby incurs God's judgment (1 Cor 11:29-30). Sixteenth century and subsequent Protestant developments whereby faith is necessary in the Christian life and sacraments is also initially ruled out by Balthasar's theological formulation—God exists and is true whether we acknowledge him or not—though as will be shown Balthasar makes faith very important in the Christian aesthetic experience.

Protestant ministers, so he saw Protestantism as short-sighted, not heretical. But he was proud of his Catholic faith, among many reasons, because he believed its focus on Christ's incarnation availed an interpretive filter constantly ignored by Protestantism. To drive home what he believed to be the privileged position of Catholicism on aesthetics, Balthasar quoted the Protestant theologian Gerhard Nebel (1903–1974): "Whoever loves beauty will ... freeze in the barns of the Reformation and go over to Rome."[21] Soon thereafter Balthasar likewise criticized the Protestant turn toward subjectivity and wrote, "If beauty is conceived of transcendentally, then its definition must be derived from God himself. Furthermore, what we know to be most proper to God—his self-revelation in history and in the incarnation—must now become for us the very apex and archetype of beauty in the world, *whether men see it or not.*"[22] So, again, Christ is the objective form of beauty for Balthasar. Let us unpack some of what that meant for him.

Nearly every sentence of Balthasar's is rich and layered, so in summarizing him it is easy to find oneself in elaborate snarls, the unraveling of which seems to risk undue damage to his overall thought. One can be, as others wrote, perplexed by Balthasar's *sui generis* complexity.[23] Obviously one cannot say everything about his theology. But should one play it safe and say nothing? Risking damage for the sake of some understanding, if we were to take a satellite picture of his theo-aesthetic we would see that Jesus Christ is a *concrete whole*. What this meant for Balthasar is that when we consider the beauty of Christ, and beauty's existence in and through Christ, we cannot reduce beauty to either his divinity or his humanity. On the latter front we cannot say that Jesus of Nazareth was just a man who lived in history,[24] or that Jesus Christ's humanity was only incidental to his being and our salvation. He *was* his humanity. He accomplished what he did precisely as Jesus of Nazareth. Of course this means he was, like us, *adamah*—of the dust—a man who suffered shame and physical pain, learned obedience, grew in wisdom and patience and character, slogged through the mud, ate bread and laughed, was hated by his enemies and forsaken by his family and friends, and was loved to the end by his mother. In this

---

21. Balthasar, *Seeing the Form*, 67, quoting Nebel's *The Event of the Beautiful*, 188.

22. Ibid., 68.

23. David Moss and Edward T. Oakes, "Introduction," in *The Cambridge Companion to Hans Urs von Balthasar*, 1. They describe Balthasar's theology as odd because it is both "intensely traditional" and "startlingly idiosyncratic," 6–7.

24. Balthasar, *Seeing the Form*, 519–20. Balthasar held disdain for the methods of the quest for the historical Jesus scholars and other reductionists like them.

regard Jesus was an ordinary man (this will be important for understanding Balthasar's theo-aesthetic anthropology below). But as Jesus this also means variously that the incarnate Word of God was a Jew, a fiery prophet who stood in continuity with a long line of fiery prophets, a man who like a good second-temple Jew attended synagogue services, studied and memorized the law, and sought to glorify God with his life. In short, Jesus was a Jew who together loved and critiqued the Judaism of his day.[25] And then on the other hand, of course, our Lord was divine. But it was not "merely the divine Logos" who was the "centre and norm of all being and history."[26] He was the eternal Word of God become incarnate. As such he was infinity become finite, eternity become temporal, the boundless one who voluntarily became limited, the all-powerful one who became willingly weak for our sake. Regarding the latter two, finitude and weakness, for the development of Balthasar's whole theology, not only his theo-aesthetics, Balthasar places a huge emphasis upon Jesus' *kenosis* (emptying; Phil 2:7). Let's explore this further.

Christ Jesus, Balthasar reasoned, can only be rightly understood as the Son of the Father. Obviously this presupposes the doctrine of the Trinity. Balthasar once put it succinctly, "The Son is the *revelation of the Trinity*."[27] Truly, we cannot much broach Balthasar's Trinitarian constructions but it is important for his aesthetic framing to note that for him God, in his immanent self (as God is to God's self), is a humble God. The Father always gives and defers to the Son. The Son reciprocates and lives to love and glorify the Father. The Spirit, for Balthasar, exists as the freely extended overflow of the love between the Father and Son, an overflow that never seeks his own but the glory of the others.[28] The Godhead is a total abandonment to erotic[29] and self-giving love. But this self-giving—like all self-giving—in-

---

25. Balthasar argued that Christ's form is "inseparable from the Old Testament," but superior to it. *Seeing the Form*, 484–5, 603, 624–5. Or, the Old Testament is like the five lines of a musical staff and Christ's unique melody plays across those lines. *Seeing the Form*, 625.

26. Healy and Schindler, "For the Life of the World," in *The Cambridge Companion to Hans Urs von Balthasar*, 53.

27. Balthasar, *The Last Act*, 121. Original italics. He regularly repeats this theme in his theology. Cf. *The Last Act*, 384.

28. Balthasar was thus an ardent proponent of the ancient Western (Catholic) Trinitarian position known as *filioque* (Latin, and the Son): the Spirit is sent, from eternity, by both the Father and the Son.

29. Erotic, as we saw with Nyssa, means that the self is involved in and enjoys the loving.

volves vulnerability and humility. True love is not true if it is forced, not even for God. True love is true only when freely offered and freely received; both of those require vulnerability and humility. Hence, it follows from God's own eternal being that that same vulnerability and humility were then made manifest in the kenotic life of the Word incarnate. Jesus' own humility, motivated by love, characterized his entire life. Indeed, the entire complex of the Christ-event is a kenotic one, a cruciform one: incarnation, lowly birth origins, rejection, scourging, mocking, crucifixion.[30] Given the profound humility of God's nature, we don't have to struggle to understand Balthasar's logic that the cross represents the "revelation of the innermost being of God."[31] But this was not merely a pragmatic humility, as though he humbled himself only for the purpose of our salvation; as though God were not in his nature truly humble, but that he just lowered himself to save us from the enemy, sin, and death. And yet it also was not a necessary humility, as though God was forced by his own nature to lower himself and love us. Rather, mirroring God's own eternal nature, the Word's humility was one freely given. Balthasar repeats the theme of freedom over and over throughout his corpus and he particularly emphasizes the role of freedom in his aesthetic construction.[32] It was beautiful that Jesus freely surrendered himself to both the Father's plan and the Spirit's abiding guidance. It was beautiful that the second person of the Trinity limited himself in kenotic abasement for his creation and humanity.[33] And it was beautiful that the Word of God took on flesh in order to become one with the universe. (Indeed, God is so free that he can do what he wills to do with his own nature!)[34] But the fact that the Word did all of those humble things was both rooted in and stemmed from his preincarnate nature and being as

---

30. For Balthasar, Jesus' incarnation is his kenosis is his crucifixion. The whole complex of the Christ event involves lowliness, rejection, humility, and suffering. *Seeing the Form*, 193, 197, 462–65; *The Last Act*, 118–131, 327–28.

31. Balthasar, *The Last Act*, 260, quoting von Speyr, *Johannes*, vol. 3, *The Farewell Discourse*, 283 and citing John 16:25, "an hour is coming when I will speak no more to you in figurative language, but will tell you plainly of the Father." Balthasar therein teaches that the Son's full revelation of the Father's identity is also cruciform. See also *The Last Act*, 478.

32. Cf. Nichols, *A Key to Balthasar*, 49–88.

33. This abasement included the forsaking of the Word's divine foreknowledge. Cf. Balthasar, *The Last Act*, 127, 258.

34. Wigley, *Balthasar's Trilogy*, 91, following Balthasar, *Theo-Drama*, vol. II, *Dramatis Personae*, 256.

Hans Urs von Balthasar (1905–1988)

God eternal, the God of eternally self-giving, self-sacrificing, and humble love.[35] All of that then, clearly, is not ordinary!

We have, with Balthasar, a paradoxical aesthetic with this concrete Jesus: he was both extraordinary God and ordinary man. Jesus was, to echo the theme, the perfect form of beauty. He was a *something more* that shined through the ordinary. Balthasar variously described Jesus' form as the "original of beauty,"[36] the "beautiful pearl to trade everything for,"[37] the form which "conditions all other experiences, both before and after it,"[38] and the "figure that both concludes and completes the universe."[39] One of his favorite ways to describe the incarnate Word was to call him the "primal form."[40] This meant that the Word is not only the first form, as God the Father's first (though eternal) or preeminent idea, but the Father's original and perfect communication. "The Incarnation," penned Balthasar, "uses created Being at a new depth as a language and a means of expression for the divine Being and essence." Jesus is "the supreme object," who takes us through himself to the Father, yet without being God the Father.[41] Ever directed to the Father, Jesus "explains the Father" (John 1:18) as the "exegesis of the Father"—Balthasar was fond of that phrase.[42] Without question, Jesus Christ, God made flesh, is the cardinal aesthetic form for Balthasar. And yet, Christ is also the source, the cause of being, for all other forms of being. "All things came into being by Him, and apart from Him nothing came into being that has come into being" (John 1:3). So there was *the*

---

35. Rowan Williams shows that for Balthasar all of reality is kenotic. God's kenotic nature, a nature that is inextricably but freely gathered in relationship, is the basis for creation's own existence and nature. All of creation is moving toward, Williams said about Balthasar, "being seen, being understood and delighted in; it has an inherent mystery, an inexhaustible quality, but not a protected hinterland of individual, unrelated essential being. Put briefly, reality is kenotic and 'ek-static', moving out of itself at every level and in every mode." "Balthasar and Trinity," in *The Cambridge Companion to Hans Urs von Balthasar*, 41. Williams, 38, clarifies that Balthasar was following the Russian theologian Sergei Bulgakov on the kenotic natures of the Trinity, Christ, and creation.

36. Balthasar, *Seeing the Form*, 20.

37. Ibid., 26, 33.

38. Ibid., 314.

39. Ibid., 465–66.

40. Ibid., 25, 28, 29, 36, 148–49, 165, 176, 197, 227, 228, 297, 376, 422.

41. Ibid., 28–29.

42. Ibid., 29, 32, 150, 167, 315, 595.

form—the Super form, as one Balthasarian scholar put it[43]—and then there are all other forms. Still again, let's dig deeper.

Jesus was a concrete self. As was implied above, Balthasar regularly processed this kind of thinking through the aesthetic category of *form*. For Balthasar beauty is not an invisible or disembodied Platonic ideal ultimately existing prior to or behind the thing, but neither is beauty only the thing itself. Rather, beauty, herself transcendent, shines in and through and as the form of the thing. Aidan Nichols quoted G. K. Chesterton to help convey Balthasar's thought hereon: "Every artist knows that the form is not superficial but fundamental; that the form is the foundation. Every sculptor knows that the form of the statue is not the outside of the statue, but rather the inside of the statue; even in the sense of the inside of the sculptor. Every poet knows that the sonnet-form is not only the form of the poem, but the poem." For Balthasar, if we remove the form there is no beauty. Beauty radiates only because of the form. Or once more Nichols, "The perceptible form of an object is the expression, under particular conditions, of its metaphysical form—its essence or nature."[44] Perhaps Davies brings further clarity hereon when he says, "Form is always material and particular." Form both reveals and conceals "depths that only emerge gradually into the field of understanding and vision."[45] For Balthasar form is "the real presence of the depths, of the whole reality, and it is a real pointing beyond itself to those depths."[46] Form is thus a quality that is truly there—it is a metaphysical something that is woven into the fabric of Being and of a being or thing—but form is not always easily discerned. We might summarize Balthasar's dynamic here, form is a depth that reveals still more depth, yet without exhausting that mysterious depth.[47] Through form, beauty together with goodness and truth, shines through existence and existences and creatures and objects as an expression of the catholicity (fullness) of the Christ-created universe. This is all a gift, an expression of love, an expression of the God who is love and who wants to be loved.

---

43. Nichols, *A Key to Balthasar*, 19.

44. Ibid., 16 and 17. The first quotation is from Chesterton's *St. Thomas Aquinas*, 188–89.

45. Quotes from Davies, "The Theological Aesthetics," 134 and 135.

46. Balthasar, *Seeing the Form*, 116.

47. In *The Last Act*, 495, following von Speyr's *Epheser* [*Letter to the Ephesians*], 131–32, Balthasar wrote, "What is revealed is the *mystery* that does not cease to be a mystery on account of being dispensed." Italics original.

Hans Urs von Balthasar (1905–1988)

Put still differently, Balthasar's emphasis on form, and beauty's appearance through form, embeds beauty within reality. Earlier we saw that Immanuel Kant, and those following him, had definitively moved beauty to the sidelines. Goodness and truth existed in the universe and were worthy of regular human consideration, but beauty, since it is *only our experience* of a subject (person, art piece, view of nature, and the like) was relegated to a psychological arena divorced from "true" reality or "real" reality. After Kant the nineteenth-century Romantics tried to rescue beauty, but having no sure metaphysical anchor they ended up seeing beauty as a mere product of our minds.[48] Methodologically, Balthasar first anchored beauty in the objective form of Christ, himself a being simultaneously finite and infinite. Second, Balthasar located beauty *as the first* of the three transcendentals (with truth and goodness) rather than the third. He once put his colossal challenge in rhapsodic form,

> Beauty is the word that shall be our first. Beauty is the last thing which the thinking intellect dares to approach, since only it dances as an uncontained splendour around the double constellation of the true and the good and their inseparable relation to one another. Beauty is the disinterested one, without which the ancient world refused to understand itself, a word which both imperceptibly and yet unmistakably has bid farewell to our new world, a world of interests, leaving it to its own avarice and sadness. No longer loved or fostered by religion, beauty is lifted from its face as a mask, and its absence exposes features on that face which threaten to become incomprehensible to man. We no longer dare to believe in beauty and we make of it a mere appearance in order the more easily to dispose of it.[49]

Methodologically, then, Balthasar prominently placed beauty back into the mix of Being and existence (beauty must be very thankful for its rightful restoration by Balthasar!). This was an enormous undertaking on both theological and philosophical lines.

Let's probe still deeper into Christ the form. Jesus was the primal form not only because of his being by nature *theos-aner*, the God-man, but because of his relationship to the Father; again, Trinitarian constructs are foundational here. Jesus did what he did and was who he was chiefly because he was uniquely attuned to the Father. The German words Balthasar

---

48. Nichols, *A Key to Balthasar*, 23.
49. Balthasar, *Seeing the Form*, 18.

repeatedly uses regarding Jesus' focus and gaze upon the Father are *stimmen*—to tune, to give the correct pitch to—and *stimmung*—disposition, attunement.[50] Jesus was attuned to his existence: the tune he was attuned to hear was suffering. He came to suffer for we his people and the entire creation.[51] Yet, Jesus' *stimmung* was not something he gave himself to do. The Father gave him this work, this mission. Jesus' faithful obedience was a perfect *stimmen* to the Father's plan of redemption. The giving of the Father was reciprocated by the receiving of the Son and both the giving and the receiving shaped Jesus of Nazareth.[52] This dynamic of being called to attunement and attuning oneself will be important for Balthasar's theo-aesthetic anthropological formulations (more below), but here we must realize that the notions of attunement and attention are important aesthetic categories. If it is necessary to fix our gaze attentively upon a subject in order to perceive its beauty, Jesus was doing that across his lifetime with the Father. If it is required that we can most fully appreciate the brilliance and radiance of a subject when we pause to apprehend and wonder at its presence, Jesus' gaze (disposition, orientation, fixedness, harmony) was ever directed toward the Father. Jesus, then, was the perfect primal form both due to his nature and his action. It was given to him by nature to be the incarnate One, but he also actively chose to obey the Father's plan.[53] Variously in his being, person, and action the Word incarnate is the Father's preeminent gift to creation.

A FRAMING FORAY: WHICH WAS FIRST, THE CHICKEN OR THE EGG, CREATION OR CHRIST? OR, JUST WHO DID JESUS THINK HE WAS?

Because Evangelicals do not quite emphasize the Word's incarnation the way Balthasar did and are generally not so christocentric as Balthasar, there may well be some confusion concerning his temporal sequence. In order to more carefully understand Balthasar on the ontological, temporal, and beauteous preeminence of Christ let's process this dynamic through a line

---

50. Ibid., 456, 463–65.

51. Ibid., 456–67. Cf. 193, 197, 462–65.

52. Williams, "Balthasar and Trinity," 45–47. Furthermore, the Father freely gave the Spirit to the Son who freely received the Spirit. Analogously, the reception of the Spirit also requires a human being's free collaboration. Cf. Balthasar, *The Last Act*, 426.

53. Dupré, "Balthasar's Theological Aesthetic," 201.

Hans Urs von Balthasar (1905–1988)

of inquiry. Did God create the world and then after the fact send Jesus Christ as a remedy for sin? Or, did God both create the world for his Son and do so such that his Son is the measure and the form of creation itself? How we fashion it matters.

The first question structures the matter following the order of the Bible: creation, fall, and redemption happen in succession. God had an original plan, as this line of thinking goes, which was subsequently marred by sin. To save people God, as a second thought, sent his Son to deal with the mess. Contrastingly, the second question above constructs the matter such that it was God the Father's plan all along to honor his Son by giving him the whole creation; the incarnation, thus, was planned from eternity, apart from sin. That Satan, sin and death entered the equation necessitated the crucifixion of God's Son, but the incarnation was destined regardless. Plainly, as we saw earlier, Balthasar argues for the latter frame: the incarnate Son is the measure, the blueprint, the archetype, the first fruits, and the *telos* for the entirety of creation. When the Father created he used the Word incarnate as the template for the rest of creation. The Father not only created with the Word (John 1:3) but through the Word (John 1:3). Jesus' form is the blueprint for the existence of all other forms. Or to risk further technical categorization, the Son's begottenness (John 1:14, 18; 3:16; origination) from the Father is the basis for all other derivations, distances, originations, sendings, and birthings in creation and existence.[54]

Still more nuanced, the objective form of Christ incarnate—real and true as it is—is, aesthetically speaking, *no mere template to stare at*. Christ's form is alive, dynamic and effective. Christ's form is so powerful that to have beheld him in his incarnate state was the beginning of the beatific vision that awaits the end![55] Effective and dynamic, the form of Christ heals all other forms. "In fact," Balthasar argued, "God's Incarnation perfects the whole ontology and aesthetics of created Being." He is a life generating Word. He is, some Evangelicals might initially be thunderstruck to process, a Word that supercedes even the Bible. Balthasar continued, "Although ever since Luther we have become accustomed to call the Bible 'God's Word', it is

---

54. Balthasar writes routinely thus. Just one example is in *The Last Act*, 62. And yet again we run into complexities: Balthasar holds the incarnate Word as the blueprint for creation, which is precisely to say that the triune God himself is the pattern for all creatures and creation. Cf. *The Last Act*, 61–109. Balthasar avers similarly on Christ as the goal of the universe in *Theo-Logic*, vol. 1, *The Truth of The Word*, 234.

55. Balthasar, *The Last Act*, 470.

not Sacred Scripture which is God's original language and self-expression, but rather Jesus Christ." More extensively,

> As One and Unique, and yet as one who is to be understood only in the context of the whole created cosmos, Jesus is the Word, the Image, the Expression and the Exegesis of God. Jesus bears witness to God as a man, by using the whole expressional apparatus of human existence from birth to death, including all the stages of life, all the states in life, the solitary and the social situations. He *is* what he expresses—namely, God—but he is not whom he expresses—namely, the Father. This incomparable paradox stands as the fountainhead of the Christian aesthetic, and therefore of all aesthetics![56]

And still more intriguingly Balthasar wants us to know that the Bible did not produce Jesus. It is not as though the disciples found Old Testament passages and prophecies and then creatively quoted them with regard to Jesus of Nazareth. (Jesus was so outstanding, so paramount, and so stupendous it is good there are four Gospels to help fill out the details and impact of his coming.)[57] Indeed, Jesus himself did not read the Old Testament and then find ways to make it applicable or amenable to his own ministry. Instead, Jesus knew who he was in relation to the Father, even if in his kenotic form he had to gradually learn that, and then began to see Old Testament passages that prefigured him, began to see that he was the completion of all manner of Jewish Scriptures, especially concerning the One who would suffer and die for the elect (Isa 53; Dan. 7). Balthasar, with his towering view of Christ, held that Christ is not merely the cause of Christianity but its center, its glue, and its meaning. For its part, in Judaism neither Abra-

---

56. Both the former quote and the blocked quote from Balthasar, *Seeing the Form*, 29, original italics.

57. About those scholars who would reduce the New Testament witness to the fragmented memories of the disciples and their colleagues von Balthasar said, "what is left is such a paltry construction ... that ... one is still left with the problem of explaining how so slight a kernel could become such a full-powered and seamless form as is the Christ of the Gospels." Ibid., 474. No, there was no conspiracy contrived by a "few isolated individuals." Indeed, the Gospels are too grand to be explained away via an ancient conspiracy. Concerning the Jesus of the New Testament Balthasar pondered, "For its part, the contemplation of two millennia finds an ever-greater unity and a fullness evermore imposing in its interrelatedness.... The inspiration of a great work of art is impenetrable and the result it achieves is not fully analyzable." Ibid., 475. At the risk of belaboring the point, Balthasar also notes that it was not the church who made Christ, but Christ who made the church. Ibid., 542.

ham, Moses, nor the prophets hold together the entire religion. But with Christianity Jesus is both the form and the content, both the revelation and its meaning. He is, therefore, the beginning and the end.[58]

Still further on Jesus' self-understanding, Evangelicals might be surprised to know also that Balthasar believed that Jesus came not to persuade people about either himself or his ministry. God, Balthasar reflected, "does not primarily communicate 'truths' about himself, but rather bestows *himself* as absolute truth and love."[59] Similarly, Jesus' goal was not to "get people to believe" that he was the Son of God or prove by force of his miracles that he had the authority to forgive sins. Contrasting those interpretive frames, Balthasar argued that Jesus came to attest (i.e., *stimmen*) to his own identity. Jesus did not like to give signs because *he himself is the sign*; Jesus wanted people to give themselves to his sign, not the signs that he did.[60] This matter-of-fact character about Jesus' coming is not what we twenty-first–century types would expect. Living in our religiously plural environs we know good and well that Jesus needs to have had an apologetic edge. He needs to have made clear his identity so people could more readily follow him. Jesus ought to have healed a blind man and said, "See, I'm who I said I was!" To many it would make far more sense if Jesus had driven out demons and then dramatically concluded, "Look, I have authority over the devil himself. You do well to heed my words and confess me as Savior." Instead, Jesus' approach tended to be other-directed (Father, Spirit, kingdom of God), other-oriented. Jesus *modus operandi* was, Balthasar reasoned, both humble and simple. But Jesus' missiological method never involved self-deprecation, self-loathing, or a worry about causing offense. He said things like, "Do not think that I came to bring peace on the earth; I did not come to bring peace, but a sword" (Matt 10:34). Jesus said his coming both would cause families to split (Matt 10:35) and people to welcome their enemies (Matt 10:36). In all of this, Jesus himself was a shocking aesthetic. Balthasar even asserted that Jesus could be simultaneously "so humble and so arrogant and self-certain; he who was at once meek and obedient as a lamb and angrily zealous for God's cause, so abrupt that he would walk away form his opponents; he ... was so unassuming and yet so all-embracing in his demands."[61] Balthasar, following Blaise Pascal (1623–1662), wrote, "his

58. Ibid., 451.
59. Ibid., 161.
60. Ibid., 648.
61. Ibid., 447.

whole behaviour is not designed to persuade anyone one way or another."[62] Jesus came, instead, to point to the truth, to embody obedience, and indeed to be a martyr: witness.

Again, all of this is far more objective than most Evangelicals would put it. Jesus was and is a totality. In Balthasar's imagination, there is a there-ness to Jesus that transcends the kind of subjective appropriation that aesthetes normally aver. "The rock-like hardness of each of his sayings," wrote Balthasar, "derives from the fact that each of them coincides with the totality of his existence: it lies in the phenomenon that he does not only remain true to his word' and is ready to die for it, but that he himself is this word."[63] If we were to ask Jesus to "prove your pre-eminent identity," or to "prove you have the authority to judge and give eternal life," Balthasar reasons that we would be asking for a standard that somehow stands outside of Jesus himself. Instead, Balthasar said, "He is not only the one who is wholly adequate: he is the measure itself." And, "Even this dynamic measure which Christ represents can be demonstrated from nowhere other than itself. How could it be otherwise, since it is God himself—the Unmeasurable who can be measured only by himself—who makes himself present here?"[64] Once more, Jesus is true for Balthasar whether we accept that or not. For Balthasar Jesus lives as the perfect form of God whether we recognize him or not. Of course, Jesus *wants us* to recognize those things and embrace him as our own perfect saving form, but Jesus, in Balthasarian framing, does not need our response, does not need our aesthetic perception in order to be true to himself and true to the Father and Spirit.

In all of this, concerning both temporal sequence and Jesus' self-consciousness Balthasar bends or warps time. In other words, Balthasar is not bothered to remain locked into sequential time as he envisions either Jesus Christ as the primal and first form or the conclusion of time. For Balthasar Jesus' identity and time both overcome our linear time. As king of the kingdom,[65] when Jesus came, "he arrives at the 'end of the world', whether or not our world-time pursues its chronological succession. His eschatology," Balthasar continued, "embraces all continuing chronological

---

62. Ibid., 471, following Pascal, *Pensées*, 637.
63. Ibid., 459.
64. Ibid., 461. Prior quote from 460.
65. Balthasar, "The whole kingdom is embodied in him, so that when people 'seek for the kingdom of God, they find the Son." *The Last Act*, 249, quoting von Speyr's *Bergpredigt* [Sermon on the Mount], 225–26.

Hans Urs von Balthasar (1905–1988)

time and qualitatively determines it. His eschatology is primary." There is some correlation both between what the ancient nation of Israel expected of the end (i.e., an unveiling that variously involved distressing cataclysmic events, persecution of the chosen, the falling away of the elect, the rise of godless forces, and God's day of judgment) and with what Jesus did and taught concerning the end, but Jesus' frame take precedence.[66] Again, the end is near because of Jesus—his coming is a novel irruption (inbreaking). The end is not near owing to the alignment of varied horizontal or temporal factors. To reiterate, the end did not produce Jesus. Jesus produces the end because he is the end, the omega of the entire universe.[67]

And for us, why do we have time? Or, what are we to do with our time? Keen to glorify the Lord, Balthasar quoted Adrienne von Speyr and said, "This little span of time is given to us so that we may affirm the eternal life that is being offered us."[68]

Before we advance, it's worth repeating that Balthasar's "beauty is objective" position is an enormous challenge to and for contemporary aesthetes, philosophers, politicians, and citizens. Here in the twenty-first century it takes just as much courage to believe in beauty as a reality as it does to believe in goodness or truth because all three have been relativized, trivialized, and privatized. Today beauty is a narrow matter of personal preference. Balthasar's formulations move against our current subjectivizing tendencies. He believed beauty in fact existed (as/in God incarnate) and exists and that there are dangerous implications of our failing to acknowledge beauty's existence. Beauty, Balthasar espoused with ancient philosophers,

---

66. Balthasar, *The Last Act*, 20–21. On correlation with Israel's eschatology see 20–24, 40–54, 194–203. Balthasar clarified that in the drama of salvation history God is the primary actor, "who else acts, who else *can* act, if God is on the stage?" *Theo-Drama*, vol. II, *Dramatis Personae*, 17. Elsewhere he wrote, "In such a context it is essential that God's action should not shrink to a single, instant, immutable point in time that is constitutive of every moment of earth-time; God's 'abiding forever' must not be seen as a 'non-time' but as a super-time that is unique to him; and this is illustrated in the fact that Christ's time mediates between God's 'time' and world-time. Christ's time recapitulates and comprehends world-time, while it also reveals God's super-time." *The Last Act*, 30. Not long thereafter in *The Last Act*, 36n3, he quotes Karl Rahner, "The Hermeneutics of Eschatological Assertions" in *Theological Investigations*, vol. 4, 342–43: "Christ himself is the hermeneutic principle of all eschatological assertions. Anything that cannot be read and understood as a christological assertion is not a genuine eschatological assertion."

67. Balthasar, *The Last Act*, 277.

68. Ibid., 113, quoting von Speyr's *Bergpredigt*, 215.

is the sister of both goodness and truth. Without beauty, goodness easily flattens into utilitarianism (doing good for the largest possible numbers) and hedonism (that pleasure is the chief end for life); without beauty "the good will involve merely the satisfaction of a need by means of some value or object." So also without beauty truth collapses into either philosophic formalism (arranging ideas "just so," without any practical outcomes) or brutish pragmatism (focusing on outcomes apart from either virtue or those outcomes' foundational commitments). Instead, Balthasar knew, truth is more than "the verification of correct facts and laws."[69] The "radiant property of truth" Wigley summarized Balthasar "is, in fact, none other than beauty."[70] To repeat, both goodness and truth need beauty. *Beauty captivates and enlivens*, but she does so with no violence. Goodness and truth are more fully themselves when beauty shines in and through them. Beauty, Balthasar wrote, "will not allow herself to be separated and banned from her two sisters without taking them along with herself in an act of mysterious vengeance."[71] Put simply, beauty is neither a nicety to be politely acknowledged nor the mere fluffy psychological frosting atop the cake of authentic reality (whatever "authentic" has come to mean in popular parlance). Beauty is inseparably woven into reality itself. If we pull beauty out of reality's fabric, to summarize Balthasar, we will find we have altogether unsewn reality itself. And just as damaging, we will find we have altogether unsewn ourselves. If existence is shorn of her beauty, if human nature is stripped of beauty, we ourselves become empty husks. Void of beauty, all that remains of our spirit is "totally dark and incomprehensible even to itself."[72] And I ask, is not that emptiness the state of postmodern mankind today?

For me, Balthasar's position, like those of the other theologians in this book, makes beauty more, not less, real. His position (beauty is objective because it is rooted in the incarnate God) intrigues me intellectually; who would have thought that answers for what vexes the contemporary aesthetic mind-set could be found in constructs so ancient, or more properly in the ancient of days? Even more, that his position is grounded in the incarnation of God enchants my heart: I want to know more sweetly the source of all

---

69. Balthasar, *Seeing the Form*, 147.
70. Wigley, *Balthasar's Trilogy*, 125.
71. Balthasar, *Seeing the Form*, 18.
72. Ibid., 19.

beauty, the beautiful one. Frankly, Balthasar makes me love both God and beauty more, not less.

NATURE AND THE ANALOGY OF BEING

Let's continue our brief review of Balthasar's theo-aesthetic. Balthasar, whereas he anchors his reflections on beauty with Christ Jesus does not stop them there. Again, owing to his Roman Catholic sensibilities—sensibilities variously informed by the church fathers and tradition, which is to say biblical study together with the histories of theology and philosophy, and the doctrines of the Trinity, the incarnation, the cross, and the resurrection—Balthasar has an appreciation for the beauty of nature.

It is critical to understand that Balthasar, again, frames and roots this love of beauty's nature in aesthetic categories. Put simply, creation's beauty reflects God's beauty. We all know from Scripture that human beings are mirrors, icons, and images of God's own self, but more broadly existence itself, the universe itself, and living nature itself all mirror God. Not only are "the heavens telling of the glory of God" (Ps 19:1), so is everything else. That we can see and sense the world around us is beautiful. Then, that the world around us is frequently beautiful is beautiful! It could have been otherwise. We could have been created deaf, mute, and blind. Creation could appear to us as a sepia-toned muddle. But God is so expressive, so brilliant, and so overflowing that he created a universe that mirrored both his own beauty and that is full of the perception of beauty. Creation is not neutral regarding God. It is not as though nature and its beauty could have caused itself to exist and as such be indifferent regarding the transcendent God. It is not as though nature may or may not attest to his glory; the very fact that it exists at all is beautiful and expresses the glory of God.[73] That kind of theo-framing of nature comes through an interpretive sieve known as the *analogia entis*, the analogy of being.

Now, the analogy of being was a concept present among ancient Greek philosophers; for that reason it has been rejected by many Christian theologians for two millennia; the concept is too philosophical, and not biblical enough, for some. This analogic concept holds that there can be "a

---

73. Balthasar, "the testimony of the cosmos attests to a single truth: 'that Jesus Christ is Lord' (Phil. 2:11)." The cosmos submits itself to its Lord in that matter can "receive and express the saving signs of grace," and "let itself be bodily permeated by God." *Seeing the Form*, 641.

relationship between two entities allowing for some similarity and equivalence without insisting on either a total identity or a total distinction." Wigley notes that this way of reasoning was already present in Christian theology as the ancient church sought to trace out Jesus' two natures.[74] We need not think long to realize the potential difficulties of the *analogia entis* position. How can finite and physical reality mirror the infinite and spiritual God? Or, how can that which seems like a mere wisp of air (Jas 4:14; Wis 2:3) mirror the eternal God? Still more and obviously, things and creatures do not make themselves, do not sustain themselves. How then can we mirror the beauty of the great "I am" (Exod 3:14; John 8:58), the uncaused One? Similarly problematic, in the dynamic of salvation, we cannot make ourselves like God by sheer moral effort, growth in virtue, or sacrificial lifestyle. And honestly, across our lifetimes, we arguably become physically less beautiful, not more. In light of all that how could Balthasar argue for some beauteous correlation between God and his creation?

In short, that aesthetic mirroring can occur if God so designed it. Nature is not, and we people are not, beautiful by necessity. But amazingly, *God is not a glory hog.* In his triune self God loves to share. The Father shares his glory with the Son and loves to love both the Spirit and the Son; and alternately so among the three members of the Trinity. That same self-sharing occurs regarding creation: God loves to share his love, goodness, truth, and beauty with non-God, that is, with nature and humankind. Many Evangelicals rightly believe that God designed the universe such that God's own fingerprints (*vestigia Dei*, the vestiges of God) are indelibly imprinted on everything he created. If people would only look carefully they would know that there is some kind of God up there, out there, who made it all. But alas, these Evangelicals lament, the human race is instead blinded by sin and unable to see those fingerprints. Such as that framing is, Evangelicals are right, but Balthasar wants us to look still more deeply.

Beauty as a fingerprint of the divine does not exist simply to "prove" God's existence. Once again Balthasar: "God does not primarily communicate 'truths' about himself, but rather bestows *himself* as absolute truth

---

74. Wigley, *Balthasar's Trilogy*, 16. The ancient church had to consider, using the biblical witness, just how it was that Jesus was human and divine. He was like us in every way, save sin. He is like God in every way save he limited (kenosis) himself for our benefit. Treitler, "True Foundations of Authentic Theology," in *His Life and Work*, summed up Balthasar hereon, "Jesus Christ is, therefore . . . the absolute analogy or the concrete analogy of being, and thus all analogy is given a Christocentric determination by Christ," 174.

Hans Urs von Balthasar (1905–1988)

and love."[75] Indeed, God loves to glorify the divine love.[76] Beauty exists as an expression of God's own excessive love. As a transcendent, beauty transcends itself; there is always more latent within and waiting to be cherished about beauty. Beauty has layers and depths that enrapture and overwhelm us. A generous overspill, beauty resides in what God has made as an emblem, a token, of God's love. Balthasar put this in many ways. Wed to form, beauty has an energy about it that is free and that freely squanders itself for us in love.[77] Nature's beauty is a copy of the divine beauty.[78] Thinking aesthetically, Balthasar wrote, "In a flower, a certain interior reality opens its eye and reveals something beyond and more profound than a form which delights us by its proportion and colour." He continued, "In the rhythm of the form of plants—from seed to full growth, from bud to fruit—there is manifested an essence, and to reduce the laws of this essence to mere utilitarian principles would be blasphemous."[79] The entirety of creation, and not just what it effects in our psyche, reflects the entirety of God; there is, as we saw above concerning Christ, a sense of the concreteness of existence, and that for both creation and God. Creation is then "a manifestation of God."[80] Beauty is drenched with eternity.[81] Like a holy ecclesial chalice which holds the wine of Christ's blood, creation's beauty is a revelation of God's presence.[82] Truly, beauty appears before us through so many varied channels. It is resplendent, elastic, and diverse.

Because it is so dynamic and elusive, many in the church are wary of beauty. They consider it dangerous. Beauty is enticing and alluring and it can lead people astray. Concerned that beauty easily leads toward idolatry, some church folk want to hide beauty in a closet. "Don't emphasize beauty," they think, "lest she detract from the glory of God." Even more, some theologians think, if we interpret beauty as a fingerprint *of* God we may confuse beauty *with* God. And so, the thinking goes, the analogy of being is itself a confusing and dangerous mode of perception. Balthasar himself was aware of both the dangers of beauty and the dangers of the *analogia entis*. "Even

---

75. Balthasar, *Seeing the Form*, 161.
76. Wigley, *Balthasar's Trilogy*, 154.
77. Balthasar, *Seeing the Form*, 22, 431.
78. Ibid., 215.
79. Ibid., 433.
80. Ibid., 420.
81 Ibid., 231.
82. Ibid., 410.

a dangerous road remains a road, perhaps one requiring special equipment and expertise, but one which does not for all that become impossible."[83] Balthasar knew that for much of the human race the experience of beauty borders on the religious.[84] Nevertheless, we can make use of the analogy of being to ponder, enjoy, and appreciate beauty. And yet, Balthasar thought, we cannot press that analogy too far. The beauty of nature glorifies God and suggests God's love—to those with the eyes of faith to see that—but nature's beauty is not God himself. "*Si comprehendis non est Deus*,"[85] Balthasar quoted Augustine—"If you can understand it then it is not God." Yes, beauty in the universe points to God, but God is always greater. Clearly, there was a mirroring of Pseudo-Dionysius' earlier mind-set with Balthasar in that our "no" about God is always greater than our "yes" about God, precisely because God transcends all our categories.[86] Balthasar was in agreement with the Roman Catholic Fourth Lateran Council (AD 1215) which decreed that "between Creator and creature no similitude can be noted, however great it may be, without noting a greater dissimilitude."[87] This side of the resurrection, our knowledge is always imperfect.[88] Sustaining the Fourth Lateran Council, Von Balthasar never argued and would never allow that we are by our being, or by the nature of being itself, analogous to God, except that God gave some capacity to us. And that takes us to the beauty of being human.

THE HUMAN PERSON AND BEAUTY

All that was said above applies now here. The beauty of God given to the human race comes through Jesus Christ. God's incarnate Son is the

83. Ibid., 37.

84. Ibid., 241.

85. Ibid., 439.

86. Though Balthasar believed that a negative theology, built on Dionysius's own scaffolding, can produce "a seeking that never arrives at is goal." Balthasar is too concrete, too optimistic that God has revealed himself and that man can indeed know God to be fully apophatic, to fully embrace a negative theological approach. Cf. Wigley, *Balthasar's Trilogy*, 129, quoting *Theo-Logic*, vol. II, 122.

87. Ibid., 17.

88. Balthasar clarified, "the *analogia entis* . . . does not imply that the finite spirit can wholly comprehend" "the relationship between finite and infinite Being." The finite spirit senses and knows that it is "encompassed by and destined for another." *Seeing the Form*, 439.

Hans Urs von Balthasar (1905–1988)

foundation, blueprint, archetype, measure, and source for the beauty of each of us. In and from the free beauty of God's triune being, he invites us into free and loving relationship. Exuberantly, yet without either violence or coercion, he shares his beauty with us. Indeed, he created us expressly to share his love, goodness, truth, and beauty. As with nature, we were not created neutral, but created with a certain God-given correspondence implanted into our very being. Because I do not believe most Christians tend to meditate on such matters let us go deeper.

God does not need anything, but wants to be loved. "God wants to be recognized," urged von Balthasar, "he must be known."[89] But God does not want to be loved merely by disembodied minds or invisible souls; Balthasar is far too aesthetic to lead us down a Gnostic path.[90] God created human beings to love the totality of whom God is from and in the totality of whom we are. Jesus of Nazareth was a concrete whole and we, created in the image of *the image*, are likewise concrete wholes. What did that mean for Balthasar?

Firstly, we are images of God, or the language of God, in our ordinariness.[91] Knowing the love of God and perceiving the beauty of God are not reserved for mystic specialists or spiritual gurus. God created ordinary man, and woman, with senses that can apprehend God, "in Christianity God appears to man right in the midst of worldly reality. The centre of this act of encounter must, therefore, lie [with] the profane human senses."[92] It follows that "the Biblical perception of God cannot be spiritualised."[93] The apostolic community, that group of people who knew and followed the

---

89. Ibid., 128.

90. Gnosticism, generally put, emphasizes the spirit over the body, unseen psychological forces over what it deems crude materiality. From the Greek *gnosis* (knowledge), Gnosticism emphasizes knowledge over deeds, or ideas over doing. Balthasar does not want us to separate our knowledge from our whole selves, or our belief that our ideas do not affect either ourselves or our ecclesial-communal constructions.

91. Balthasar, *Seeing the Form*, 446.

92. Ibid., 357.

93. Ibid., 305. Hereon Balthasar believed that the Christ-affirming church is thus the guardian of metaphysics. Nichols put it thus, "only an orthodox Christian mind and heart can bridge the gap between, on the one hand, an acosmic spirituality—a religiosity concerned merely with salvation in some other realm, private, interior, extra-mundane, and, on the other hand, a present world consigned to domination by positivists for whom all that exists is only organized matter. Revelation can be a therapy for a metaphysical malaise that has, at the moment, no other medicine available." Nichols, *A Key to Balthasar*, 12–13.

incarnate Logos, were, like all human beings, characterized by *sensoriness*. Specifically, they heard, saw, and touched Jesus.[94] It was not their soul that had an encounter with the Nazarene but their whole selves. The Bible does not espouse a Platonic dualism that splits the soul from the body; the soul and the body are one self.[95] Women and men were created for encounter with each other and the living God. Materiality was not a problem at creation, and it is not a problem today. Again, the Bible views humankind as fashioned by God such that we are by creation oriented "toward the Grace of the Covenant." The human body, flesh and blood and bone, is a God-created receptacle for God's breath, the Holy Spirit. "The body is an inspirited frame, a world which opens out to the world."[96] The human self was created to perceive, experience, and encounter. And again, we do all that sensorially. True, we can perceive and encounter God more readily by receiving God's gift of faith (we'll note more thereon momentarily), but even sinful men perceive God, though they do so poorly; besought by sin, they do not even like to be perceived by God.[97]

Balthasar even takes us on a sensory tour of the human organs. The heart is our very center. From and with it we pine for one another, and hunger for rest and God and love. The heart is not only a means of perception, it is a means of embrace. Indeed, it is "an enveloping womb" that takes life in and embraces it. With our eyes we see images, images that for good and/or bad shape our identity.[98] Even though our sin-produced guilt occludes our vision,[99] sight, for Balthasar the "crown of the 'tree of senses,'"[100] enables our ability to perceive the life and color and movement of things. Sight, guided by the heart's orientation and the brain's analytic machinery, allows us to distinguish, compare, illumine, and order the world around us. Touch is a dear sensation, with it Thomas placed his fingers in the wound of the resurrected (not ghostly) Jesus' side.[101] Touching, Mary first held the baby in her womb and then later held her son in her arms.[102] Touch, in

94. Balthasar, *Seeing the Form*, 301.
95. Ibid., 371–5.
96. Ibid., 376, where Balthasar follows Barth, *Church Dogmatics*, vol. 3, 344–66.
97. Ibid., 378–80.
98. Ibid., 387, former quote from page 386.
99. Ibid., 509.
100. Ibid., 385, following Aquinas.
101. Ibid., 206, 339.
102. Ibid., 332. Balthasar reasoned that the experiences of the faithful (Old Testament

Hans Urs von Balthasar (1905–1988)

part, makes profound the experience of water baptism.[103] And yes, there is soulish, or spiritual touch; a sensation with which we discern the presence of the Lord.[104] With our ears we hear, most importantly, God's word; Christianity is first a religion of hearing the preached word.[105] But hearing also enables us to hear life, a kind of musical score played for our benefit.[106] Taste, too, is a gift. We receive Christ in the Eucharist with our mouths, and encounter him in the profoundly simple act of eating.[107] And finally, if briefly, smell also is a means of encounter. Odor is a "precious essence" that expresses the radiance and intoxication of being and existence.[108]

Of course, that we are created with sensorial capacity to encounter and perceive the universe and its beauty does not necessitate that we are able to encounter and rightly perceive God; indeed, we can err about our perception of natural goodness, truth, and beauty, let alone do the same concerning God.[109] What is necessary is God's further gift; we may even think of it as a gift given atop our created giftedness. Faith is "God's witness in us"[110] and "the light of God becoming luminous in man, for, in his triune intimacy, God is known only by God."[111] We cannot rightly see apart from faith. Just as a spectator wrongly views a work of art without an appreciation for both craftsmanship and beauty, the human person wrongly views Christ Jesus apart from faith. Faith is prerequisite to rightly perceiv-

---

theophanies together with the eyewitnesses' experiences of Jesus himself) are events that happened not only for the original persons, but for the whole household of faith. In other words, they were given experiences of God that were intended to bless us all. *Seeing the Form*, 330–56.

103. Ibid., 563.
104. Ibid., 356–69, 398–407.
105. Ibid., 568, 577.
106. Ibid., 394.
107. Ibid., 557–58.
108. Ibid., 394.
109. Balthasar believed that those in other religions are indeed perceiving truth, goodness, and beauty but that those perceptions, devoid of Christ's revelation and the indwelling of the Holy Spirit, fall short. *Seeing the Form*, 490–96. Dupré qualifies that Balthasar's "own treatment reflects more judgment than redemption." Comparing Christianity to other religions, Balthasar paints "the contrasts in rather harsh tones." Balthasar was, Dupré wrote, especially hard on Hinduism and Buddhism. Dupré, "Balthasar's Theological Aesthetic," 203. Along more generous lines, Balthasar viewed the other religions as hungry for truth and even sometimes true, and anticipatory of Christ Jesus.
110. Balthasar, *Seeing the Form*, 152.
111. Ibid., 151.

ing and loving God. To be a good aesthete, "one must possess a spiritual eye capable of perceiving the forms of existence with awe." To realize that the precious pearl of the kingdom is worth sacrificing everything requires eyes of faith.[112] Similarly, to rightly see and appreciate beauty, indeed if one is to capture beauty in astonished wonder, the only right and fitting response to true beauty, requires the eyes of faith. "There is a moment in which the bursting light of spirit as it makes its appearance completely drenches external form in its rays," Balthasar noted. But that moment will be missed without the right kind of eyes, the eyes of faith.[113] Faith is not first human generated. The believer's response to God's revelation is not something she calls up by herself. Christ both shows himself to a person and enables, by the work of the Holy Spirit, that person to rightly see Christ. So then, faith is infused by God in a way that corresponds to, rather than does violence to, our created nature.[114] And yet, we indeed can develop faith.

Earlier we saw that Balthasar believed Christ Jesus was a man rightly attuned to the Father. By obediently receiving what the Father had for him, Jesus was on the same wavelength (*stimmung*) as the Father. Jesus' dispositions were the same as the Father's. And so the Christian, herself a true aesthete because she confesses and serves God's Son, can attune herself to the Lord. Yet, this is not some merely psychological effort; aesthetic attunement to God is not achieved by positive confession, healthy self-talk, or building one's self-esteem. The whole self is involved in what Balthasar insisted is "strictly theological."[115] We are, again and again, concrete selves responding to the concrete self, Jesus, God from Nazareth.[116] "The senses are the exteriorisation of the soul, and Christ is the exteriorization of God,"[117] Balthasar reasoned. *Stimmung*, attunement, involves our saying yes to God's yes for us, our obeying the Lord's ways for us. "The first prerequisite for understanding," Balthasar noted, "is to accept what is given just as it offers itself."[118] That means this is not an act of imaginative fabrication; we are responding to God's revelation of and as Jesus Christ.[119]

112. Ibid., 26, former quote from page 24.
113. Ibid., 32.
114. Ibid., 173.
115. Ibid., 118.
116. Ibid., 455.
117. Ibid., 397.
118. Ibid., 454.
119. Ibid., 166, 171, 175.

Hans Urs von Balthasar (1905–1988)

Christian aesthetic-attunement involves our loving response to God's first movement toward us, love.[120] Through faithfulness, worship, obedience,[121] prayer, Christian fellowship, we cooperate with the grace of God that is at work in us. What God really wants from us is in all of this, Balthasar again expressed in aesthetic categories, is openness. Attuned-to-God aesthetes, we know to be ready to perceive what God has for us. Balthasar reasoned that the aesthete has eyes that are always open to seeing, ears that are always open to hearing.[122] Is this openness, this aesthetic peering, a matter of affective wonder or a matter of critical mindedness? Both. There is, in aesthetic seeing, a twofold dynamic. There is simultaneously an "involuntary and spontaneous" response stemming from astonishment, and wonder and a wise and calculated approach to one's seeing. This experience is, Balthasar waxed, like something that occurs between two lovers. In their mutual love they are enrapt with one another, but they do not get stuck in a chamber of infatuation. With openneness and felicity the two lovers genuinely know and understand one another, but they do not exhaust themselves in critical analysis of one another. This is all somewhat mysterious, but it is a mystery that evokes love and joy, not one that summons secret or esoteric knowledge.[123] Or to put it still differently, we can on the one hand err by looking wrongly at both Christ and our life in him; we can thus err by making the Christian aesthetic way of being only a matter of affectivity and emotion. On the other hand, we err when we do not look long enough at the truth of who Jesus Christ really is; our critical attention was not enough fixed.[124] Our aesthetic apprehension of Jesus Christ necessitates both loving wonder and thoughtful reflection.

What is the aim of all of this aesthetic reflection? What does Balthasar want for us? Or, what does he believe God wants for us? Fascinatingly, but consistent with his overarching aesthetic, Balthasar believes that the greatest proof for God's existence, love, and beauty are not ideas, not even biblical ideas. Rather, he believes the best arguments for God are *saints*. He wrote, "It is not dry manuals (full as these may be of unquestionable truths) that express with plausibility for the world the truth of Christ's Gospel; it is

---

120. Ibid., 118.

121. He commented, "The more obediently [the theologian] thinks, the more accurately will he see." Ibid., 160.

122. Ibid., 384.

123. Ibid., 434–35.

124. Ibid., 454, 474.

the existence of the saints who have been grasped by Christ's Holy Spirit. And Christ himself foresaw no other kind of apologetics (John 13:35)."[125] Saints are those who perceive the true form; of course that presupposes that the saint is attuned to Christ, full of the Holy Spirit, and exhibiting high moral quality.[126] And, finally, lest the reader erroneously assume that sainthood is achieved through some regimen of moral or ascetic rigor, Balthasar quoted Augustine and said, "What is Christian about the Christian is Christ himself."[127] In the end, the Christian is, like her master, "precisely a form."[128]

WRAP-UP

With Hans Urs von Balthasar we have reached an theo-aesthetic construction that is thus far the zenith of Christian theology. He neither only spoke about theology in light of the preeminence of God's Son, nor did he singularly get buried down inside of the complexities of aesthetic vocabulary. On the one hand Balthasar did not keep his reader at a satellite's view of theology, focusing only on theoretical abstraction. On the other hand, Balthasar did not force his students' noses deep down into the furrows of technical aesthetic philosophy and analysis. In an unprecedented way, he wove together both theology and aesthetic reflection that opens up fresh ways for perceiving and framing this way of ours in Christ.

Particularly fascinating for our study, Balthasar shows us that salvation itself profoundly involves beauty. Yes, of course, God himself is beautiful, particularly in and as the incarnate form, Jesus of Nazareth. But Balthasar, with his emphasis upon concrete wholes—Christ as a concrete self, the human person as a concrete self, and even the church as a concrete entity[129]—is emphatic that the whole of reality is involved in God's plan of redemption for the universe. Any Gnosticizing understanding of salvation, in other words one wherein the human body and/or the physical elements of creation are ignored or are unredeemable, is implicitly and unilaterally rejected. With Balthasar then, if Jesus Christ, the original of beauty, is the

---

125. Ibid., 482.
126. Ibid., 194–97.
127. Ibid., 608.
128. Ibid., 27–28.
129. Balthasar constantly describes the church in both her strengths and weaknesses. She is at once the body and bride of Christ, and a body full of sinners. Ibid., 411–13, 508, 510, 517, 529.

omega intended for the whole of reality, we can hope for tangible and tactile eternal life together in his presence. And, we will only mention, the implications for ethics, aesthetics, and earth care this side of eternity are all established: since God intends to beautify and redeem whole selves in the wholeness of the universe our work now should ever move toward the same.

WHAT BALTHASAR TEACHES US TO SEE:

- We can benefit from the past
- Christ Jesus surpasses all other forms of beauty
- Beauty exists objectively in Jesus Christ
- Jesus is a concrete whole that cannot be reduced
- God's Son is a revelation of the Trinity
- The triune God is humble and shares his glory
- The universe was created for Jesus of Nazareth
- There is no beauty without form
- Goodness and truth (and reality) need beauty
- We can be attuned to God like Jesus was
- Jesus is Lord over time
- God created the whole of nature and whole human persons for relationship with him
- Nature's beauty, like human beauty, mirrors God
- Beauty exemplifies, rather than detracts from, God's own beauty
- God created people with the sensory capacity to experience God
- Faith is necessary to see both Christ and his beauty
- Christians who live their lives for Christ are the best argument for God's existence
- Salvation is not only beautiful but incorporates beauty into its very fabric

Bibliography

"18th Century German Aesthetics." http://plato.stanford.edu/entries/aesthetics-18th-german/.
Artz, Frederick B. *The Mind of the Middle Ages: An Historical Survey*. 3rd ed. New York: Alfred A. Knopf, 1959.
Athanasius. "The Incarnation of the Word of God," 54, in *Patrologiae Cursus Completus, Series Graecae*. 168 vols., edited by I. P. Migne. Reprint. Turnholti, Belgium: Typographi Brepols, 1978.
Augustine. *The City of God*. Translated by Marcus Dods. New York: Modern Library, 1950.
———. *Questions for Simplicianius*, I. In *The Essential Augustine*, translated and edited by Vernon J. Bourke, 45. Indianapolis, IN: Hackett, 1964, 1974.
———. *Saint Augustine's Confessions*. Translated by Henry Chadwick. Oxford: Oxford University Press, 1991.
———. *The True Religion*. Translated by C. A. Hangartner, *De vera religione (Chapters 1–17)*. St. Louis University Master's Thesis, 1945.
———. *The Works of Saint Augustine: A Translation for the 21st Century*. New York: New City, 1990.
"Average home has more TVs than people." *USA Today*. http://usatoday30.usatoday.com/life/television/news/2006-09-21-homes-tv_x.htm.
Balas, David L. "Deification." In *The Brill Dictionary of Gregory of Nyssa*, edited by Mateo-Seco Lucas Francisco and Guilio Maspero, 210–13. London: Brill, 2010.
Balthasar, Hans Urs von. *The Glory of the Lord*, vol. 1 of 7, *A Theological Aesthetics: Seeing the Form*. 2nd ed. Translated by Erasmo Leiva-Merikakis, edited by Joseph Fessio and John Riches. San Francisco: Ignatius, 2009.
———. *The Glory of the Lord*, vol. 2 of 7, *Studies in Theological Style: Clerical Styles*. Translated by Andrew Louth, edited by Francis McDonagh, Brian McNeil, and John Riches. San Francisco: Ignatius, 1983.
———. *Theo-Drama*, vol. 2 of 5, *Dramatis Personae: Man in God*. Translated by Graham Harrison. San Francisco: Ignatius, 1990.
———. *Theo-Drama*, vol. 5 of 5, *The Last Act*. Translated by Graham Harrison. San Francisco: Ignatius, 1998.
———. *Theo-Logic*, vol. 1, *The Truth of the Word*. Translated by Adrian J. Walker. San Francisco: Ignatius, 2000.
———. *The Theology of Henri de Lubac*. Translated by Joseph Fessio and Michael M. Waldstein. San Francisco: Ignatius, 1991.

Bibliography

Barasch, Moshe. *Icon: Studies in the History of an Idea*. New York: New York University Press, 1995.

Bauer, Walter. *A Greek-English Lexicon of the New Testament*. 2nd ed. Translated by William F. Arndt and F. Wilbur Gingrich. Chicago: University of Chicago Press, 1979.

Baumgarten, Gottlieb. "Aesthetics." http://plato.stanford.edu/entries/aesthetics-18th-german/.

Bauerschmidt, John C. "Adultery." In *Augustine Through the Ages: An Encyclopedia*, edited by Allan D. Fitzgerald, 11. Grand Rapids: Eerdmans, 1999.

Baxandall, Michael. *Painting and Experience in Fifteenth Century Italy: A Primer in the Social History of Pictorial Style*. Oxford: Oxford University Press, 1972.

Beck, Lewis White, ed. *Kant: Selections*. New York: Macmillan, 1988.

Begbie, Jeremy. *Beholding the Glory: Incarnation through the Arts*. Grand Rapids: Baker Academic, 2000.

———. *Resounding Truth: Christian Wisdom in the World of Music*. Grand Rapids: Baker Academic, 2007.

———. *Theology, Music and Time*. Cambridge: Cambridge University Press, 2000.

Bloesch, Donald. *God The Almighty: Power, Wisdom, Holiness, Love*. Downers Grove, IL: InterVarsity, 1995.

Bourke, Vernon J., ed. *The Essential Augustine*. First ed. Indianapolis, IN: Hackett, 1964.

———. *The Pocket Aquinas*. New York: Washington Square, 1960.

Bouwsma, William. *John Calvin: A Sixteenth Century Portrait*. New York: Oxford University Press, 1988.

Burch Brown, Frank. *Good Taste, Bad: Aesthetics in Religious Life*. Oxford: Oxford University Press, 2000.

Brown, Peter. *Augustine of Hippo, A Biography*. Berkeley, CA: University of California Press, 1967.

Burnham, Douglas. *Internet Encyclopedia of Philosophy: Immanuel Kant: Aesthetics*. http://www.iep.utm.edu/kantaest/.

Bussanich, John. "Happiness, *Eudaimonism*." In *Augustine Through The Ages: An Encyclopedia*, edited by Allan D. Fitzgerald, 413–14. Grand Rapids: Eerdmans, 1999.

Campenhausen, Hans von. *The Fathers of the Greek Church*. Translated by L. A. Garrard. London: Adam & Charles Black, 1963.

Calvin, John. *Commentaries on the First Book of Moses Called Genesis*. Translated by John King. Edinburgh: Calvin Translation Society, 1847.

Catholic Encyclopedia. "Manichaeism." http://www.newadvent.org/cathen/09591a.htm.

Charles-Murray, Sister. "Art and the Early Church." *Journal of Theological Studies* 18:2 (1977) 303–45.

Chesterton, G. K. *St. Francis of Assisi*. New York: Image, 1990.

———. *St. Thomas Aquinas*. London: Sheed and Ward, 1933.

Christensen, Carl C. *Art and the Reformation in Germany*. Athens, OH: Ohio University Press, 1979.

Clapp, Rodney. *Tortured Wonders: Christian Spirituality for People, Not Angels*. Grand Rapids: Brazos, 2004.

Clark, Elizabeth A. "Asceticism." In *Augustine Through The Ages: An Encyclopedia*, edited by Allan D. Fitzgerald, 67–71. Grand Rapids: Eerdmans, 1999.

Coakley, Sarah, and Charles M. Stang, eds. *Re-Thinking Dionysius the Areopagite*. Oxford: Wiley-Blackwell, 2009.

Bibliography

Copleston, Frederick. *A History of Philosophy*, vol. 2, book 1, *Medieval Philosophy*. New York: Image, 1985.

———. *A History of Philosophy*, vol. 3, *Ockham to Suarez*. New York: Image, 1985.

Coulton, G. G. *The Fate of Medieval Art in the Renaissance & Reformation*, part II of *Art and the Reformation*. New York: Harper Torchbooks, 1958.

Daniélou, Jean, ed. *From Glory to Glory: Texts from Gregory of Nyssa's Mystical Writings*. Crestwood, NY: St. Vladimir's Seminary Press, 1997.

———. *Platonisme et théologie mystique: essai sur la doctrine spirituelle de saint Grégoire de Nysse*. Paris: Aubier, 1944.

Davidson, Bruce W. "Narcission: The Root of All Hypocrisy in the Theological Psychology of Jonathan Edwards." *Journal of the Evangelical Theological Society*, 57:1 (2014) 135–45.

Davies, Oliver. "The Theological Aesthetics." In *The Cambridge Companion to Hans Urs von Balthasar*, edited by Edward T. Oakes and David Moss, 131–142. Cambridge: Cambridge University Press, 2004.

De Lubac, Henri. *The Mystery of the Supernatural*. Translated by Rosemary Sheed. New York: Crossroad, 1998.

———. "A Witness to Christ in the Church: Hans Urs von Balthasar. In *Hand Urs von Balthasar: His Life and Work*, edited by David Schindler, 271–88. San Francisco: Ignatius, 1991.

Dewey, John. *Art as Experience*. New York: Penguin Group, 1934.

Duffy, Stephen J. "Anthropology." In *Augustine Through The Ages: An Encyclopedia*, 447–51, edited by Allan D. Fitzgerald. Grand Rapids, MI: Eerdmans, 1999.

Dupré, Louis. "The Glory of the Lord: Hans Urs von Balthasar's Theological Aesthetic." In *Hans Urs von Balthasar: His Life and Work*, edited by David Schindler, 183–206. San Francisco: Ignatius, 1991.

Dyrness, William. *Reformed Theology and Visual Culture: The Protestant Imagination from Calvin to Edwards*. Cambridge: Cambridge University Press, 2004.

———. *Visual Faith: Art, Theology, and Worship in Dialogue*. Grand Rapids: Baker Academic, 2001.

Eco, Umberto. *The Aesthetics of Thomas Aquinas*. Translated by Hugh Bredin. Cambridge, MA: Harvard University Press, 1988.

Edwards, Jonathan. "God Glorified in Man's Dependence etc." In *The Works of Jonathan Edwards*. vol. 2, edited by Edward Hickman, 169–78. Banner of Truth Trust, 1974.

———. *The Works of Jonathan Edwards*. Edited by Edward Hickman. Banner of Truth Trust, 1974.

———. *Works Online*. At the Jonathan Edwards Center at Yale University Yale.

Elwood, Douglas. *The Philosophical Theology of Jonathan Edwards*. New York: Columbia University Press, 1960.

Evdokimov, Paul, *The Art of the Icon: A Theology of Beauty*. Translated by Steven Bigham. Redondo Beach, CA: Oakwood, 1996.

———. *Orthodoxy*. Translated by Jeremy Hummerstone and Callan Slipper. London: New City, 2011.

Ewing, Keith H. "The Hidden Pentecostal Doctrine: A Modern Gnosticism—Reflections on the Uncertainties in Dealing with Creative Types in the Fine Arts." Unpublished paper presented to the Lewis Wilson Institute for Pentecostal Studies, Vanguard University, Costa Mesa, California, November 10, 2000.

Bibliography

Ferguson, George. *Signs and Symbols in Christian Art: With Illustrations.* New York: Oxford University Press, 1966.

Fitzgerald, Allan D., ed. *Augustine Through the Ages: An Encyclopedia.* Grand Rapids, MI: Eerdmans, 1999.

———. "Habit (*Consuetudo*)." In *Augustine Through the Ages: An Encyclopedia*, edited by Allan D. Fitzgerald, 409–10. Grand Rapids: Eerdmans, 1999.

Follett, Ken. *The Pillars of the Earth.* New York: Penguin, 1990.

Garside, Charles, Jr. *Zwingli and the Arts.* New Haven, CT: Yale University Press, 1966.

Gaustad, Edwin S., ed. *A Documentary History of Religion in America: To the Civil War.* Grand Rapids: Eerdmans, 1982.

Gero, Stephen. "Byzantine Iconoclasm and the Failure of a Medieval Reformation." In *The Image and the* Word, edited by Joseph Gutmann, 27–62. Missoula, MT: Scholars, 1977.

Gladwell, Malcom. *Blink: The Power of Thinking Without Thinking.* New York: Back Bay, 2005.

Grant, James. "Aesthetics and the Philosophy of Art: Kant's Critique of Judgment, Lectures 1 and 2." University of Oxford Faculty of Philosophy online podcasts. http://media.podcasts.ox.ac.uk/philfac/aesthetics/2011-03-09-grant-aesthetics-4.mp3?CAMEFROM=podcastsGET.

Gregory of Nyssa. *Song of Songs.* Translated by with an introduction by Casimir McCambley. Brookline, MA: Hellenic College Press, 1987.

Gunton, Colin E. "Creation and Re-creation: An Exploration of Some Themes in Aesthetics and Theology." *Modern Theology* 2:1 (1985) 1–19.

Guyer, Paul. *Kant.* New York: Routledge, 2006.

Harrison, Carol. *Beauty and Revelation in the Thought of Saint Augustine.* Oxford: Oxford University Press, 1992.

Hart, David Bentley. *The Beauty of the Infinite: The Aesthetics of Christian Truth.* Grand Rapids: Eerdmans, 2003.

Healy, Nicholas, and David L. Schindler. "For the Life of the World: Hans Urs von Balthasar on the Church as Eucharist." In *The Cambridge Companion to Hans Urs von Balthasar*, edited by Edward T. Oakes and David Moss, 51–63. Cambridge: Cambridge University Press, 2004.

Henrici, Peter. "Hans Urs von Balthasar: A Sketch of His Life." In *Hans Urs von Balthasar: His Life and Work*, edited by David Schindler, 7–43. San Francisco: Ignatius,1991.

Hill, Edmund, trans. *The Works of Saint Augustine*, vol. 3. Brooklyn: New City, 1992.

Hopko, Thomas. "The Trinity in the Cappadocians." In *Christian Spirituality: Origins to the Twelfth Century*, edited by Bernard McGinn and John Meyendorff, 260–76. New York: Crossroad, 1985.

Huizinga, Johan. *Waning of the Middle Ages.* Translated by F. Hopman. Harmondsworth, England: Penguin, 1965.

James, William. *Principles of Psychology*, vol. 1. New York: Dover, 1950.

Janz, Dennis R., ed. *A Reformation Reader: Primary Texts with Introductions.* Minneapolis: Fortress, 1999.

Jenson, Robert W. *The Triune Identity.* Minneapolis: Fortress, 1982.

Kannengiesser, Charles. "The Spiritual Message of the Great Fathers." In *Christian Spirituality: Origins to the Twelfth Century*, edited by Bernard McGinn and John Meyendorff, 61–88. New York: Crossroad, 1985.

Bibliography

Kant, Immanuel. *Critique of the Power of Judgment*. Translated by Paul Guyer and Eric Matthews. Cambridge: Cambridge University Press, 2000.

———. *Critique of Aesthetic Judgment*. Translated by J. C. Meredith. Oxford: Clarendon, 1928.

Kemal, Salim. *Kant's Aesthetic Theory: An Introduction*. 2nd ed. New York: St. Martin's, 1997.

Krautheimer, Richard. *Early Christian and Byzantine Architecture*. 4th ed. New Haven, CT: Yale University Press, 1986.

———. *Rome: Profile of a City, 312–1308*. Princeton, NJ: Princeton University Press, 1980.

Kristeller, Paul Oskar. "The Modern System of the Arts." In *Aesthetics*, edited by Susan Feagin and Patrick Maynard, 90–102. Oxford Readers Series. Oxford: Oxford University Press, 1997.

Krivocheine, Basil. *In the Light of Christ: St Symeon the New Theologian*. Translated by A. Gythiel. Crestwood, NY: St. Vladimir's Seminary Press, 1986.

Latourette, Kenneth Scott. *A History of Christianity*, vol. 1, *Beginnings to 1500*. Rev. ed. San Francisco: Harper & Row, 1975.

Lee, Sang. *The Philosophical Theology of Jonathan Edwards*. Princeton, NJ: Princeton University Press, 1988.

Lossky, Vladimir. *In the Image and Likeness of God*. Edited by John H. Erickson and T. E. Bird. Crestwood, NY: St. Vladimir's Seminary Press, 1974.

———. *The Vision of God*. Translated by Asheleigh Moorhouse. 2nd ed. Bedfordshire: The Faith, 1973.

Louie, Kin Yip. *The Beauty of the Triune God: The Theological Aesthetics of Jonathan Edwards*. Eugene, OR: Pickwick, 2013.

Lucas Francisco, Mateo-Seco, and Guilio Maspero, eds. *The Brill Dictionary of Gregory of Nyssa*. Translated by Seth Cherney. London: Brill, 2010.

Ludlow, Morwenna. *Gregory of Nyssa: Ancient and [Post]modern*. Oxford: Oxford University Press, 2007.

Luther, Martin. *Luther's Works*. Edited by Helmut T. Lehmann. Philadelphia: Muhlenberg, 1957.

Manent, Pierre. "Between Athens and Jerusalem." *First Things*, no. 220 (February 2012) 35–39.

"Manichaeism." *Catholic Encyclopedia*. http://www.newadvent.org/cathen/09591a.htm.

Marsden, George. *Jonathan Edwards: A Life*. New Haven, CT: Yale University Press, 2004.

McClymond, Michael J., and Gerald McDermott. *The Theology of Jonathan Edwards*. Oxford: Oxford University Press, 2012.

McDermott, Gerald R. *The Great Theologians: A Brief Guide*. Downers Grove, IL: InterVarsity, 2010.

———. "The Emerging Divide in Evangelical Theology." *Journal of the Evangelical Theological Society*, 56:2 (2013) 355–77.

McGinn, Bernard. *The Doctors of the Church: Thirty-Three Men and Women Who Shaped Christianity*. New York: Crossroad, 1999.

———. *The Foundations of Mysticism*, vol. 1 of *The Presence of God: A History of Western Christian Mysticism, Origins to the Fifth Century*. New York: Crossroad, 1999.

McGrath, Alister. *Reformation Thought: An Introduction*. 4th ed. Oxford: Wiley-Blackwell, 2012.

Meyendorff, John. *Catholicity and the Church*. Crestwood, NY: St. Vladimir's Seminary Press, 1983.

Bibliography

———. *Eastern Christian Thought*. Crestwood, NY: St. Vladimir's Seminary Press, 1987.

———. *Rome, Constantinople, Moscow: Historical and Theological Studies*. Crestwood, NY: St. Vladimir's Seminary Press, 1996.

Miles, Margaret R. *Image as Insight: Visual Understandings of Western Christianity and Secular Culture*. Eugene, OR: Wipf and Stock, 1985.

Mitchell, Louis J. *Jonathan Edwards on the Experience of Beauty*. Princeton, NJ: Princeton Theological Seminary, 2003.

Moeller, Bernd. "Piety in Germany Around 1500." In *The Reformation in Medieval Perspective*, edited by Steven E. Ozment, 50–75. Chicago: Quadrangle, 1971.

Moltmann, Jürgen. *The Source of Life: The Holy Spirit and the Theology of Life*. Minneapolis: Fortress, 1997.

Moss, David, and Edward T. Oakes. "Introduction." In *The Cambridge Companion to Hans Urs von Balthasar*, edited by Edward T. Oakes and David Moss, 1–8. Cambridge: Cambridge University Press, 2004.

Moxey, Keith. *Peasants, Warriors and Wives: Popular Imagery in the Reformation*. Chicago: University of Chicago Press, 1989.

National Vital Statistics Reports, Volume 61, Number 6: "Deaths: Preliminary Data for 2011." The U.S. Center for Disease Control and Prevention, http://www.cdc.gov/nchs/data/nvsr/nvsr61/nvsr61_06.pdf.

Nemoianu, Virgil. "An Appreciative review of Peter Kivy, *The Seventh Sense: Francis Hutscheson and Eighteenth-Century British Aesthetics*." *The Review of Metaphysics*, 58:2 (December 2004) 445–47.

Newbigin, Lesslie. *The Gospel in a Pluralist Society*. Grand Rapids: Eerdmans, 1989.

Nichols, Aidan. *A Key to Balthasar: Hans Urs von Balthasar on Beauty, Goodness and Truth*. Grand Rapids: Baker Academic, 2011.

O'Donohue, John. *Beauty: The Invisible Embrace*. New York: Harper Perennial, 2005.

Panofsky, Erwin. *Abbot Suger on the Abbey Church of St.-Denis*. Princeton, NJ: Princeton University Press, 1946.

Palmquist, Stephen R. "Kant's Religious Argument for the Existence of God: The Ultimate Dependence of Human Destiny on Divine Assistance." *Faith and Philosophy*, 26:1 (2009) 3–22.

Payne, Robert. *The Holy Fire: The Story of the Early Centuries of the Christian Church in the Near East*. New York: Harper & Brothers, 1957.

Pearcey, Nancey R., and Charles B. Thaxton, *The Soul of Science*. Turning Point Christian Worldview Series. Wheaton, IL: Crossway, 1994.

Pelikan, Jaroslav. *The Emergence of the Catholic Tradition (100–600)*, vol. 1 in *The Christian Tradition: A History of the Development of Doctrine*. Chicago: University of Chicago Press, 1975.

———. "Introduction." In *Pseudo-Dionysius: The Complete Works*. Translated by Colm Luibheid. Foreword, notes, and translation collaboration by Paul Rorem. Mahwah, NJ: Paulist, 1987.

Phan, Peter C. *Culture and Eschatology: The Iconographical Vision of Paul Evdokimov*. New York: Peter Lang, 1985.

Phillips, John. *The Reformation of Images: Destruction of Art in England (1535–1560)*. Los Angeles: University of California Press, 1973.

Plekon, Michael. *Jacob's Well*. "A Theologian of God's Beauty, A Life of Service," sponsored by the Orthodox Church in America. http://jacwell.org/Summer_2002/a_theologian_of_god's_beauty.htm.

Bibliography

Plekon, Michael, and Alexis Vinogradov, eds. and trans. *In the World, of the Church: A Paul Evdokimov Reader*. Crestwood, NY: St. Vladimir Seminary Press, 2001.

Potts, Timothy. "Director's Foreword." In *Picturing the Bible: The Earliest Christian Art*, edited by Jeffrey Spier, xi-xii. Fort Worth, TX: Kimbell Art Museum, 2007.

Prothero, Stephen. *God Is Not One: The Eight Rival Religions that Run the World—and Why Their Differences Matter*. New York: HarperOne, 2010.

Pseudo-Dionysius. *Pseudo-Dionysius: The Complete Works*. Translated by Colm Luibheid. Foreword, notes, and translation collaboration by Paul Rorem. Mahwah, NJ: Paulist, 1987.

———. *The Divine Names*. Translated by C.E. Rolt. London: SPCK, 1940.

Putnam, Caroline Canfield. *Beauty in the Pseudo-Denis*. Washington, DC: The Catholic University Press, 1960.

Quenot, Michel. *The Icon: Window on the Kingdom*. Translated by a Carthusian Monk. Crestwood, NY: St. Vladimir's Seminary Press, 1991.

"Quotes about taste." Goodreads. http://www.goodreads.com/quotes/tag/taste.

Rahner, Karl. "The Hermeneutics of Eschatological Assertions." In *Theological Investigations*, vol. 4, translated by Kevin Smyth, 323–46. London: Darton, Longman, and Todd, 1974.

Ramelli, Ilaria. "Good/Beauty." In *The Brill Dictionary of Gregory of Nyssa*, edited by Lucas Francisco Mateo-Seco and Guilio Maspero, 356–63. Translated by Seth Cherney. London: Brill, 2010.

Rausch, Thomas P. *Catholicism at the Dawn of the Third Millennium*. Collegeville, MN: Liturgical, 1996.

Riordan, William K. *Divine Light: The Theology of Denys the Areopagite*. San Francisco: Ignatius, 2008.

Rist, John. *Augustine: Ancient Thought Baptized*. Cambridge: Cambridge University Press, 1994.

Rookmaaker, H.R. *Modern Art and the Death of a Culture*. Wheaton, IL: Crossway, 1994.

Romanowski, William D. *Eyes Wide Open: Looking for God in Popular Culture*. Grand Rapids: Brazos, 2001.

Russell, Jeffrey Burton. "Hell, Damnation." In *Augustine Through the Ages: An Encyclopedia*, edited by Allan D. Fitzgerald, 422. Grand Rapids: Eerdmans, 1999.

Russell, D. S. *The Method and Message of Jewish Apocalyptic 200 BC–100 AD*. London: SCM, 1964.

Rybarczyk, Edmund J. *Beyond Salvation: Eastern Orthodoxy and Classical Pentecostalism on Becoming Like Christ*. Carlisle, Cumbria, UK: Paternoster, 2004.

———. "Jonathan Edwards on Aesthetics: Low-Hanging Fruit for Pentecostals." In *From Northampton to Azusa: Pentecostals and the Theology of Jonathan Edwards*, edited by Amos Yong and Steven M. Studebaker. Yale University Press, forthcoming.)

———. "Pentecostalism, Human Nature, and Aesthetics: 21st Century Engagement," *Journal of Pentecostal Theology*, 21, Fall 2012, 1–20.

———. "Reframing Tongues: Apophaticism and Postmodernism." *Pneuma: The Journal of the Society for Pentecostal Studies*, 27:1 (Spring 2005) 83–104.

———. *The Spirit Unfettered: Protestant Views on the Holy Spirit*. Brewster, MA: Paraclete, 2010.

———. "What Are You O Man?: Theo-Anthropological Similarities in Classical Pentecostalism and Eastern Orthodoxy." In *Ancient and Postmodern Christianity:*

Bibliography

Paleo-Orthodoxy in the 21st Century, edited by Kenneth Tanner, 83–105. Downers Grove, IL: InterVarsity, 2002.
Ryken, Leland. "The Original Puritan Work Ethic." *Christian History*, 89 (2006). http://www.christianitytoday.com/ch/2006/issue89/7.32.html?start=1.
Saint Francis. "Canticle of Brother Sun." AD 1224. http://www.franciscanfriarstor.com/archive/stfrancis/stf_canticle_of_the_sun.htm.
Sammon, Brendan Thomas. *The God Who Is Beauty: Beauty as a Divine Name in Thomas Aquinas and Dionysius the Areopagite*. Princeton Theological Monograph Series. Eugene, OR: Pickwick, 2013.
Schindler, David, ed. *Hans Urs von Balthasar: His Life and Work*. San Francisco: Ignatius, 1991.
Scruton, Roger. *Kant*. Past Masters Series. Oxford: Oxford University Press, 1982.
Severance, Diane. "Magnificent Medieval Cathedrals." http://www.christianity.com/church/church-history/timeline/901-1200/magnificent-medieval-cathedrals-11629780.html.
Sherry, Patrick. *Spirit and Beauty: An Introduction to Theological Aesthetics*. 2nd ed. London: SCM, 2010.
Spier, Jeffrey, ed. *Picturing the Bible: The Earliest Christian Art*. Fort Worth, TX: Kimbell Art Museum, 2007.
Stanford Encyclopedia of Philosophy. http://plato.stanford.edu/entries/plotinus/.
Stang, Charles. "Dionysius, Paul and the Significance of the Pseudonym." In *Re-Thinking Dionysius the Areopagite*, edited by Sarah Coakley and Charles M. Stang, 11–25. Oxford: Wiley-Blackwell, 2009.
Stark, *The Rise of Christianity*. San Francisco: HarperSanFrancisco, 1997.
———. *The Victory of Reason*. New York: Random House, 2005.
Studebaker, Steven. *From Pentecost to the Triune God: A Pentecostal Trinitarian Theology*. Grand Rapids: Eerdmans, 2012.
"Technology in the Medieval Age." http://www.mastep.sjsu.edu/history/middle.htm.
Thiessen, Gesa E., ed. *Theological Aesthetics: A Reader*. Grand Rapids: Eerdmans, 2004.
"Transcendental Idealism." http://www.britannica.com/topic/transcendental-idealism.
Treitler, Wolfgang. "True Foundations of Authentic Theology." In *Hans Urs von Balthasar: His Life and Work*, edited by David Schindler, 169–82. San Francisco: Ignatius, 1991.
Ugolnik, Anthony. *The Illuminating Icon*. Grand Rapids: Eerdmans, 1989.
Vajta, Vilmos. *Luther on Worship*. Philadelphia: Fortress, 1958.
Van Bavel, Tarscicius. "Love." In *Augustine Through the Ages: An Encyclopedia*, edited by Allan D. Fitzgerald, 509–10. Grand Rapids: Eerdmans, 1999.
Viladesau, Richard. *Theological Aesthetics: God in Imagination, Beauty, and Art*. Oxford: Oxford University Press, 1999.
Ware, Kallistos. "The Human Person as an Icon of the Trinity." *Sobornost* 8:2 (1986) 6–23.
———. *The Orthodox Church*. Baltimore, MD: Penguin, 1964.
———. *The Orthodox Way*. Crestwood, NY: St. Vladimir's Seminary Press, 1995.
Wenzel, Christian Helmut. *An Introduction to Kant's Aesthetics: Core Concepts and Problems*. Malden, MA: Blackwell, 2005.
Wigley, Stephen. *Balthasar's Trilogy: A Reader's Guide*. New York: T&T Clark, 2010.
Williams, Rowan. "Balthasar and Trinity." In *The Cambridge Companion to Hans Urs von Balthasar*, edited by Edward T. Oakes and David Moss, 37–50. Cambridge: Cambridge University Press, 2004.
Wills, Gary. *Saint Augustine: A Life*. New York: Penguin, 1999.

Bibliography

The Works of Jonathan Edwards. Online at the Jonathan Edwards Center at Yale University.

The Works of Saint Augustine. Vol. 3.4, Translated by Edmund Hill. Brooklyn: New City, 1992.

Wright, N. T. *Surprised by Hope: Rethinking Heaven, the Resurrection and the Mission of the Church.* San Francisco: HarperOne, 2008.

Zachman, Randall C. *Image and Word in the Theology of John Calvin.* Notre Dame, IN: University of Notre Dame Press, 2007.

www.ingramcontent.com/pod-product-compliance
Lightning Source LLC
Chambersburg PA
CBHW031732230426
43669CB00007B/330